the classroom
reading program
in the
elementary school

the classroom reading program in the elementary school,

assessment, organization and management

J. David Cooper

Ball State University

Thomas W. Worden

Auburn University

Macmillan Publishing Co., Inc.
New York

Collier Macmillan Publishing Co., Inc.
London

Macmillan Publishing Co., Inc.
866 Third Avenue, New York, New York 10022

Collier Macmillan Canada, Inc.

Library of Congress Cataloging in Publication Data

Cooper, J. David (James David), Date:
   The classroom reading program in the
elementary school.

   Bibliography: p.
   Includes index.
   1. Reading (Elementary)   2. Classroom
management.   I. Worden, Thomas W.   II. Title.
LB1573.C5563   1983   372.4   82-7797
ISBN 0-02-324660-X   AACR2

Printing: 1 2 3 4 5 6 7 8   Year: 3 4 5 6 7 8 9 0

ISBN   0-02-324660-X

Grateful acknowledgment is hereby made for permission to reproduce collages of reading test materials, as follows:

Page 48: *Iowa Silent Reading Tests*, Manual of Directions, Level 1. Copyright © 1973 by Harcourt Brace Jovanovich, Inc.

Metropolitan Achievement Tests, Primary II. Copyright © 1969 by Harcourt Brace Jovanovich, Inc.

Durrell Listening-Reading Series, Intermediate Level. Copyright © 1969 by Harcourt Brace Jovanovich, Inc.

Gates-MacGinitie Reading Tests, Second Edition. Copyright © 1978 by Hougthon Mifflin Company.

Page 49: *Reading Diagnostic Tests*, Second Edition, by Gates, McKillop, and Horowitz. Copyright © 1981 by Teachers College, Columbia University.

Analytical Reading Inventory, Second Edition, by Woods and Moe. Copyright © 1981 by Charles E. Merrill Publishing Co.

Basic Reading Inventory, Pre-Primer–Grade Eight, Second Edition, by Jerry L. Johns. Copyright © 1981 by Kendall/Hunt Publishing Co.

Diagnostic Reading Inventory, Second Edition, by Jacobs and Searfoss. Copyright © 1979 by Kendall/Hunt Publishing Co.

Informal Reading Assessment, by Burns and Roe. Copyright © 1980 by Rand McNally College Publishing Co.

Durrell Analysis of Reading Difficulty, Third Edition. Copyright © 1980 by The Psychological Corporation, a Subsidiary of Harcourt Brace Jovanovich, Inc.

Page 51: *The Wisconsin Tests of Reading Skill Development*. Copyright © 1974 by The Board of Regents of the University of Wisconsin System for the Wisconsin Research and Development Center for Cognitive Learning.

preface

Teaching children to read is one of the most significant roles of the elementary school. Teachers today know more about the teaching of reading and are doing a better job of performing this task than was done before. However, there is always room to improve.

This text was written to help preservice elementary teachers develop the knowledges and skills needed to organize and direct the reading program *in the elementary classroom*. To accomplish this goal we have focused on assessment, organization, and management rather than on detailed knowledge of reading content and methods of teaching. The text was written with several basic assumptions in mind:

1. The persons using this text will have had at least one course in the teaching of reading.
2. This *is not* a textbook on clinical diagnosis or reading problems.
3. The majority of the teachers in the United States will use a basal reader to teach reading. Therefore, a major goal of preservice reading-methods courses should be to help them learn how to use this tool effectively.
4. The core of the reading program in the elementary school must center around the classroom teacher, not on a special reading teacher.
5. Although this text draws from the extensive body of research in reading, it is not a compendium of reading research.
6. No single textbook can or should cover all aspects of the teaching of reading because they cannot be thoroughly developed in any single given course.

We are deeply indebted to Dr. Nancy Kiger, Northeast Missouri State University, Kirksville, Missouri, for the hours of editorial work throughout the development of this manuscript. Her comments and insights helped us develop a more readable and practical text.

Special thanks go to Tasha Worden for her work in typing and proofreading the manuscript and to the editorial staff of the Macmillan Publishing Co., Inc., for the assistance in putting together the final copy.

J. D. C.
T. W. W.

contents

section ‖ assessment   69

3   PLACING A STUDENT IN BASAL MATERIALS   71

ASSESSING SPECIFIC SKILLS   109

section organization

ORGANIZING THE CLASS FOR INSTRUCTION   127

section IV management 185

RELATING THE READING PROGRAM TO ALL AREAS
OF THE CURRICULUM   255

the classroom reading program in the elementary school

section 1

background

The two chapters in this section of the text are a preparation for the guidelines and procedures that are suggested throughout the book for organizing and managing the reading program in the elementary school. It is assumed that students using this text have had at *least one* basic course in the teaching of reading and are aware of some basic instructional procedures. The information given on tests, testing, and factors related to reading growth has been written with the classroom teacher in mind.

chapter 1

the classroom reading program

objectives

As a result of reading this chapter, one will be able to

1. Identify the components of an effective reading program.
2. Define diagnostic teaching as it relates to classroom instruction.
3. Identify a diagnostic teacher in the classroom.
4. Know the information needed by a diagnostic classroom reading teacher.

overview

The concept of a reading program as opposed to merely having a collection of materials for instruction will be developed. The components of an effective reading program will be identified and related to the program concept. Diagnostic teaching will be presented and defined as it relates to the total classroom operation of a reading program. The specific steps for diagnostic teaching will be related to the teaching of reading utilizing a basal text. The teacher reading this chapter can draw on his/her knowledge of the reading process and the teaching strategies appropriate to help children develop the needed skills and abilities to become proficient readers.

READING ACHIEVEMENT IN THE U.S. TODAY

During the past ten years numerous studies have been conducted that have attempted to determine how children and young adults are reading today (5, 6, 7, 8, 13, 14, 15, 23). By examining the evidence gathered in these studies one quickly sees a trend that leads to the conclusion that *children and young adults in the United States today demonstrate better reading skills than their predecessors demonstrated.* Not only are children *able* to read but they *do* read (7).

Another area to examine in relation to reading is that of the technological advancements of today's world. When one looks around, what does one notice about the technology of our society? All of the gadgets, machines, and devices that help to make life more efficient, enjoyable, and relaxing have been developed by an educated person—a person who can read. Without the ability to read, humans could not have advanced so far so quickly. Although some may argue that many human creations are not advancements, most persons would agree that what the human being has accomplished in terms of technology is indeed a wonder when compared to life in the past.

Reading studies together with the evidence of modern technology are striking indications that children are leaving school reading better than ever before, despite some opinions to the contrary (3). Who deserves the credit for this situation? As a bumper sticker used by several professional organizations states, "IF YOU CAN READ THIS, THANK A TEACHER." It is the creative, enthusiastic teacher who is doing a better job of teaching children to read. It is this teacher who is responsible for American students' improved reading ability.

USING THIS BOOK

The person using this book has already learned a lot about teaching and especially teaching reading. It is the purpose of this book to help the teacher further develop his/her skills of teaching reading in the best possible ways. This book provides the most practical, up-to-date information that is known about teaching reading in the elementary school. It will help a teacher walk into a classroom with the skills needed to do an effective job of assessing the students' needs and of organizing and managing the reading program.

In the beginning of this chapter were sections marked "Objectives" and "Overview." These two sections will appear at the beginning of each chapter. The objectives will state what the teacher can expect to learn or accomplish as a result of reading each chapter. The overview will alert one to major points to be covered and will relate important background information on which to draw. At the conclusion of each chapter are a summary, thought and discussion questions, activities to help apply what one has learned, and a bibliography for further reading. Taking advantage of all of these features will help the teacher to improve his/her teaching methods while using this text.

THE ROLE OF READING INSTRUCTION IN TODAY'S SCHOOLS

One of the most important tasks that the elementary classroom teacher performs is that of teaching children to read. More is known about teaching reading than ever before, but it is mandatory to strive to be better. In today's schools, the role of reading instruction continues to be a significant one. The reading program and reading related activities take a major portion of the instructional day. To be effective, classroom reading teachers must make certain that they see this role in its proper perspective and understand certain assumptions about it.

The Teacher

The key to effective reading instruction is the classroom teacher. The enthusiastic, well-organized classroom teacher will make more difference in how children learn to read than any other single factor (11). The methods, materials, and classroom environment do not influence the child's reading achievement nearly as much as the classroom teacher. What one does as a classroom teacher in teaching children to read is of first importance in organizing and managing the classroom reading program. Therefore, as one continues to improve one's skills as a teacher, it is important to be sure to learn the best techniques possible for communicating with children and providing technical excellence in instruction. Accepting the assumption that the classroom teacher is the most significant factor in determining how children will learn to read means that the teacher will be continuously devoting his/her professional time and energies to improving her/his knowledge and skills as a classroom reading teacher. An effective classroom reading teacher is (10)

1. Enthusiastic.
2. Well organized.
3. Able to communicate with children.
4. Knowledgeable about reading and reading instruction.
5. Able to evaluate critically instructional situations and decisions.

Each of these characteristics requires many different skills and abilities on the part of the classroom teacher. It is the purpose of this text to help one develop and refine those skills and abilities because one's skills and abilities as a teacher of reading will do more to bring about improved reading instruction than any other factors.

The Reading Program in the Classroom

Where should reading be taught in the elementary school? Should reading instruction be the primary responsibility of the classroom teacher? Is a reme-

dial program needed? Should some types of learners be sent out of the classroom to special programs? These questions have been discussed frequently. Although the answers to them are not absolute, there are some very important points that must be considered in developing an effective elementary reading program.

The base for a child's reading instruction must be the elementary classroom. It is within this classroom that the bulk of a child's formal elementary education takes place and if one is to do the most effective job possible of teaching him/her to read, every aspect of the reading program must be centered around the classroom instruction. For years, schools sent children out of the classroom for special reading instruction. Some schools still do this. Often this was termed "remedial reading" or "reading improvement." During this period of time out of the classroom, the child usually worked on some skills, played a game, did some type of reading, or drilled on an area of weakness. At the end of the period, the child returned to the classroom with its reading program and other activities. Little or no coordination existed between the old concept of a "remedial" program and the classroom. The reasons for this situation included a lack of communication between teachers, insufficient time on the part of teachers for planning, and a general program concept that supported the idea of the classroom program and the remedial program being separate and independent. The effectiveness of such programs has not been proved (11). Because of the existing evidence on effective reading programs and what one has seen in schools, one must conclude that the elementary reading program must be focused around the classroom with the classroom teacher being the person responsible for coordinating all aspects of instruction. This does not mean that special reading teachers are no longer needed. It does mean however, that the roles of such individuals must be redefined, possibly to become a resource teacher model or resource person for the classroom teacher.

If children are to be removed from the classroom for special reading instruction, this instruction should be coordinated with the content and procedures used in the classroom reading program. This rule should apply for all special reading programs, learning disabilities, or remedial reading programs. In all cases, reading instruction implemented away from the classroom should be coordinated with and supportive of the classroom reading program.

The classroom reading program must be designed so that it accounts for all types of learners—average students, less able readers, learning-disabled students, gifted, talented, and creative readers, and a variety of mainstreamed learners. Planning the reading program around the needs of these various types of individuals requires, more than ever, that the teacher assume the role of a decision maker.

Placing the major emphasis of the reading program in the classroom does not exclude the use of specialists and resource teachers from outside the classroom. These individuals provide the classroom teacher needed and valuable support, but the activities carried on by these persons in terms of reading instruc-

tion must be correlated with the classroom program. The two programs for reading cannot be developed and operated independent of each other.

The Basal Reader

The majority of elementary classroom teachers who teach reading make use of a basal reader in their instruction (16) and many school systems in the United States require elementary teachers to use a basal reader. This does not mean that other approaches to reading instruction cannot or will not be used. It is simply stating the situation as it exists.

Some authorities are very critical of basal series. Many of the criticisms relate to the ways in which basals have been used in the classroom. The evidence that is available on the effectiveness of various approaches to teaching reading indicates that there is no one best approach or method (2, 10). As already pointed out, the teacher is the single most important factor in determining how children learn to read. Therefore, to be an effective classroom reading teacher one must learn to make sound professional decisions about how each individual child should be taught to read. This is not an easy task but neither is it an impossible one. Making such decisions requires that one learn to use effectively whatever basal series is part of one's program and base decisions about individual children on information gained from their performance in the series.

Mrs. Word's Enthusiasm Makes Reading Exciting in This Classroom.

Basal readers are effective teaching *resources* (1). They provide teachers with valuable guidelines that should serve to help them make the best professional decisions possible about teaching children to read. It is how basal readers are used that determines the role they play in the reading program. Therefore, a major thrust of this text will be to help the teacher learn to use more effectively a basal reader to meet the needs of individual learners in the classroom.

Reading and the Total Curriculum

Many times reading instruction is viewed as a separate subject in the elementary curriculum. Certainly there is a need for and should be a time for providing children direct instruction in reading. But the concept of the reading program must be such that it encompasses opportunities to develop reading abilities in all areas, whether math, science, social studies, art, physical education, or whatever. It is too narrow a concept to think of the reading program as being *only* the reading period. Rather, the reading program must be viewed in terms of all the places where reading can be taught and used.

The content areas of the elementary curriculum provide valuable opportunities to teach specific types of reading and reading skills as well as instances in which one can apply all reading skills that have been taught. One of the most important things that a student must do as he/she learns to read is to apply in a variety of situations what is being learned. The math text, the science book, directions for a project—all of these areas provide opportunities for the teaching and extension of reading. To be effective, a reading teacher must see to it that these areas are not only viewed as a part of the reading program *but are actually* implemented as an integral part of the instruction.

A READING PROGRAM

If most elementary teachers were asked to describe their reading program they would probably name the company that publishes their basal series, such as Ginn, Houghton Mifflin, Macmillan, or some other publisher. In other words, they see their reading program as the basal series from which they teach.

One point stressed throughout this text is that the basal series is *not* the reading program and to regard it as such is one of the main reasons that basal readers have been so misused. If, from the beginning of their careers, elementary teachers were to view basal readers differently and have a *clearer* concept of the reading program, much of the misuse of basals would diminish.

The basal reading series are nothing more than collections of materials. They are like the many thousands of other materials that are available for teaching reading. They comprise the resources that the elementary classroom

reading teacher has to draw from as instructional decisions are made for children. Basal series are generally composed of a well-organized, sequential set of materials that allow and require the teacher to make a variety of decisions about what should be done in teaching children to read. Although many schools may use one basal series as the core of their reading program, this does not mean that other series and materials will not be needed to teach children to read. *No one basal series will ever be complete enough to teach all children to read.*

Basal readers and other instructional materials are the resources and tools from which the classroom reading teacher must draw as each child's reading program is planned. They do not make up the total program. Basals and other materials should be regarded by the teacher much as a mechanic views his tools and handbooks or as a chef sees his various spices and ingredients. These professionals draw from their resources as the conditions demand. The effective classroom reading teacher draws from the basals and other materials as the needs of learners require.

Many reading programs will depend heavily on one basal series to form the core of their reading instruction, but they will use other series and materials as the needs of children indicate. Reading programs that use their materials in this correlated manner have developed a clear concept of a program. Teachers in this type of program will not "blindly" follow one series page after page or book after book.

The Reading Program Defined

Exactly what is a reading program? The various dictionary definitions of the word *program* all indicate that it is *a plan of what is to be done.* This would imply that a *reading program is a plan of what is to be done in teaching children to read.*

A reading program has four component parts:

1. Objectives. Knowing exactly what one wants to accomplish and what one wants the students to learn.
2. Needs of Learners. Being able to account for the characteristics, interests, abilities, and needs of the children being taught.
3. Instructional Procedures. This includes all of the decisions relating to "how to teach," excluding materials.
4. Resources. The materials, books, games, and whatever else will be used.

Figure 1-1 presents a graphic model for the reading-program concept.

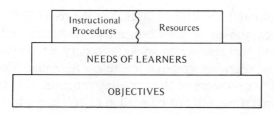

FIGURE 1-1.   Reading Program Model.

Objectives

In every reading program teachers must know exactly what is going to be accomplished. This requires careful identification of overall goals and objectives. These goals and objectives are sometimes identified on a building level or school-system basis and are written down in a format called a curriculum guide. The goals and objectives for the reading program will include statements that indicate what the teacher wants students to learn generally in reading, such as being able to read critically as well as specific statements of what is expected in terms of reading skills.

The portion of the program objectives relating directly to reading skills is referred to as the *scope and sequence* of the reading program. This identifies the specific skills to be taught and gives a suggested order for teaching them. The listing does not constitute an absolute list and sequence of skills but presents one that is based on the best and most current thinking of reading teachers in terms of what should be included in the act of reading. The definition of reading that an individual teacher and school system have developed will definitely influence what is included and how it fits into the scope and sequence.

Some schools develop their scope and sequence of skills by adopting and revising the scope and sequence of a particular basal series to fit their needs. There is nothing wrong with this approach as long as the adopted basal scope and sequence are critically reviewed and revised to fit the needs of the population being served. This means that the school will have to study such matters as the background of the students, their language development, and other factors that would influence the skills that would need to be taught in reading. There are certain advantages to this approach in that adopting a scope and sequence from a particular series being used makes it much easier for teachers to correlate skills instruction with the other components of the reading program. Table 1-1 presents a portion of a scope and sequence from one basal series. One should note that skills are identified and grouped in a suggested order for teaching.

TABLE 1-1. Sample Scope and Sequence from the Houghton Mifflin Reading Series, 1981. Reprinted by permission.

Decoding

D1 Words Unfamiliar in Form
1. Recognizing that a word is missing in spoken context and using that
   context to predict the missing word (D1 · 1)   Level A.
2. Distinguishing letter forms (D1 · 2)   Levels A–B, D.
   a. Recognizing similarities and differences between both capital
      and lower-case letters (D1 · 2a)   Level A.
   b. Recognizing both capital and lower-case letters by name (D1 · 2b)   Levels A–B.
   c. Distinguishing between consonant and vowel letters (D1 · 2c)   Level D.
3. Associating consonant letters with the beginning sounds they
   represent (D · 3)   Levels A–B.
   a. Learning what is meant by the terms "beginning sound" and
      "beginning letter" (D1 · 3a)   Level A.
   b. Understanding that a beginning consonant letter represents a
      sound that is part of a word (D1 · 3b)   Level A.
   c. Distinguishing between beginning consonant sounds (D1 · 3c)   Levels A–B.
4. Learning the sounds represented within words by specific single
   consonant letters (D1 · 4)   Level A.
5. Associating consonant letters with magic key pictures as an aid in
   remembering letter-sound associations (D1 · 5)   Level A.

Comprehension

C2 Getting Meaning of Phrases and Special Expressions
1. Learning that an idiom is a phrase or group of words that is used
   with a special meaning that is different from its literal meaning and
   using context clues to get the appropriate meaning of an idiom
   (C2 ∘ 1)   Levels K–O.
2. Learning that a simile is a fully stated comparison of two things that
   are very different from each other in almost all respects in order to
   stress or highlight one way in which they might be thought to be
   alike (C2 · 2)   Levels K–O.
   a. Learning to recognize a simile by noting words such as like or as
      which may signal a simile (C2 · 2a)   Levels K–O.
   b. Interpreting a simile by determining what things are being com-
      pared and what similarity between the two is being stressed
      (C2 · 2b)   Levels K–O.
   c. Understanding the difference between a simile and an ordinary
      comparison (C2 · 2c)   Levels K–O.
3. Learning that a metaphor is like a simile except that the comparison
   is implied by saying that one thing is another, instead of being fully
   stated and including words such as like or as (C2 · 3)   Levels K–O.
   a. Interpreting a metaphor by determining what things are being
      compared and what similarity between the two is being
      stressed (C2 · 3b)   Level K.
   b. Recognizing that a metaphor may be expressed by a single
      word (C2 · 3b)   Levels L–O.

TABLE 1-1. (Continued)

Comprehension

4. Understanding that personification is a special form of metaphor
   in which a lifeless object or abstract idea is represented as having
   one or more characteristics of a person; recognizing a personification; and deciding why the writer decided to personify the object
   or idea (C2·4)   Levels M–O.

Comprehension Application

CA5 Drawing Conclusions and Making Inferences
1. Listening to a short selection or riddle and answering a question that
   requires drawing a conclusion from given facts (CA5·1)   Levels A–F.
2. Reading a paragraph and answering a question that requires the
   drawing of a conclusion (CA5·2)   Levels B, D–H, J.
3. Understanding what clue words are and noting the clue words that
   point to a conclusion (CA5·3)   Levels B–D.
4. Listening to two or more paragraphs and answering oral and written
   questions that require the drawing of a conclusion; also noting the
   clue words that helped lead to that conclusion (CA5·4)   Level I.
5. Reading one or more paragraphs and answering written questions
   that require the drawing of a conclusion; also noting the clue words
   that helped lead to the conclusion (CA5·5)   Levels J–O.
6. Understanding that a writer often does not state every fact but
   expects the reader to draw certain conclusions based on what the
   writer has stated or implied (CA5·6)   Levels J–O.
   a. Listening to or reading a passage and concluding from what is
      stated or implied in the passage that word or words would be
      stressed in a subsequent sentence to be consistent with the
      meaning of the passage (CA5·6a)   Levels J–O.
   b. Listening to or reading a passage and concluding from what is
      stated or implied how a story character would have spoken a
      subsequent sentence (CA5·6b)   Levels K–O.

Reference and Study

R1 Learning to Use the Library
1. Using the card catalog in a library (R1·1)   Levels L–O.
   a. Learning that a card catalog is a special aid provided in most
      libraries for locating desired books (R1·1a)   Levels L–O.
   b. Understanding that for every book in a library, there are at least
      two cards in the card catalog: one by author's last name, one by
      title and, for some books, a third card by subject matter, all
      filed alphabetically in the drawers of the catalog (R1·1b)   Levels L–O.
   c. Learning how the letters on a label at front of each drawer in
      the card catalog help one to locate a desired card (R1·1c)   Levels L–O.
   d. Learning what kinds of information appear on an author card,
      how the information is arranged, and understanding when to
      use an author card (R1·1d)   Levels L–O.

TABLE 1-1.   (Continued)

Reference and Study	
e. Learning what kinds of information appear on a title card, how the information is arranged, and understanding when to use the title card (R1 · 1e)	Levels L–O.
f. Learning that title cards are filed alphabetically by the first word —other than A, An, or The—in the title (R1 · 1f)	Levels L–O.
g. Learning what kind of information appears on a subject card, how it is arranged, and understanding when to use a subject card (R1 · 1g)	Levels L–O.
2. Understanding the organization of a library (R1 · 2)	Levels M–O.

Needs of Learners

A second major component of the reading-program concept is what is called the "needs of learners." This programmatic aspect includes those characteristics of children that must be considered in planning instruction and those procedures that the teacher must use to obtain certain information about each child's reading in order to develop the program.

The characteristics that must be considered in instructional planning include the learner's background, interests, attitudes, language development, reading ability, and general style of learning. This is the component of the reading program in which one identifies the procedures and techniques that will be used to determine these characteristics in students. One will determine the specific items to look for from the objectives of one's program. This is frequently referred to as the diagnostic aspect of the reading program, but it is more encompassing than the traditional diagnosis because it also enables one to determine the general learning characteristics of the students that will need to be known in order to plan appropriate instructional procedures.

Instructional Procedures

The instructional-procedures portion of the reading program includes the identification of how the teacher will organize for instruction, manage the program, and actually teach reading. One's teaching decisions will be closely related to the program objectives and the needs of one's learners. The instructional procedures of the program will not be specifically determined until one knows the students. The more general policies related to organization and management should be determined on a school-wide or system-wide basis.

The teacher's manual of a basal series will be a valuable resource within this program component. One of the major items to be considered in instructional procedures is their systematic nature. Effective reading instruction is sys-

tematic. As one plans exactly how to teach a specific skill or aspect of reading, one will need to refer to the teacher's manual for assistance.

Resources

Finally, the reading-program concept includes the identification of the materials (books, games, records, films, tapes, and so on) that will be used to accomplish one's objectives. If the teacher knows the objectives of the program and has identified the specific needs of the learners in relation to those objectives, it should be possible to select the materials needed to carry out the appropriate instructional procedures that have been identified. Too frequently, teachers start by selecting materials and trying to make the materials fit the learner. In this type of situation, there is no program, only a set of materials.

The interrelatedness of the components of a reading program is evident. At this point one may still feel uncertain as to how they all work together. That is what the remaining chapters of this text are about.

AN EFFECTIVE READING PROGRAM

Now that the concept of a reading program has been given, the specific characteristics of what an effective reading program is should be discussed. In the field of reading there is an abundance of research on this subject, much of which is contradictory. However, there is enough consistency in terms of identifying the overall characteristics of an effective reading program that they can be considered in this text. The characteristics of an effective reading program can be divided into two categories, programmatic and instructional (9, 10, 11, 12, 22, 24). Every one of these characteristics may not be present to the same degree in every program, but most, if not all, will be found in any effective reading program.

Programmatic Characteristics

Programmatic characteristics relate to the overall reading program operation and includes the following:

1. Strong administrative support and leadership.
2. Teachers involved in the planning.
3. An atmosphere of success expectation.
4. An acceptable pupil-teacher ratio.
5. Dollar resources for personnel and personnel improvement.
6. Teacher aides involved in instructional tasks.

First, an effective reading program has *strong administrative support and leadership.* Just as the teacher makes the difference in how children learn to read within the classroom, the school administration, specifically the principal, makes a difference in how successful the reading program is on a building-level or system-wide basis. The principal must be viewed as the curricular leader at the school. He/she must coordinate the plans of the reading program from staff member to staff member. Special in-service programs will assist principals in assuming this responsibility. From the point of view of an elementary classroom reading teacher, this means that one should work closely with the principal in planning a classroom program. Keeping the principal informed and working through her/him is important as one's instruction is carried out throughout the school year.

An effective reading program has *teachers involved in the planning* and adopts a two- to three-year plan for program improvement. The teacher must assume some responsibility in relation to the program and serve on any committees and attend the meetings when asked to do so. Sometimes teachers will be asked to volunteer to serve on committees. Taking on these duties in the long run will help one in teaching and help the school. It is only through one's input and the input of one's colleagues that the concerns of teachers and the current needs of the students can be dealt with in program planning. Since the teacher is a major component of the reading program, he/she must feel a certain amount of proprietorship over it.

A third important component of an effective reading program is that it operates in *an atmosphere of success expectation* with emphasis on quality of education. Anyone who has started a college or high-school class in which the instructor mentioned how hard the course was going to be, or that it was unlikely that everyone would pass, remembers how difficult it was for anyone to succeed. The same situation will hold true in the reading program in the elementary school. If one wants children to learn to read, then one must *expect* them to learn and create an atmosphere that conveys this expectation. Only the teachers and principal working together can do this.

Within the reading program, each teacher must have *an acceptable pupil-teacher ratio.* This means that each teacher must have the number of students that will permit the teacher's skills to accommodate their needs. This does not mean that one should have only one group. The times when this possibility would occur are really nonexistent because within any group there are always individual needs to be met.

The effective reading program also uses its *dollar resources for personnel and personnel improvement.* If the teacher is the most significant factor that influences how children are going to learn to read, the school should spend its dollar resources on helping the teacher improve her/his teaching skills. Money spent on more materials and hardware is not the answer to program improvement. The major funds available for the reading program need to be spent on effective in-service and other professional-development opportunities that will help teachers improve their skills of teaching.

Teacher's aides or adequate support personnel are viewed as an important part of the effective reading program and should be *involved in instructional tasks.* Aides should help with directing practice activities or doing follow-up under the teacher's direction.

These characteristics indicate what is important on a programmatic level in an effective reading program. The classroom reading teacher must be concerned about these items even though, at times, one may feel that they are not as important as the instruction. They can and will influence what happens within one's classroom.

Instructional Characteristics

As already pointed out, there is no one best method of teaching reading and the teacher is the most significant factor in influencing how children learn to read. But there are also four additional instructional characteristics of an effective reading program that must be considered.

First, an effective reading program *identifies the reading skills that should be taught.* There is agreement among teachers as to which skills will be covered; these skills are not absolutes. Some may be appropriate for some children and some may have to be changed or added as we learn new information about reading. What is important is that the school agrees to a listing of skills and is willing to use it as a set of guidelines to direct what will be taught. This is a portion of the "Objectives" section of the reading-program concept that was presented earlier.

The second instructional characteristic of the effective reading program is that the school agrees to *a sequence for teaching the reading skills* that it has identified. Again, this is not an absolute sequence, but it is the best that can be determined at a particular time. The needs of the children may necessitate changing the sequence but at least there is some general agreement about the one selected that will serve as a guide for the program.

An effective reading program also has an *agreed-upon level of mastery that leads to continuous diagnosis* for all learners. This component of the program gives the classroom reading teacher the tools needed to monitor continuously each child's progress in reading. It is essential for doing an effective job of planning instruction based on the needs of learners. This characteristic of an effective reading program relates to the "Needs of Learners" section of our reading-program definition.

The fourth and final instructional characteristic of an effective reading program is that there are ample opportunities for *direct instruction* by the teacher. Research evidence leads one to the conclusion that the achievement of learners is directly related to the amount of direct instructional time provided by the teacher in the reading program (10, 21, 22). In other words, if students are to learn to read then the program must provide enough opportunities for

direct teaching and not just give learners one series after another of practice-oriented assignments.

These four instructional characteristics along with the six programmatic characteristics that were mentioned before must be considered as critical elements to be included in any reading program. The concept of a reading program that was developed earlier in this chapter accounts for and includes these components. While there are many effective ways to approach reading instruction—any of which are likely to be successful in producing effective readers—they must in some way include procedures that incorporate these characteristics. The remaining portions of this chapter and the other chapters in the text will be devoted to developing the concepts and procedures needed by the elementary classroom reading teacher to become the type of teacher who operates with a program concept that includes the critical characteristics that have been described.

DIAGNOSTIC TEACHING

The development and operation of an effective classroom reading program requires that the teacher operate in a continuing role as a decision maker. Thinking about classroom reading instruction within a framework such as this gives the teacher the needed structure and direction to continuously determine the needs of each individual student and decide upon appropriate instructional strategies to help the student improve in reading regardless of his/her level of functioning. This type of teaching is called *diagnostic teaching.*

The diagnostic teaching of reading is nothing more than a systematic way of determining the needs of individual students and providing the learning opportunities that will help the students improve their reading ability. As the name implies, diagnosis takes place during teaching with testing serving as a part of the diagnostic teaching process. The processes of diagnostic teaching are equally dependent upon diagnosis through testing and diagnosis through teaching, and this will be discussed in greater detail later.

Steps in Diagnostic Teaching

One of the first things to learn about the process of diagnostic teaching is the steps involved. There are five basic steps (4), and Figure 1-2 illustrates how these steps function together. Step 1 is to *gather relevant background information.* In this step the teacher is concerned about finding out what the students are able to do in reading in relation to the objectives of the program. This is the major step involving testing in the process because at this point the teacher is usually trying to gather information on an entire class of students and it is

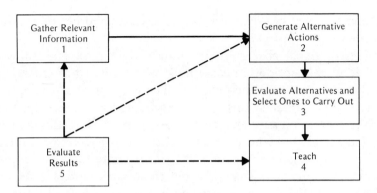

FIGURE 1-2. Diagnostic Teaching Model.

more efficient to use tests than rely on informal observations or work samples alone.

After gathering the relevant background information, the teacher should examine it and *generate alternative actions* (Step 2). At this point one is concerned about deciding what to teach, how to organize to teach, and how one will teach. The possibilities are numerous. The teacher must examine his/her scope and sequence of reading skills along with the needs of the students to determine what is important to teach. What one is trying to do is to consider a number of different instructional activities that one could do to guide the students to improved reading.

After considering several possibilities, the teacher must make a decision as to which ones are best and *evaluate alternatives and select ones to carry out* (Step 3). The decisions one makes at this point are based on

1. The needs of the students.
2. What one considers the best approach for them at this time.
3. What one can do best in teaching after considering the first two points.

Completion of Step 3 does not insure correct answers. It only insures that the teacher will have considered various types of information in making his/her decisions.

Next, one is ready to do what the entire process is about—*teach* (Step 4). The fourth step requires the teacher to put into action the alternatives that were selected in Step 3. This is where one will employ diagnosis through teaching.

After completing one's instruction, it is time to move on to Step 5 and *evaluate results*. What did the children do? Is there evidence that they have learned what one has taught? Does something need to be retaught? Does the teacher need more information? Does the teacher need to generate new alternatives? These and other questions must be answered. By examining Figure 2,

one can see that there are three possible directions to go. The results can indicate that one needs to reteach, that one needs more or different information, or that one needs new or changed alternatives. The direction that the teacher goes will depend on what she/he learns when evaluating the results.

Diagnostic teaching is an ongoing process that allows the teacher to be thinking constantly in terms of the students' needs. A diagnostic classroom reading teacher will learn to internalize these five steps and do them automatically as a part of effective teaching.

Diagnostic Teaching and the Reading Program Concept

One should now think back to the definition of a reading program presented earlier in this chapter. How does it relate to the concept of diagnostic teaching?

The objectives of one's reading program make one aware of what one wants to accomplish and gives direction in terms of deciding some of the types of relevant background information that are needed. The needs of learners help the teacher to identify how to find out the relevant information and what learning characteristics need to be considered in generating alternatives and selecting the ones to carry out. The instructional procedures and resource components aid the teacher in generating the alternatives and in teaching.

The concept of a reading program presented in this book and the process of diagnostic teaching are very compatible. Diagnostic teaching sets up the framework that helps insure that the teacher has a reading program and not just a collection of materials. Diagnostic teaching is not a method of teaching but a way of thinking about and organizing for instruction. By developing this style of thinking one is in a position of always being able to approach reading instruction from a programmatic point of view.

The Basal Reader in the Diagnostic Reading Program

As already stated, a basal series will probably be used by most elementary teachers to teach reading. The important thing is that the teacher learn how to utilize the resources of the basal series to achieve the reading-program concept and implement diagnostic teaching. Teachers are familiar with one or more basal series and the resources that are available in them. Table 1-2 shows how the resources of a basal series fit into the steps of diagnostic teaching. As one can see by examining the listing, the resources of the basal series provide the teacher much of what is needed to help make the necessary decisions in a diagnostic reading program. While the resources from series to series vary, the items listed are usually available. As one works to develop skills in teaching reading, it will become more apparent how to use the resources of basal series to implement the diagnostic teaching concept.

TABLE 1-2.   The Basal Series and Diagnostic Teaching.

Steps in Diagnostic Teaching	Basal Resources
1. Gather Relevant Background Information	Scope and sequence
	Tests (pre-tests, post-tests, placement tests)
	Group-skill tests
	Record cards
2. Generate Alternative Actions	Teacher's manual
	Scope and sequence
	Workbook
	Pupil's book
	Other supplementary materials
3. Evaluate Alternatives and Select Ones to Carry Out	Information obtained from the resources by Step 1 helps one do this.
4. Teach	Teacher's manual
	Pupil's books
	Workbooks
	Supplementary materials
5. Evaluate Results	Objectives in scope and sequence
	Tests, group and individual
	Records of progress

THE ROLE OF THE CLASSROOM TEACHER IN DIAGNOSTIC TEACHING

As noted before, the classroom teacher is the single most important factor in the classroom reading program, and research supports this (2). In a diagnostic reading program the teacher becomes even more important because of the need for him/her to make many decisions about objectives, needs of learners, instructional procedures, and resources. The classroom teacher must assume this key responsibility of decision maker.

As a decision maker in the diagnostic reading program, the teacher must consider all the alternatives related to meeting the needs of individuals. The decision-making role of the teacher is the one that transforms the basal readers and other materials available for instruction into a program rather than just a collection of materials. Learning how to make the decisions necessary in such a reading program is the primary emphasis of this book.

Any decision-making process requires an element of judgment. This includes the teacher's decision-making role in the diagnostic reading program. It, too, requires teacher judgment. Tests, instructional materials, curriculum guides, and other resources are available for the teacher's use, but certain elements of judgment must be employed by the teacher in making the needed decisions. For example, a child's reading teacher will frequently need to decide what level of material should be used for instruction. The teacher will use certain test results, but he/she must also rely on his/her judgment through observations of the child's work in actual reading situations.

The teacher's role in the diagnostic reading program is a significant one as a decision maker who must make use of judgment to meet the needs of each individual student. The diagnostic reading teacher will be called upon frequently to make all types of decisions.

DIAGNOSTIC TEACHING VERSUS DIAGNOSTIC TESTING

The diagnostic reading program uses both teaching and testing situations for diagnostic purposes. The tests provide the teacher valuable resources for getting information in a less subjective manner than does teaching. Tests also make it possible for the teacher to gather a larger quantity of needed information in a shorter period of time. In this sense, the tests help to make the teacher's role of gathering relevant information a more efficient one.

Teaching is also a source of valuable information to the teacher in diagnostic teaching. The results of each teaching or practice activity allow the teacher to know how a student is learning in a particular aspect of reading. By utilizing teaching activities diagnostically, the teacher is continuously assessing each student's progress.

Too often teachers think of the diagnostic aspect of diagnostic teaching as only the testing. When this happens the tests become too important and teachers soon find themselves feeling that they are doing more testing than teaching. An effective diagnostic teacher will want to avoid this by making certain that teaching and testing are so combined that one can get the maximum diagnostic value from them.

KNOWLEDGE AND SKILLS NEEDED BY THE DIAGNOSTIC CLASSROOM READING TEACHER

The effective classroom reading teacher needs a variety of information and skills to make the decisions required in the diagnostic reading program, including the following:

1. An understanding of the reading process.
2. The ability to use basic assessment procedures.
3. Techniques for organizing a class for instruction.
4. Skill in selecting and using appropriate instructional strategies and materials.
5. Management skills.

Each of these areas includes a number of components. Developing the needed knowledge and skills related to each component is important.

The Reading Process

Reading is a complex process. Some authorities define reading from a skills point of view (17), including elements of decoding and comprehension. Decoding refers to the ability of the reader to figure out words and associate the correct sounds with appropriate symbols. Comprehension is the ability of the reader to associate meaning with these symbols. Usually included in the skills definition of reading is the category of study skills, the tool skills of reading which include reading graphs, maps, charts, and other items. From the skills point of view, each of these broad categories has many subskills (17).

Another way to think about reading is from a psycholinguistic point of view (18, 19, 20). From this standpoint, reading is viewed as an interaction between thought and language. The field of psycholinguistics has added much to our understanding of reading but has not provided us with a complete understanding of the process.

As reading is understood today, it appears to be a skills process that is based on language and thinking. While skills are important, they are not an end in themselves. Viewing reading in these terms means that there will be skill teaching that will consider the reader's language and thinking base. Language is the foundation on which thinking and reading are built.

In this text it is assumed that the teacher has already developed some background in the reading process. From previous course work, the teacher has read about and discussed various definitions of reading and has probably started to develop her/his own definition of reading. The teacher will need to draw from this information in using this text and developing her/his skills as a diagnostic reading teacher.

Basic Assessment Procedures

The diagnostic classroom reading teacher must have a thorough understanding of what to assess as well as how to assess. The areas that need to be considered in assessment include interests, attitudes, reading levels, skill development, oral language development, background, and other related factors such as health, vision, and hearing. The procedures used for assessment must be appropriate to classroom use. Developing an understanding of these procedures will help the teacher account for the reading-program component known as "needs of learners." Chapters 2, 3, and 4 will help one develop the knowledge and skills needed in this area.

Organizing for Instruction

An effective classroom reading teacher is organized for instruction. This involves knowing how to meet individual needs, keeping track of individual stu-

dent progress, and having materials organized so that they can be readily used. Chapters 5, 6, and 7 are devoted to these topics.

Instructional Strategies

The teacher using this text has already learned many instructional procedures for teaching reading that will be of benefit in continuing to develop one's skill as a diagnostic reading teacher. In this text one will learn more about how to use these procedures diagnostically and how to make them vital components of an effective management system. Chapter 8 will cover this area.

Management

The key to effective operation of the diagnostic reading program is a sound management system. Management entails much more than record keeping. It involves developing time schedules, promoting independence on the part of learners, utilizing instructional strategies appropriately, and taking advantage of all areas of the curriculum where reading can be developed. Chapters 8, 9, and 10 will help the teacher develop the knowledge and skill needed in this area.

SUMMARY

Children and young adults in the United States are reading better today than they have ever read before. This is attributable to the single most important factor in the instructional program—the teacher.

The reading program in the elementary school is a systematic plan for teaching reading that includes *objectives, needs of learners, instructional procedures,* and *resources.* This program should center around classroom instruction and should not follow a remedial concept. There are certain programmatic and instructional characteristics of the effective reading program that should be considered in deciding what a school will do to improve its reading instruction.

The framework within which the classroom reading program should operate is the diagnostic teaching concept, which is an ongoing five-step process that includes (1) gathering relevant background information, (2) generating alternative actions, (3) evaluating and selecting alternatives to carry out, (4) teaching, and (5) evaluating the results to determine the next steps needed. Diagnostic teaching is a systematic process that depends on the teacher as a decision maker who uses teaching and testing as diagnostic tools.

An effective diagnostic teacher understands the reading process, uses a variety of assessment procedures, has many organizational patterns to follow, is able to select from a variety of instructional strategies and materials appropri-

ate to student needs, and has a management system that encompasses more than record keeping.

THOUGHT AND DISCUSSION QUESTIONS

1. How would one defend the statement "Children are reading better today than ever before"?
2. How does the concept of diagnostic teaching compare to the way reading was being taught in the past?
3. Why is it important for the classroom reading teacher to accept the reading-program concept as being more than a basal reader or a collection of materials?
4. How can the diagnostic teaching of reading be implemented in an elementary school? What factors will influence its success?

APPLYING WHAT YOU HAVE LEARNED

1. Spend a portion of a day in an elementary school. Observe the teachers, talk to the students, and interview the principal and resource personnel. Try to find out how many of the characteristics of an effective reading program are present.
2. Select two different basal series. Examine them to determine what resources they have available and make a chart like the "Basal Series and Diagnostic Teaching" table in this chapter to show how these resources will relate to the diagnostic teaching concept. Is one series better than the other for diagnostic teaching?
3. Make an outline of what you need to know in order to become a diagnostic classroom reading teacher. Indicate for yourself the areas that you feel need the greatest improvement. Use this as a guide for yourself as you work in this course.

BIBLIOGRAPHY

1. Aukerman, Robert C. *The Basal Reader Approach to Reading*, New York: John Wiley & Sons, Inc., 1981.
2. Bond, Guy L., and Dykstra, Robert. "The Cooperative Research Program in First Grade Reading." *Reading Research Quarterly*, 2 (summer 1967).
3. Copperman, Paul. *The Literacy Hoax.* New York: William Morrow and Company, Inc., 1978.
4. Cooper, J. David, et al. *Decision Making for the Diagnostic Teacher.* New York: Holt, Rinehart & Winston, 1972.

5. Falletta, John, and Sheffield, James. *Pupil Reading Achievement in New York City.* New York City Public Schools, Dec. 1978.

6. Farr, Roger; Tuinman, Jaap; and Rowls, Michael. *Reading Achievement in the United States: Then and Now.* Bloomington, Ind.: Indiana University, 1974.

7. Farr, Roger, and Blomenberg, Paula. "Contrary to Popular Opinion . . ." in *Thoughts on Reading.* River Forest, Ill.: Laidlaw Brothers, No. 7, June 1979.

8. Gadway, Charles, and Wilson, H. A. *Functional Literacy: Basic Reading Performance.* Denver: National Assessment of Educational Progress, 1976.

9. Guthrie, John T., et al. *A Study of the Locus and Nature of Reading Problems in the Elementary School.* Final Report, ED 127 568, 1976.

10. Huitt, William G., and Segars, John K. "Characteristics of Effective Classrooms." Research for Better Schools, Inc., Philadelphia, Oct. 1980.

11. *The Information Base for Reading.* U.S.O.E., Mimeographed, Project No. 0-9031, 1971.

12. Kean, Michael H., et al. *What Works in Reading?* Office of Research and Evaluation, School District of Philadelphia, 1979.

13. Maeroff, Gene. "Reading Achievement of Children in Indiana Found As Good As in '44." *The New York Times*, Apr. 15, 1976, p. 10.

14. Oklahoma State Department of Education. *Oklahoma Educational Status Study: Reading and Math Grades 3, 6, 9, 12, Year 1978-79,* 1979, ED 179 587.

15. Oklahoma State Department of Education. *Oklahoma Educational Status Study: Reading and Math Grades 3, 6, 9, 12, School Year 1978,* 1978, ED 179 588.

16. Osborne, Jean. "The Purposes, Uses and Contents of Workbooks and Some Guidelines for Teachers and Publishers." Champaign, Ill.: Center for the Study of Reading, Aug. 1981, Report No. 27.

17. Otto, Wayne, et al. *Focused Reading Instruction.* Reading, Mass.: Addison-Wesley Publishing Co., Inc., 1974.

18. Ruddell, Robert B. "Psycholinguistic Implications for a Systems of Communication Model," in Harry Singer and Robert B. Ruddell, eds., *Theoretical Models and Processes of Reading,* 2nd ed. Newark, Del.: International Reading Association, 1976.

19. Singer, Harry, and Ruddell, Robert B., eds. *Theoretical Models and Processes of Reading,* 2nd ed. Newark, Del.: International Reading Association, 1976.

20. Smith, Frank. *Reading Without Nonsense.* New York: Teachers College Press, 1978.

21. Smith, B. Othaniel. *Research in Teacher Education: A Symposium.* Englewood Cliffs, N. J.: Prentice-Hall, 1978.

22. Stallings, June. "Allocated Academic Learning Time Revisited or Beyond Time on Task." *Educational Researcher*, Vol. 9, No. 11 (Dec. 1980), pp. 11–16.

23. Tierney, Robert J., and Lapp, Diane. *National Assessment of Educational Progress in Reading.* Newark, Del.: International Reading Association, 1979.

24. Venezky, Richard L., and Winfield, Linda F. *Schools That Succeed Beyond Expectation in Teaching Reading.* Final Report, NIE Grant, NIE-G-78-0027, University of Delaware, 1979.

FOR FURTHER READING

Cheek, Martha Collins, and Earl H. Cheek, Jr. *Diagnostic Prescriptive Reading Instruction,* Dubuque, Iowa: William C. Brown Company, Publishers, 1980, Chapters 1 and 2.

Harris, Larry A., and Carl B. Smith. *Reading Instruction: Diagnostic Teaching in the Classroom,* 2nd ed. New York: Holt, Rinehart & Winston, 1976, Chapters 2 and 3.

chapter 2

what classroom teachers need to know about diagnosis and tests

objectives

As a result of reading this chapter, one will be able to

1. Relate to classroom instruction existing evidence on factors influencing reading.
2. Identify the types of information needed by the diagnostic classroom reading teacher.
3. Identify and define various types of reading tests.
4. Identify, define, and interpret selected types of reading test scores.
5. Discuss with parents ideas related to the interpretation of tests.

overview

The types of information and background that are needed by the effective diagnostic classroom reading teacher are identified and discussed. These items are presented in relationship to the diagnostic teaching model introduced in Chapter 1. The evidence relative to factors that influence reading is reviewed with emphasis on its relationship to the classroom reading program.

Classroom teachers must first have a certain amount of information about tests in order to use them effectively. Types of tests will be identi-

fied and defined. The information needed to interpret the tests effectively will be presented. Ideas on how to discuss test results with parents will be reviewed. The thrust of this chapter will be to help classroom teachers develop a working knowledge about tests. This will serve as background to the steps of diagnostic teaching.

An effective diagnostic classroom reading teacher needs to know what information is needed to organize and operate a reading program. She/he must not only know what information is needed but also must have efficient ways to obtain it. In addition, the teacher must have some understanding of tests and testing in order to use these tools and interpret the results.

A major concern for the classroom reading teacher is understanding those factors that influence reading. These include vision, hearing, language development, family and educational background, general health, and emotional factors. Each of these contributes to a student's success in reading and must be understood by the classroom teacher. Efficient, effective teaching of reading is based on the teacher understanding the factors that influence reading and knowing how to use the information in planning and implementing instruction. Having this background is essential before the diagnostic decision-making process can begin.

FACTORS RELATED TO GROWTH IN READING

Reading growth is dependent upon many different factors. When the research in this area is examined the major conclusion that can be drawn is that no single factor creates the condition for successful reading nor does any single factor cause reading difficulties (26). It is a combination of factors interacting together that create the conditions for a person to learn to read successfully. At the same time it can be said that it is a combination of interacting factors that appears to cause certain reading problems. Many times it is almost impossible to pinpoint the specific cause of an individual's inability to learn to read.

The research in this area is voluminous. No attempt will be made to present complete coverage. A summary of the major conclusions that can be drawn regarding the most significant factors related to reading growth will be presented.

At this point in one's development a diagnostic classroom reading teacher should know the relationship of the various factors to learning to read. He/she must be concerned about how to use this information in planning an effective reading program.

Visual Factors

Visual factors to be considered in relation to reading include visual acuity and visual discrimination. Visual acuity refers to how well the student is able to see, his/her clarity of sight. Visual discrimination refers to the student's ability to detect likenesses and differences.

It is obviously important for the individual learning to read to have good, clear vision in order to see the print. While some research suggests that certain types of visual defects are more related to reading difficulty than are others (4,

9, 10, 26, 33), no clear pattern of evidence exists suggesting that a specific visual problem creates a condition that leads to poor reading (28).

A diagnostic classroom teacher should observe students for signs of visual problems, such as the following:

1.   Tilting the head to read.
2.   Holding the book too close to face.
3.   Frequent rubbing of the eyes.
4.   Moving the head while reading.
5.   Extreme tension or nervousness while doing visual work.

If these or other signs are noted in students, they should be referred to the school nurse or other appropriate person for visual screening. It is very important that the teacher makes certain that the students have the best vision possible so as to facilitate learning conditions. All children should have periodic visual screening throughout their elementary school years to detect potential problems before they become too serious.

Visual discrimination is important to reading (23) but it must focus on the discrimination of letters and words not geometric shapes. Therefore, assessing a student's ability to discriminate various designs, shapes and/or patterns is not going to tell the teacher anything of real value related to reading. The assessing and/or training of visual discrimination should be done using materials comprised of letters and words.

Auditory Factors

When considering auditory factors and learning to read, one must first distinguish between auditory acuity—the ability to hear—and auditory discrimination—the ability to detect slight differences between sounds. There is some evidence that impaired auditory acuity may affect the child's ability to learn to read (4, 32). A child who cannot hear adequately may not be able to follow directions, listen, or discriminate sounds. This could have a definite influence on his/her ability to learn decoding skills as well as learning other general skills where listening is required. While the conclusions to be drawn concerning auditory factors in reading are not absolute, the diagnostic teacher should look for signs that the children are having difficulty hearing or discriminating sounds. Again, one should be concerned about eliminating any problems that might produce conditions unfavorable to learning.

In observing students for possible hearing problems one should look for the following signs:

1.   Frequent complaints about earache or hearing difficulties.
2.   Moving close to the person speaking.

3. Tilting an ear toward person speaking.
4. A frequent misunderstanding of directions.
5. Constant requests for directions to be repeated.

If a repeated pattern of signs of hearing problems is detected, the child should be seen by the school nurse for possible referral to a physician.

Language Development

There is a definite relationship between a child's language development and his/her ability to learn to read (18, 27). Of all the factors that influence reading, language development may be one of the most significant (26). A diagnostic reading teacher needs to be aware of the oral language development of one's students. Do they have good speaking vocabularies? Are their listening skills well developed? Do they come from a language background that is different from the one in which they are being taught (such as Spanish or a regional dialect, for example)? Many times students will need instruction in oral language before they can be taught to read more effectively (28). For this reason an examination of oral language skills is a vital part of the diagnostic teaching of reading. Through observations and informal testing procedures the teacher will want to assess the oral language background of his/her students. The checklist presented in Figure 2-1 can be used to record the information one gains from such observations.

Informal observations of students are the best way to assess their oral language skills. Situations can be set up where small groups of children are playing, telling stories (not reading), or working together on some project. The teacher should have a checklist on each student in the group. In observing them, one should concentrate on one or two areas at a time, such as vocabulary. Then the results can be recorded on a sheet. It may take several days or weeks to get all the information needed, but using situations like this allows for better observations of a student's realistic use of language. The teacher should extensively observe children's speech wherever language is used freely such as in the playground, lunchroom, halls, or other places.

Background and Environmental Factors

In discussing a child's ability, his/her family and educational background must be considered. Both will have an effect on the way he/she learns to read (4, 30).

The educational experience that a student has prior to entering the teacher's class can influence how he/she will learn to read. A teacher needs to know what has been taught and how it was taught. A student's reading behavior and

Name _____ Grade _____ Date _____

Teacher _____

	Yes	No	Comments
Speaking			
1. Speaks in complete sentences.			
2. Uses correct sentence constructions in speaking			
3. Uses a variety of sentence constructions in speaking.			
4. Vocabulary Above Average Below Average Average			
5. Uses concrete words in speaking—car, tree, etc.			
6. Uses more abstract words in speaking—on, in, under			
Listening			
7. Follows simple directions.			
8. Follows more complex directions.			
9. Comprehends at least 75% of a short story.			
10. Has good listening vocabulary.			

FIGURE 2-1. Oral Language Checklist.

attitude can be greatly influenced by previous teaching. Much of the information the teacher obtains relative to educational background will have to be gathered through examining records and informal discussions with previous teachers and the principal.

Background in terms of the types of experiences a child has at home influences his language development. The home environment can definitely affect the way a child learns. A home that is filled with tension, frustration, and conflict may produce a child who has difficulty learning. However, one cannot conclude that a child's background or his/her home environment is the single cause of his reading difficulty or inability to learn to read.

A classroom teacher can do little to control background or environmental factors. The teacher must be aware of them and try to account for them when planning instruction. Just because a child comes from a certain type of family

background or environment, one cannot assume that she/he will or will not learn to read.

Health and Nutrition Factors

An unhealthy or hungry child cannot work as well as she/he should. A child who misses lots of school due to illness of any type misses the opportunity to learn. A child who is hungry has difficulty paying attention and focusing on the task at hand. Often glandular misfunction, especially that associated with thyroid deficiency, has been associated with difficulties in learning to read (29). Health and nutrition factors can affect the way a child learns, but they should not be assumed to be the sole cause of a reading problem (4, 26).

It is the responsibility of the classroom teacher to look for signs of health and nutrition problems—not diagnose them. If there is a suspicion of any type of problem in these areas, one should talk with the parents and suggest that the child have a check-up by the family physician.

Emotional Factors

An emotionally well-adjusted child is likely to learn more readily than one who is not (4, 30). When reading difficulties and emotional difficulties of various types are studied it is hard to say which came first, the reading problem or the emotional difficulty (26, 30). A classroom teacher should also watch for signs of emotional difficulties. If these are present in a child the teacher should refer him/her to the school nurse, guidance counselor, or child's parents.

Emotional difficulties can be recognized by signs of moodiness, extreme shyness, sudden or unusual changes in behavior, or being withdrawn. In any case where there appears to be an emotional difficulty the teacher should talk with the principal or other appropriate person in the school. Caution should always be exercised in jumping to conclusions about a child's emotional difficulty affecting his/her reading.

INFORMATION NEEDED TO ORGANIZE A DIAGNOSTICALLY BASED READING PROGRAM

Diagnostic teaching of reading is based on a continuous process of the teacher carefully examining and evaluating each student's growth in reading and altering instruction in light of what is learned. Sometimes the information is gained from testing and sometimes it comes from teacher observations. When a reading program is initially developed for a child the teacher must look at most of the significant areas, if not all, to have the appropriate information for

making decisions about what to teach and how to teach it. The following are the areas that the classroom reading teacher must understand and examine in planning the diagnostic reading program:

1. Reading levels.
2. Skill development.
3. Interests and attitudes.
4. Capacity.

These four areas coupled with the teacher's knowledge of the factors that influence reading provide the classroom teacher with appropriate information to plan and implement a highly individualized reading program for each student.

Reading Levels

A student has three reading levels about which a teacher must be concerned:

Independent Reading Level.   This is the level at which a student can read with ease and comprehend what is read. As the term *independent* implies, the student reads on his/her own without help from the teacher or anyone else.

Instructional Reading Level.   The level at which a student is placed for instruction in reading is the instructional reading level. At this point the student misses some words and does not comprehend the material with 100 per cent accuracy. At this level the student needs instruction from the teacher to be completely successful and continue to grow in reading ability. Students should be placed for basal instruction at this level.

Frustration Reading Level.   At this point the student's reading breaks down because the material to be read is too difficult. The student misses too many words and fails to comprehend most of what has been read. A student given material at his/her frustration level will not grow in reading ability.

Reading levels are usually discussed in terms of grade level, such as first-grade level, second-grade level, and so on. This is simply a way of indicating the student's reading performance in relation to material difficulty. In some schools the materials used are numbered in sequence and the students' reading levels given accordingly. The number does not reflect the grade level but rather the level or number of the book the student is reading.

Understanding that a student has three different reading levels is very important. Sometimes a student will have a range of reading levels as shown in Table 2-1.

Sue, a second grader, is independent at levels one and two. This means that she can comfortably read and comprehend by herself at both levels. Jeff

TABLE 2-1. Reading Levels.

Student	Grade	Independent Reading Grade Level	Instructional Reading Grade Level	Frustration Reading Grade Level
Sue	2	1–2	3	4
Jeff	4	4	5–6	7
Ann	6	3	4–5	6

can handle material instructionally at the fifth- or sixth-grade level while Ann, a sixth grader, can read instructionally at either the fourth- or fifth-grade level. For an individual student to have such a range of reading levels is very normal and must be considered by the classroom teacher when planning instruction.

Determining a student's reading levels is one of the most crucial elements in planning an effective reading program. Too many learners are placed in materials that are either too difficult or too easy for them to read. In either case, little or no growth will take place.

There are many ways to determine a student's reading levels. Some of the more commonly used ones include the following:

The Informal Reading Inventory (IRI)

The IRI is a series of passages graded in difficulty. Each passage has a set of questions for checking comprehension. This test is the best way to accurately determine a student's reading levels (11). Even though it has to be administered individually, it is the classroom teacher's most useful diagnostic instrument.

Basal Placement Tests

Most basal reading series have group placement tests that accompany them. These tests can be administered to the entire group at one time but frequently misplace children in materials that are either too difficult or too easy.

Informal Assessments

Informal assessments are materials that are developed by the teacher. These include a set of passages taken from the reading materials that are available for instruction. The teacher then has the student read the material and answer some questions. This procedure is much like the IRI but is much less structured. The teacher can think of this as "trying on" a piece of reading material to see if it fits.

TABLE 2-2. Sample Cloze Test* Reprinted by permission.

Directions to the teacher:
Discuss the answers (following the paragraph) with the children and explain how to find clues or exact words in the context. Lessons on function words and their role in grammatical structure will be easily motivated by these exercises. A copy of the test is in Appendix II.

Directions to the children:
Put one word in each blank. Try to find out what word goes in each blank by looking at the other words in the paragraph. If you can't figure out one answer, skip over it and fill in as many blanks as you can. Then go back and fill in the ones you didn't do.

Bill and Sally live in the same house. They are brother and _____. They both go to _____. When they come home _____ school, they sit at _____ table and have milk _____ cookies. Then they have _____ to play outdoors until _____. When it is time _____ dinner, their mother calls _____. They eat dinner with _____ mother and help her _____ dishes because she _____ very tired from working.

Answers: sister, school, from, the, and, time, dinner, for, them, their, wash, is

---

*Taken from Potter and Rae, *Informal Reading Diagnosis*, 2nd ed. (Englewood Cliffs, N.J.: Prentice-Hall, Inc., 1981) p. 112 (24).

Cloze Tests

Cloze tests are made up of a series of passages in which certain words have been deleted. The students read the passages and write in the word. Following some given criteria, the teacher is able to determine the students' reading levels. This procedure can be utilized in a group. A sample cloze test is presented in Table 2-2.

Procedures for placement will be discussed in more detail in Chapter 3.

Specific Skill Development

One aspect of a student's reading growth is his/her specific skill development. As a student grows in his/her overall ability to read, he/she also grows in his/her ability to use specific skills. However, she/he may not grow evenly in both of these areas. In other words, a student might reach one level in her/his ability to read but not the same level in skill development and vice versa. Learning specific skills does not insure growth in reading, but because the more effective reading programs systematically emphasize skills (13), this is an area that should be understood and assessed by the teacher. In developing one's skill as a diagnostic classroom reading teacher, it is necessary to work to understand the relationship between specific skill development and actual reading growth.

There are four areas of specific skill development that the teacher should understand and assess in planning a classroom reading program. These include

Tina Is Given a Skills Test to Determine Needs.

Tina's Teacher Checks Her Reading to See If She Uses the Skills in Reading.

prereading, word attack or decoding, comprehension, and study skills. If a review of the content of any or all of these areas is needed, one should refer to one of the references at the end of this chapter under the section "For Further Reading."

Specific skill development may be assessed in many ways. Group tests, individual tests, games, work samples, or actual reading may be used to determine a student's ability to use skills. Caution should be exercised, however, in testing skills in isolation and not looking to see how the student actually uses the skill in a real reading situation. Too much emphasis on skills in isolation is just as bad or worse than no emphasis on skills at all. One should remember that the only reason for a student to learn a specific reading skill is to become a better reader. If skills are learned in isolation and never used in reading, there is no reason to learn them.

Interests and Attitudes

Determining a student's interests in and attitudes about reading is an important component of the diagnostic reading program. Although it is not possible to always give a student just what he or she wants to read, knowledge about interests and attitudes can be helpful in selecting materials for students, determining groupings, and generally planning instruction. The procedures used for gathering this information need not be elaborate. Several simple techniques will enable a teacher to gather the needed information with minimal time and effort.

Observations.   Observing and listening to students as they work, play, eat, and talk will instruct the teacher about their interests and their attitudes. Routine school occurrences can be used in making observations or situations set up where students must make some kinds of choices. The teacher can put out magazines and books on different topics. One should notice which ones students select. The students should be given the opportunity to do certain types of activities—read, listen to records, view filmstrips, do art and craft work, or play games. By observing the choices made, the teacher can learn more about a student's interests and attitudes.

Records of observations can be kept simply by having a sheet on one's desk like the one in Table 2-3. Observations can be noted on it for future reference.

Checklists.   A teacher-developed checklist can be used to record information about student interests and attitudes. A type of checklist like the one in Table 2-4 can be used by the teacher to structure observations or it can be adapted for students. Whenever a checklist is being completed by students with limited reading ability the items should be read aloud by the teacher to insure that student responses are not influenced by lack of reading ability.

TABLE 2-3.   Sample Observation Sheet.

Names	Interests	Attitudes
Mark	Sports	+most of the time
Beth		
Tim	Space travel; wants to fly	+ always happy
Fred		
George		
Ron		
Lou	Has no *real* interests	− never seems to like school
		+ = positive − = negative

Interest Inventories.   Another way to gather information about a student's interests and attitudes is through some type of inventory like the one presented in Table 2-5. There are many such inventories available in other texts (24) or the teacher can construct her/his own. The main thing to keep in mind is that the inventory should be simple to use and at the same time provide useful information for planning the reading program.

Incomplete Sentences.   Another version of the interest inventory is the incomplete-sentence technique. Students are given sentence starters and are asked to complete them. This procedure is sometimes helpful in determining student attitudes because it is possible with the sentence starters to get students to express their feelings more. Table 2-6 presents a sample set of incomplete sentences.

Collage.   Art techniques are also very valuable in helping the teacher determine the interests and attitudes of students. A simple, enjoyable activity is to give students magazines and a piece of construction paper and have them make a collage about what they like to do, where they like to go, what they would like to be, and so on. This activity requires no artistic ability but at the same time provides a creative, fun way to gain some important information about student interests and attitudes. From looking at the collage pre-

TABLE 2-4.   Sample Teacher Observation Checklist to Determine Student Interests and Attitudes.

	Jackie	Mark	Jeff	Lou Ann	Melissa	Sammy	Rhonda	David	Betty
1. Interests									
Animals									
Sports									
Space travel									
Mystery									
Adventure									
Music									
Art									
Dancing									
————									
————									
2. Enjoys reading									
3. Reads during free time									
4. Brings books to school									
5. Sticks to reading a book once started									

sented in Table 2-7, what does it appear that this student would enjoy reading about?

This is the type of activity that the teacher can do with the entire class at one time. It is important to be sure that a variety of magazines are used so that students can express their individual interests. The teacher should not use only sports magazines, for example, because everyone will not be interested in sports. After a few months of working with the students it is sometimes possible to match up the collage with the person without really knowing who made it.

TABLE 2-5.   Sample Interest Inventory.

Name

Date

Grade

INTEREST INVENTORY RECORD

1. What sports do you like to play? (Circle the answers.) What sports do you like to watch? (Underline the answer.)

   a. Roller skating   d. Baseball   g. Bowling
   b. Skiing   e. Basketball   h. Horseback riding
   c. Football   f. Swimming   i. Boating

2. Do you have pets? What kinds? _____

   _____

   _____

3. Do you collect things?

   a. Foreign money   c. Rocks   e. Dolls
   b. Stamps   d. Butterflies   f. ——— (Other)

4. Do you have hobbies and pastimes? (Circle the answers.)

   a. Writing letters   _____

   b. Sewing or knitting   _____

   c. Dancing   _____

   d. Singing or playing a musical
      instrument   _____

   e. Playing cards   _____

   f. Working on cars   _____

   g. Repairing things   _____

   h. Drawing and painting   _____

   i. Driving a car   _____

   j. Cooking   _____

   k. Making things with tools   _____

   l. Experimenting in science   _____

   m. Going for walks   _____

   n. Fishing   _____

TABLE 2-5. (*Continued*)

  o. Making things   _____

  p. Other   _____

  _____

  _____

(Comments)

5. Suppose you could have one wish that might come true. What would you wish for? ___

6. What school subject do you like best? _____

7. What school subject do you like least? _____

8. What is the best book you ever read? _____

9. Do you enjoy reading? _____

10. Do you like someone to read to you? Who? _____

11. Apart from lessons, about how much time each day do you spend reading? _____

12. Do your parents encourage you to read at home? _____

13. What are the names of some books you have been reading lately? _____

14. Do you have a card for the public or school library? _____

15. How many books do you have of your own? _____

16. How many books have you borrowed from friends during the last month? _____ Give the titles of some. _____

17. How many books have you loaned to friends during the last month? _____ Give the titles of some. _____

TABLE 2-5. (*Continued*)

18. About how many books do you have in your home? _____

   Give the titles of some. _____

   _____

19. From what sources, other than your home, libraries, and friends do you obtain books?

   a. Buy them? _____   c. Rent them? _____
   b. Gifts? _____   d. Exchange? _____

20. What kinds of reading do you enjoy most? (Circle the answer.)

   a. History   h. Novels
   b. Travel   i. Detective stories
   c. Plays   j. Fairy tales
   d. Essays   k. Mystery stories
   e. Adventure   l. Biography
   f. Science   m. Music
   g. Poetry   n. Other _____

21. What kind of work do you want to do when you finish school?

   _____

22. What newspapers do you read? _____

23. What sections of the newspaper do you like best? (Circle the answer.)

   a. Sports   d. News
   b. Funnies   e. Editorials
   c. Stories   f. Other _____

24. What magazines are received regularly in your home? _____

   _____

25. Name your favorite magazine. _____

26. Name the comic books you read. _____

27. Where do you get your magazines and comic books? _____

   _____

28. Name some movies you last saw. _____

   _____

29. What are your favorite television programs? _____

   _____

30. Name some other states (or some countries) you have visited.

   _____

31. Which of the following have encouraged you to read? (Circle the answer.)

   a. Parents   e. Friends
   b. Teacher   f. Club leader
   c. Librarian   g. Relative
   d. Hobby   h. Other _____

Taken from *Decision Making for the Diagnostic Teacher.* Cooper, J. David, et al., Holt, Rinehart and Winston, 1972 (6). Reprinted by permission.

TABLE 2-6. **Sample Incomplete Sentences**

1. My favorite thing to do is _____.

2. I am happiest when _____.

3. I like to read _____.

4. Boys _____.

5. Girls _____.

6. My favorite subject in school is _____.

7. When my mom gets mad I _____.

8. When my dad gets mad I _____.

9. If I had three wishes _____.

10. When I get mad I _____.

(The teacher can add other sentence starters that will elicit the type of information wanted.)

TABLE 2-7. **Collage.**

Capacity for Learning to Read

Each child has a certain capacity or potential for learning to read, and this is sometimes referred to as reading expectancy. A child's reading capacity is the prediction of the level of reading he/she should be able to attain provided all circumstances for learning are optimum. One can think of reading capacity as an educated guess about the approximate level a child should be able to achieve in reading. At the beginning reading level this is likely to be several levels above actual reading.

Much of what is known about reading capacity is of a theoretical nature and is not absolutely supported by research (15, 29). However, cautious use of capacity information can be helpful to the classroom reading teacher.

Reading capacity is usually determined by one of two basic procedures: an intelligence score used with a formula for predicting reading capacity or a listening comprehension score. While many authorities in reading support the use of both of these procedures (15), the use of some type of listening score as a capacity measure seems preferable for the classroom teacher because learning to read is based on an oral-language foundation. Listening comprehension parallels reading comprehension in terms of certain similarities of process (15) and also indicates whether a child has the concepts sufficient to understand material at a given level. Therefore, comparing listening comprehension with a reading score should provide some indication of whether or not a student is reading up to present capacity. The following information on some students provides an example of this comparison:

TABLE 2-8. Third-Grade Students.

	Instructional Reading Level	Listening Comprehension
Mark	3	2
Sara	3	6+
Lee	3	3

All three students have the same instructional reading level. However, by considering their listening comprehension scores as indicators of reading capacity, the teacher can see significant differences in terms of needs for instructional planning. Sara's listening score would lead us to believe that she has considerable potential for reading growth. At least this indicates that she has a good oral-language foundation as measured by listening comprehension.

Mark and Lee have listening-comprehension scores that are lower than or equal to their instructional reading levels. This would indicate to the teacher that these students need a strong component of oral-language development as well as increased experiential background and listening comprehension built into their reading program in order to increase their potential to learn to read.

Sometimes teachers refer to students like Mark as overachievers because a comparison of his listening score and his reading score seems to indicate that he is reading at a level that would not be expected from the level of his listening score. Such a misinterpretation stems from a lack of understanding of the capacity concept.

Listening comprehension is a possible indicator of a student's capacity for learning to read (29). Used as has been demonstrated, it will help identify those students who need to have some type of oral-language instruction as a part of their reading program. The diagnostic classroom reading teacher should consider this information as tentative, however, and not rely on it entirely.

Other measures of reading capacity or general learning capacity are based on some type of intelligence measure. While these are very useful in working with students who have learning difficulties, they are not as useful for classroom reading teachers. Therefore, for additional information on capacity, the teacher should refer to other sources on clinical diagnosis (5).

Chapter 3 will focus in detail on how to administer, score, and interpret listening comprehension tests. Because the classroom reading teacher needs to work with groups of students, emphasis will be placed on such procedures.

THE ROLE OF TESTS IN DIAGNOSTIC TEACHING

One criticism frequently leveled against reading programs, and especially diagnostic reading programs, is that too much time is devoted to testing. In some instances this may be true. However, appropriate and judicious use of tests gives the classroom reading teacher a set of tools for gathering information and evaluating students efficiently. Tests are ONLY INDICATORS of a student's performance and should be used in comparison to work samples from a variety of areas.

Some educators are critical of testing because teachers frequently accept test data as gospel and judge students accordingly (11). A student's performance on *any* test is only an *indicator* of what he/she can do on that particular test. However, the effective diagnostic reading teacher must be able to use test information along with other information to make appropriate decisions about a student's reading instruction. In order to do this the teacher must understand how to interpret the different types of tests and test scores.

Mastery and Retention

Tests are frequently used to determine a student's knowledge of reading skills through a concept known as *mastery learning*. Two terms are important to the understanding of mastery learning: *mastery* and *retention*.

Mastery means that a student has achieved a particular level of performance in relation to a given skill or area. For example, the teacher might want

the students to be able to read a given set of paragraphs and select the main idea with 80 per cent accuracy, which is usually the level used to determine mastery (2, 3). When a reading program uses a mastery-learning concept, certain areas or skills are identified for instruction and are taught for a given period of time. At the conclusion of this time a test is usually given or some sample of work is taken to determine whether the student has achieved the expected mastery level. If mastery is not attained, reteaching takes place. If the skill or area has already been retaught, then the teacher must decide whether to move on to a new area or try more reteaching.

A second important term in mastery learning is retention, which refers to longer-term learning. Once a student has mastered a given skill or area, for it to be of use to him/her, he/she must be able to maintain it or keep it. This is retention. Mastery *does not* insure retention of reading skills unless opportunities to practice or apply the skills are provided. The teacher can probably think of several skills in his/her life that were mastered at one time. However, since they have not been used recently or continuously, mastery of them may not have been retained.

In applying the concept of mastery to reading skills it must be understood that decoding and study skills are more likely to be mastered than comprehension skills. The skills that comprise comprehension are such that they always must be taught, practiced, and applied because as the level of the material changes and the content changes, the reader's ability to use the comprehension skills also changes. Therefore, it is likely that comprehension is never completely mastered in the same way as decoding and study skills.

In reading instruction the concepts of mastery and retention are very important. If a student has achieved mastery of a given set of skills, he/she must have opportunities to *apply* them in real reading situations in order for them to be maintained.

TYPES OF READING TESTS

There are many different types of reading tests. Some of them will be more useful to the classroom teacher than others. Each is designed for a different purpose.

Group Tests

Group tests are those that can be administered to a large number of students at one time. These are especially useful to classroom reading teachers. It is difficult to construct a group test to measure certain skills or abilities. Therefore, group tests are frequently limited in what they can measure. An example of a group test that a teacher might be using in the classroom is the Gates-MacGinitie Reading Tests (21).

Individual Tests

There are tests that must be administered to one student at a time. From the classroom teacher's point of view, individual tests are less feasible to use because they require so much time, particularly when one has a class of twenty-five or thirty students. However, there are many aspects of reading that can be measured only through an individual test. Even for the classroom teacher a certain amount of individual testing must be done. An informal reading inventory, which was mentioned earlier as a procedure for determining reading levels, is an example of an individual test.

Sample Group Reading Tests.

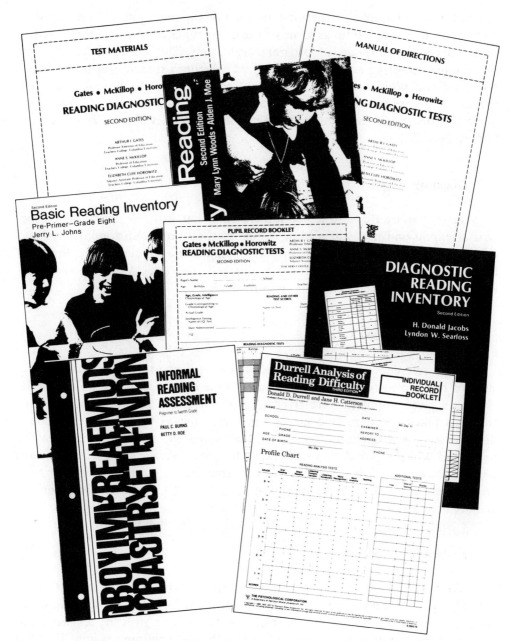

Sample Individual Reading Tests.

Achievement Tests

Achievement tests are designed to measure the overall performance of students in a given area such as reading. Usually achievement tests are group administered. They are more useful in terms of looking at program growth as

opposed to determining instructional needs. For the classroom teacher, achievement tests are not as useful as some of the other types of tests but they need to be given for the purposes of program evaluation. The classroom teacher can make some use of an achievement test by analyzing a student's errors to determine specific problems. Since so many tests are now machine-scored using special answer sheets, this is not always possible. An example of an achievement test that might be used is the Metropolitan Achievement Tests: Reading Survey Test (25).

Diagnostic Tests

Tests that are diagnostic give information that will reveal a student's specific strengths and needs in reading. Some of these are group administered and others are individually administered. An example of each type is the Stanford Diagnostic Reading Test (17) for a group and the Gates McKillop Horowitz Reading Diagnostic Tests (12) for an individual.

Norm-Referenced Tests

Norm-referenced tests compare students against other students. The results of normed tests let the teacher know how the students are doing in relation to a given population (referred to as the norming sample or population) that has taken the test. One factor that must always be remembered about normed tests is that students are being compared and ranked one against the other and half the population will always be above average and half will always be below average. This is the nature of normed tests. Most achievement tests are normed tests. The Stanford Achievement Test (19) is a well-known normed achievement test.

Criterion-Referenced Tests

Criterion-referenced tests are designed to compare students against an arbitrarily, predetermined objective. These tests usually focus on specific skills. As compared to a norm-referenced test, a criterion test gives the teacher more specific information about a student's strengths and needs in reading. The skill tests that accompany most basal reading series are examples of criterion-referenced tests.

Standardized Tests

A standardized test is one that is given under set conditions. The time limits, directions for administration, and procedures are all consistent and are

Criterion Referenced Tests.

TABLE 2-9. Types of Tests.

	Norm Referenced	*Criterion Referenced*
Group	Standardized Achievement Diagnostic	Standardized Diagnostic Informal
Individual	Standardized Diagnostic	Standardized Diagnostic Informal

to be carried out in the same manner every time the test is administered. Achievement tests are examples of standardized tests.

Informal Tests

Tests that are usually teacher made and nonstandardized are informal tests. Sometimes basal-reader publishers provide teachers with informal measures that can be used to check specific skill progress.

Each of these different types of tests have different purposes. One test might fit into several of the above categories. Table 2-9 summarizes the different types of tests and shows the overlap in categories. Table 2-10 also lists some of the more commonly used published reading tests and indicates the categories into which they fit. These are tests that can be used easily by the classroom teacher.

TYPES OF TEST SCORES

Interpreting tests and using them correctly requires that one know something about the various types of scores and what they mean.

Raw Score

This is simply the number of items the student got correct. Some tests have a factor to compensate for guessing. This is usually the number right minus some proportion of the number wrong (such as number right minus 1/4 the number wrong). Raw scores are of little value to the teacher because there is no way to know what the score means. For example, if the teacher knows that one of his/her students got a raw score of 31 on a reading comprehension test, he/she would really know very little.

Grade Scores

Grade scores are among the most commonly used scores because teachers have generally felt that they are easy to understand and interpret. This, however, is not really so. Table 2-11 shows the reading-grade scores for a second-grade class. When looking at the scores for Tony, Chuck, and Betty, one sees that Tony has a score of 1.3 which is read as first grade, third month. This means that Tony read the second-grade test as well as the average first grader in the third month of school would have read it. Chuck, on the other hand, read the same test as well as the average third grader in the eighth month of school, and Betty read about as well as the average second grader in the seventh month of school. These scores *do not* reflect the actual instructional reading level for these students. More than likely, most standardized reading test scores such as these represent the students frustration level (9). Another problem with grade scores is that they do not represent equal interval scores. When examining the portion of the test manual given in Table 2-12, the teacher will notice that a student taking this test could score 545 and get a grade score in reading of 1.9. If he/she made thirteen more raw score points his/her grade score would jump .1 (or to 2.0). However, if she/he made an additional twelve more raw score points her/his grade score would move to 2.1. The change in raw score points is not on an equal-interval scale. Because of the problems with interpretation and meaning, there is a move on the part of the International Reading Association to discourage the use of grade scores (22).

Percentiles

Percentile scores tell the teacher how a student ranks assuming that 100 people have taken the test. Table 2-13 presents examples of some percentiles.

Mark scored at the 71st percentile. This means that he did better than 70 per cent of the people in his grade who took the test. Or one could say 29 per cent of the people who took the test did better than Mark. In either case the teacher can tell how well Mark did by comparing him with the other people who took the test. Percentile scores are useful to the classroom teacher in that they reveal how a student compares with others who took the test. They do not, however, help in determining reading level.

Standard Scores

Standard scores are designed to overcome the problems related to grade scores and percentiles; they are based on equal units. To use and interpret standard scores, the teacher needs to understand two factors: the mean and the

TABLE 2-10. Tests for Use by the Elementary Classroom Teacher.

	Group	Normed	Criterion	Diagnostic	Achievement	Standardized
California Achievement Tests: Reading CTB/McGraw Hill, 1978 Grades K.O–12.9 Measures general reading achievement	X	X			X	X
Durrell Listening Reading Series The Psychological Corp., 1968–1970 Grades 1–9 Measures general reading and listening achievement. May be used for determining student capacity for reading	X	X			X	X
Metropolitan Achievement Tests: Reading Survey Test The Psychological Corp., 1979 Grades K–12 Measures general reading achievement	X	X			X	X
Gates-MacGinitie Reading Tests (Second Edition) Walter H. MacGinitie Houghton Mifflin Company, 1978 Grades Primary–12 Measures general achievement in reading	X	X			X	X
Gates-MacGinitie Reading Test: Readiness Skills Arthur I. Gates and Walter H. MacGinitie Houghton Mifflin Company, 1968 Grades K–1 Assesses selected readiness areas	X	X				X

Test						
Metropolitan Readiness Tests Joanne R. Nurss and Mary E. McGauvran The Psychological Corp., 1976 Grades K–1 Measures selected readiness skills	X		X			X
Metropolitan Reading Instructional Tests The Psychological Corp., 1979 Grades K–9.9 Assesses student mastery of selected reading skills	X	X	X	X	X	X
Murphy-Durrell Reading Readiness Analysis The Psychological Corp., 1964–1965 Grades K–1.5 Measures selected readiness skills	X		X	X		X
Prescriptive Reading Inventory CTB/McGraw Hill, 1977 Grades K.0–6.5 Assesses student mastery of specific skills	X		X	X		X
Reading Yardsticks The Riverside Publishing Company, 1981 Grades K–8 Assesses mastery of selected reading skills				X		X
Stanford Diagnostic Reading Test The Psychological Corp., 1978 Grades 1.6–13 Diagnoses selected reading skills			X	X		X
Wisconsin Tests for Reading Skill Development Interpretive Scoring Systems, 1972–1977 Grades K–6 Measures mastery of selected reading skills, word attack, comprehension and study skills			X	X		X

TABLE 2-11.   Reading Grade Scores for a Second-Grade Class from a Test Administered in April.

Students	Total Reading
Tony	1.3
Larry	2.7
Susan	3.1
Leroy	2.6
Phyllis	1.9
Joan	1.6
Chuck	3.8
Jim	7.0
David	2.1
Betty	2.7
Mary	2.3

standard deviation. The mean of the test refers to the average score of all the people who took the test. In other words, it is the arithmetic average. This should be reported in the test manual. The standard deviation is the average deviation of the scores away from the mean. This statistic is also reported in the test manual. With regard to the test data presented in Table 2-14, the mean (X is the symbol for mean) for the test is 50 and the standard deviation (SD is the symbol sometimes used for standard deviation) is 10. Edward scored 87 on the standard-score scale. This means that he scored 3 and approximately 2/3 standard deviations above the average which is 50. One should now look at the diagram of the normal or bell curve presented in Figure 2-2.

This shows how the scores on any given test would fall if a random sample of the population took the test. Most of the scores would pile up in the middle of the scale, which is the mean or midpoint of the curve. Figure 2-2 also shows the per cent of cases under each section of the curve, and relates stanines (which will be covered in a later section), percentile scales, and the normal curve scale which is a type of standard score that has been discussed. By examining Figure 2-2, one can see how these various types of scores relate to each other.

In the example of Edward, his score was 87, and he scored almost four standard deviations (3 2/3) above the mean. This indicates that he ranked very high in the group that took this particular test. Ann's score, on the other hand, was 23. This means that she scored a little more than three standard deviations below the mean.

There is a special standard score scale that is found in many currently used tests called the stanine scale. Stanine means that it is a standard scale of nine points with a mean of five and a standard deviation of two. In looking back at Figure 2-2, one can see how stanines compare to other scores that have been discussed. Table 2-15 presents some sample stanine scores in a sixth-grade class.

TABLE 2-12. Portion of Test Manual.

TABLE A-3
Scaled Score to Grade Equivalent (GE) Conversion Table

SCALED SCORES

GE	Reading	Mathematics	Language	Science	Social Studies	Basic Battery	Complete Battery	GE
PHS*	843	813	828	807	861	824	843	PHS*
12.9	841	812	827	805	858	822	840	12.9
12.8	839	811	825	804	855	820	837	12.8
12.7	837	810	824	803	852	818	834	12.7
12.6	836	809	822	801	849	817	832	12.6
12.5	835	808	821	799	846	816	830	12.5
12.4	834	807	819	798	844	815	828	12.4
12.3	833	806	818	797	841	814	826	12.3
12.2	831	805	816	795	838	813	824	12.2
12.1	830	804	815	793	836	812	822	12.1
12.0	828	803	813	792	833	811	820	12.0
11.9	827	802	812	791	830	810	818	11.9
11.8	825	801	810	789	827	809	816	11.8
11.7	824	800	809	788	824	808	814	11.7
11.6	822	799	808	786	821	807	811	11.6
11.5	821	798	806	785	819	806	809	11.5
11.4	819	797	805	783	816	805	807	11.4
11.3	818	796	804	782	813	804	804	11.3
11.2	816	795	802	780	811	803	802	11.2
11.1	815	793	801	779	808	802	800	11.1
11.0	813	792	800	777	805	801	797	11.0
10.9	812	791	798	776	803	800	795	10.9
10.8	810	789	797	774	800	798	793	10.8
10.7	809	788	796	773	797	797	791	10.7
10.6	807	787	794	771	795	796	788	10.6
10.5	805	785	793	770	792	795	786	10.5
10.4	803	784	791	768	789	793	784	10.4
10.3	801	782	790	766	786	791	781	10.3
10.2	799	781	788	765	784	790	779	10.2
10.1	797	779	787	763	781	788	777	10.1
10.0	795	778	785	761	778	787	775	10.0
9.9	793	776	784	760	776	785	772	9.9
9.8	791	775	782	758	773	783	770	9.8
9.7	789	773	780	756	770	781	768	9.7
9.6	787	772	778	754	767	779	766	9.6
9.5	785	770	776	752	765	777	764	9.5
9.4	783	769	774	750	762	775	761	9.4
9.3	781	767	772	748	759	772	759	9.3
9.2	779	765	770	746	756	770	756	9.2
9.1	778	763	768	744	753	768	754	9.1
9.0	776	762	766	742	750	766	751	9.0
8.9	774	760	764	740	747	764	749	8.9
8.8	772	758	762	737	744	761	746	8.8
8.7	770	756	760	735	741	758	744	8.7
8.6	768	753	757	732	738	756	741	8.6
8.5	766	751	755	730	735	753	738	8.5
8.4	764	748	753	727	731	751	735	8.4
8.3	762	746	750	725	728	748	732	8.3
8.2	760	743	748	722	725	745	729	8.2
8.1	758	741	746	719	721	742	726	8.1
8.0	756	738	743	716	718	739	723	8.0
7.9	754	736	741	713	715	736	720	7.9
7.8	753	733	738	710	711	733	717	7.8
7.7	751	731	736	707	708	730	714	7.7
7.6	750	728	733	704	705	728	711	7.6
7.5	748	725	730	700	701	725	708	7.5
7.4	747	722	728	697	698	722	705	7.4
7.3	745	719	725	694	694	720	702	7.3
7.2	744	716	722	690	690	717	699	7.2
7.1	742	713	720	687	687	714	696	7.1
7.0	740	710	717	684	683	711	692	7.0
6.9	738	707	714	680	679	708	689	6.9
6.8	736	704	711	677	676	705	686	6.8
6.7	734	700	708	674	672	702	652	6.7
6.6	732	696	705	670	669	699	679	6.6
6.5	730	692	702	667	665	696	676	6.5
6.4	728	688	699	664	662	693	672	6.4
6.3	726	684	696	661	659	690	669	6.3
6.2	724	680	693	657	655	687	665	6.2
6.1	723	676	690	653	652	684	662	6.1
6.0	721	672	686	649	648	681	658	6.0

SCALED SCORES

GE	Reading	Mathematics	Language	Science	Social Studies	Basic Battery	Complete Battery	GE
5.9	719	668	682	645	645	678	654	5.9
5.8	717	664	678	641	641	675	651	5.8
5.7	715	660	674	637	638	671	647	5.7
5.6	713	656	670	632	634	668	644	5.6
5.5	711	651	666	628	631	665	640	5.5
5.4	709	647	662	624	627	662	637	5.4
5.3	707	642	657	619	624	659	634	5.3
5.2	705	638	652	615	620	655	630	5.2
5.1	703	633	647	610	616	652	627	5.1
5.0	701	629	642	605	613	649	623	5.0
4.9	700	624	638	600	609	646	620	4.9
4.8	698	619	634	595	605	642	616	4.8
4.7	696	614	630	591	601	639	612	4.7
4.6	694	609	625	586	597	635	608	4.6
4.5	692	604	620	582	593	632	604	4.5
4.4	689	599	615	577	589	628	600	4.4
4.3	687	594	610	572	585	624	596	4.3
4.2	684	589	605	567	580	620	592	4.2
4.1	682	584	600	562	575	616	587	4.1
4.0	679	579	595	557	570	612	582	4.0
3.9	676	574	590	552	565	607	577	3.9
3.8	673	569	584	547	560	602	572	3.8
3.7	670	564	579	541	555	597	567	3.7
3.6	667	559	574	536	550	592	562	3.6
3.5	664	553	568	530	545	587	557	3.5
3.4	660	547	562	525	540	582	551	3.4
3.3	656	541	556	519	534	577	545	3.3
3.2	651	535	550	514	528	572	539	3.2
3.1	646	528	543	508	522	566	533	3.1
3.0	641	521	536	502	516	560	527	3.0
2.9	635	513	529	495	510	554	520	2.9
2.8	629	505	522	489	504	547	513	2.8
2.7	623	496	515	482	497	540	506	2.7
2.6	616	487	507	476	490	533	499	2.6
2.5	608	478	499	469	483	525	491	2.5
2.4	599	469	491	462	476	517	483	2.4
2.3	590	460	482	455	469	508	475	2.3
2.2	580	450	472	448	462	499	467	2.2
2.1	570	440	462	441	455	489	459	2.1
2.0	558	430	452	434	448	479	451	2.0
1.9	545	420	441	426	441	468	443	1.9
1.8	531	410	430	418	434	456	434	1.8
1.7	516	401	418	410	426	443	425	1.7
1.6	500	392	405	402	418	429	417	1.6
1.5	483	383	392	393	410	414	408	1.5
1.4	465	375	378	383	401	398	399	1.4
1.3	447	368	363	373	392	381	390	1.3
1.2	428	360	349	363	383	365	381	1.2
1.1	409	352	336	352	374	350	372	1.1
1.0	391	345	323	341	364	336	363	1.0
K.9	374	338	311	330	353	323	354	K.9
K.8	358	331	300	319	341	311	344	K.8
K.7	342	323	290	307	329	300	334	K.7
K.6	327	316	281	295	317	291	324	K.6
K.5	314	308	273	282	304	283	314	K.5
K.4	302	301	266	268	290	275	303	K.4
K.3	291	293	259	254	275	268	293	K.3
K.2	281	284	253	241	260	261	283	K.2
K.1	272	274	247	228	244	255	272	K.1
K.0	264	264	242	215	227	250	262	K.0
PK**	256	253	237	202	210	245	251	PK**

* PHS = Post-High School

** PK = Pre-Kindergarten

If a particular Scaled Score does not appear on these tables, read to the next higher Scaled Score.

Taken from *Metropolitan Achievement Tests*, Teachers Manual for Administering and Interpreting (The Psychological Corporation, 1978), p. 77 (25). Reprinted by permission.

TABLE 2-13.   Sample Percentile Scores.

Student	Reading Percentiles
Mark	71 percentile
Ann	25
Morse	88
Lynn	92
Linda	74

TABLE 2-14.   Sample Standard Score Test Data.

Student	Total Reading Score	
	Raw Score	Standard Score
Edward	120	87
Lou Ann	95	70
Joe	85	63
Tom	65	50
Ann	25	23
Marcia	20	20

Test mean: 50
Standard deviation: 10

Nancy scored a 7 which means that she scored one standard deviation above the mean on the stanine scale. This is just another type of standard score.

In the school where one will be teaching, there will probably be some type of testing program. To make full use of the test results the teacher must understand the scores and their limitations. Each test that is used will have slightly different types of scores. It will always be necessary for the teacher to read the

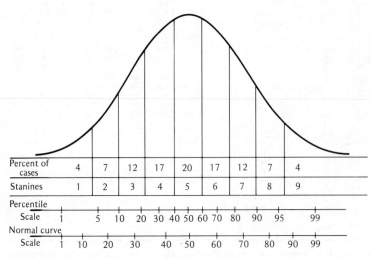

Percent of cases	4	7	12	17	20	17	12	7	4
Stanines	1	2	3	4	5	6	7	8	9

Percentile
Scale   1   5   10   20 30 40 50 60 70 80   90   95   99

Normal curve
Scale   1   10   20   30   40 50   60   70   80   90 99

FIGURE 2-2.   Bell Curve.

TABLE 2-15.   **Stanine Scores in a Sixth-Grade Class.**

Student	Total Reading Score
Ted	5
Nancy	7
Sandy	3
Blanche	1

test manual carefully to determine the scores used with each test. The basic information presented here should be helpful in assisting a teacher to understand whatever scores are used.

INFORMATION NEEDED TO INTERPRET TEST RESULTS

Interpretation of test scores and test results requires an understanding of certain technical items about tests. These include reliability, validity, standard error of measure, and norming population information. It is not necessary to have all the details relative to each of these items but a basic understanding is required.

Reliability

Test reliability refers to how accurately a test measures what it does measure. Statistical procedures are used to determine reliability which is reported in numerical terms as a reliability coefficient. If a test had perfect reliability—that is, one always got the exact same score or scores when the test was given—its reliability would be 1.0. Since no test is that perfect, no reliability coefficient is 1.0. Most reliability coefficients for reading tests range between .70 and .90. The closer the score is to one, the more reliable the test. One should always look for the reliability of any standardized tests one gives. This information should be found in the test examiner's manual.

Standard Error of Measurement

Another statistic that the teacher should understand to interpret test scores is the standard error of measurement. This is the statistically estimated amount of error that would occur if an individual retook the same test several times. Therefore, one can add and subtract the standard error of measurement to an individual's test score in order to determine the range of his/her true score on that test. This statistic can also be found in the test manual. Table

TABLE 2-16. Standard Errors of Measurement.

Test	Standard Error in Grade Scores
Test X	.5
Text Y	.8
Text Z	.4

2-16 presents the standard error of measurement in grade scores for three hypothetical reading tests.

If a third-grade student scored 3.1 on all three tests, one could figure his/her true score with approximately 66 per cent accuracy by adding and subtracting one standard error of measurement. For approximately 95 per cent accuracy one would add two standard errors. Table 2-17 provides further data on standard errors of measurement.

One can see that the higher the standard error the more likely the student's true score will be in a broader range. For example, Test Y is likely to have the greatest amount of error in determining a student's true score. Knowledge of this information alerts one to the fact that the test score is not absolute and should be used cautiously.

Validity

Validity is the degree or extent to which a test actually measures what it says it is supposed to measure. A test could be very reliable and still not be valid. The examiner's manual of the tests one uses should report validity information. Different types of tests report different types of validity.

Norming Population Information

A final item that the teacher should examine when using a standardized test is the information provided in the manual on the norming population. This is the group that was used by the test constructors to determine the norms for the test. The makeup for this group should be similar to the makeup of one's group for the test to be considered appropriate. For example, if one is teaching children in a rural area, one should use a test that has included children from a

TABLE 2-17. Standard Errors Added to Given Scores.

	Score	± 1 SEM	± 2 SEM
Test X	3.1	2.6–3.6	2.1–4.1
Test Y	3.1	2.3–3.9	1.4–4.7
Test Z	3.1	2.7–3.5	2.3–3.9

similar area in the norming sample. It is important for the norming sample of a test to match the student population that one is teaching. A teacher may not be able to control the selection of the tests but at least she/he can be aware of this information and be cautious in interpretation if the test-norming population does not match her/his group.

In summary, all of these factors—reliability, standard error of measurement, validity, and norming-population information—should be considered as one interprets test results. If one is given the opportunity as a classroom teacher to help select tests, these factors along with others should also be considered in making decisions.

ADMINISTERING STANDARDIZED TESTS

Administration of standardized tests will be one of many aspects of one's job as a classroom reading teacher. Correct procedure is important because the way a test is administered can influence the results one gets. Each standardized test is slightly different from the other. Therefore, the teacher should review the test manual carefully before using the test. Standardized test results depend upon being administered as the authors intended them to be. For this reason the guidelines for administration of each particular test should be followed. The following general guidelines should be helpful in learning to administer different standardized tests in reading and other areas.

Guidelines for Using and Administering Standardized Tests

1. The teacher should review the test, manual, answer sheet, and any other items that come with the test. Before using any test, one should read the manual, study the directions, examine the pupil booklet, and look over the answer sheet if one is used. The teacher should be sure to know exactly what the students will have to do when they take the test. In studying the manual, one should look for items such as reliability and validity. The teacher should notice the types of scores given by the test.

2. Prior to the time that one is going to administer the test all of one's materials should be gathered together and organized. The test booklets, answer sheets, and manual should be ready for use. Some tests require special pencils. These should be sharpened and ready.

3. In administering the test the directions should be followed *exactly as the manual instructs one to do.* Following the directions exactly is very important in using a standardized test. Time limits should be observed. The teacher should read the directions aloud to students care-

STUDENT DIAGNOSTIC REPORT

THE RIVERSIDE PUBLISHING COMPANY

Test: **READING YARDSTICKS**	Teacher: **MRS. ECKLAND**
Level: **11** Date: **10/81**	Form: **1** Process No.: **000-1429-002**
Sex: **F** Grade: **5**	Norms: **FALL** System: **KENNON**
Building: **KENNON MIDDLE**	

STUDENT RECORD FOR

RITA FINNEGAN

Criterion-Referenced Interpretation — Performance on Objectives

*= DID NOT REACH MASTERY LEVEL OF 60 % AS SET BY SCHOOL DISTRICT

Part / Subtest / Objective	NUMBER OF ITEMS	NUMBER ATTEMPTED	NUMBER CORRECT	PERCENT CORRECT FOR THIS STUDENT	BUILDING AVERAGE PERCENT CORRECT
VOCABULARY	40	38	36	90	67
SYNONYMS	10	9	8	80	51
ANTONYMS	10	10	9	90	55
MULTI-MEANING WORDS	10	10	10	100	82
PRONOUN REFERENTS	10	10	9	90	80
COMPREHENSION	60	58	41	67	52
LITERAL READING COMPREHENSION	13	12	11	82	79
VISUALIZING	3	2	2	67	63
DETAILS	5	4	4	80	77
SEQUENCE	5	5	5	100	81
INTERPRETIVE READING COMPREHENSION	19	19	14	73	71
MAIN IDEA	8	8	8	100	76
DRAW CONCLUSIONS	5	5	3	60	54
CAUSE AND EFFECT	9	9	7	78	63
EVALUATIVE READING COMPREHENSION	14	14	8	*57	49
PREDICT OUTCOMES	5	5	3	60	52
FACT VS. OPINION	5	5	3	60	53
CHARACTER TRAITS	14	13	8	*50	51
LANGUAGE COMPREHENSION	14	13	8	*56	62
SIMILES AND METAPHORS	3	3	2	67	59
IDIOMS	3	3	1	*33	42
PUNCTUATION, PERIOD, QUESTION MARK	4	4	2	*50	50
PUNCTUATION, QUOTATION MARKS	4	3	3	75	73
STRUCTURAL ANALYSIS	55	45	35	64	62
WORD PARTS	55	45	35	64	64
PLURALS	5	5	3	60	62
POSSESSIVES	5	4	4	80	81
SYLLABICATION; NUMBER OF SYLLABLES	10	8	6	60	56
SYLLABICATION; WORD DIVISION	5	5	3	60	51
BASE WORDS	10	8	6	60	78
AFFIXES; WORD MEANING	10	7	5	50	65
CONTRACTIONS	55	49	38	66	53
STUDY SKILLS	39	35	28	73	70
REFERENCE MATERIAL					
DICTIONARY, ALPHA ORDER, GUIDE WORDS	3	3	3	100	92
ALPHA ORDER, SECOND-FOURTH LETTERS	5	5	4	80	71
DICTIONARY; CHOOSING DEFINITIONS	5	5	3	60	58
PRONUNCIATION KEY	4	4	3	75	80
ENCYCLOPEDIA	3	3	2	67	62
CARD CATALOG	4	3	2	*50	50
PARTS OF BOOKS	5	5	4	80	77
CHOOSING REFERENCE SOURCES	5	5	4	80	85
MAPS	16	14	10	63	61
ORGANIZATIONAL STUDY SKILLS					
TOPIC	4	3	3	75	74
TOPIC; SUBTOPICS	4	3	3	75	74
TOPIC; RELEVANT DETAILS	4	4	3	*50	80
FOLLOWING DIRECTIONS	4	3	2	*50	75
TEST TOTAL	210	204	150	71	69

LEGEND: RS = Raw Score (Number of test items correct); SS = Standard Score; LCL PR = Local Percentile Rank; NAT SMP PR = National Sample Percentile Rank; GE = Grade Equivalent; NCE = Normal Curve Equivalent

Norm-Referenced Interpretation — Scores / Profile

Subtest	RS	PR	Profile (Below Average / Average / Above Average)
VOCABULARY	36	76	/////////////
LITERAL READING COMPREHENSION	11	60	////////
INTERPRETIVE READING COMPREHENSION	14	52	//////
EVALUATIVE READING COMPREHENSION	8	53	//////
LANGUAGE READING COMPREHENSION	8	24	//
WORD PARTS	35	49	//////
REFERENCE MATERIAL STUDY SKILLS	28	50	//////
ORGANIZATIONAL STUDY SKILLS	10	46	/////

LC Average: 1   25   50   75   99 Above Average

RITA'S ESTIMATED ITBS SCORES ARE AS FOLLOWS:

	OCTOBER 1981	MAY 1982	SEPTEMBER 1982
VOCABULARY			
GE	63	70	74
PR	76	76	76
NCE	65	65	65
SS	137	146	151
READING COMPREHENSION			
GE	51	57	61
PR	49	49	49
NCE	50	50	50
SS	124	130	136
WORK-STUDY SKILLS			
GE	52	58	62
PR	50	50	50
NCE	50	50	50
SS	124	131	137

* NOTE THAT IN ADDITION TO A DESCRIPTION OF WHERE SHE IS NOW, RITA'S PROJECTED GROWTH IS REPORTED FOR THE COMING YEAR.

Narrative Interpretation

HOW WELL IS RITA DOING IN READING? TO HELP ANSWER THIS QUESTION, RITA TOOK READING YARDSTICKS IN OCTOBER 1981. HER TEST RESULTS ARE SHOWN ON THE LEFT.

LET'S GO OVER THE RESULTS FOR RITA. WE START AT THE FAR LEFT, UNDER THE SECTION HEADED "CRITERION-REFERENCED INTERPRETATION." THE FIRST SUBTEST IN READING YARDSTICKS IS VOCABULARY. UNDER VOCABULARY, FOUR OBJECTIVES ARE MEASURED. THE FIRST OBJECTIVE IS SYNONYMS. RITA ATTEMPTED 9 OF 10 TEST EXERCISES UNDER SYNONYMS. SHE GOT 8 OF THEM CORRECT. HER PERCENT CORRECT IS 80. THIS COMPARES WITH THE BUILDING PERCENT CORRECT OF 51, WHICH WAS BASED ON 247 FIFTH GRADE STUDENTS WHO TOOK THE TEST WITH RITA. RITA'S PERCENT CORRECT IN SYNONYMS IS HIGHER THAN THE BUILDING PERCENT CORRECT. THIS MEANS THAT RITA MAY BE STRONGER IN SYNONYMS THAN OTHER FIFTH GRADE STUDENTS IN THE BUILDING. USING THIS APPROACH, WE CAN LOOK AT HOW RITA DID ON EACH OF THE READING OBJECTIVES.

HOW DID RITA DO COMPARED WITH OTHER STUDENTS? WE ALREADY HAVE SOME INFORMATION, BUT THE SECTION ON THE LEFT UNDER "NORM-REFERENCED INFORMATION" GIVES MORE. FOR EXAMPLE, RITA'S PERCENTILE RANK IN VOCABULARY IS 76. THIS MEANS THAT RITA SCORED HIGHER THAN 76 PERCENT OF THE FIFTH GRADE STUDENTS IN THE BUILDING. ON THE OTHER HAND, 24 PERCENT SCORED AS WELL OR BETTER. RITA SEEMS TO BE SOMEWHAT ABOVE AVERAGE IN VOCABULARY COMPARED TO OTHER FIFTH GRADE STUDENTS. LET'S SEE HOW RITA DID ON THE OTHER SUBTESTS. RITA HAS SOMEWHAT ABOVE AVERAGE IN LITERAL READING COMPREHENSION, ABOUT AVERAGE IN INTERPRETIVE READING COMPREHENSION, ABOUT AVERAGE IN EVALUATIVE READING COMPREHENSION, SOMEWHAT BELOW AVERAGE IN LANGUAGE, ABOUT AVERAGE IN WORD PARTS, AVERAGE IN REFERENCE MATERIAL STUDY SKILLS, AND ABOUT AVERAGE IN ORGANIZATIONAL STUDY SKILLS.

LET'S LOOK AT RITA'S HIGH AND LOW POINTS IN READING FOR DIAGNOSTIC PURPOSES. WE LOOK AT EACH PAIR OF TEST SCORES, TO SEE IF THERE IS BETTER THAN A 50 PERCENT CHANCE THAT THE OBSERVED DIFFERENCES BETWEEN THEM ARE RELIABLE ONES. RITA IS HIGHER IN VOCABULARY THAN IN WORD PARTS, IN LITERAL READING COMPREHENSION THAN IN LANGUAGE, AND IN WORD PARTS THAN ORGANIZATIONAL STUDY SKILLS.

RITA'S LEVEL OF PERFORMANCE ON THE IOWA TESTS OF BASIC SKILLS (ITBS) IS ESTIMATED ON THE LEFT, FOR VOCABULARY, READING COMPREHENSION, AND WORK-STUDY SKILLS. GRADE EQUIVALENTS (GE), NATIONAL PERCENTILE RANKS (PR), AND NORMAL CURVE EQUIVALENTS (NCE) ARE ESTIMATED FOR BOTH CURRENT STATUS AND PROJECTED FOR A YEAR FROM NOW. THE PROJECTED GROWTH IS AN AVERAGE GROWTH. SOME STUDENTS WILL GROW MORE AND SOME LESS. RITA CAN BE RETESTED IN MAY 1982 OR SEPTEMBER 1982 WITH THE ITBS OR YARDSTICKS AND HER ACTUAL SCORES COULD THEN BE COMPARED WITH THE PROJECTED GROWTH SCORES.

COULD RITA BENEFIT FROM SPECIAL HELP IN READING? ALL OF THE FIFTH GRADE STUDENTS WHO WERE TESTED WITH RITA WERE COMPARED WITH ONE ANOTHER ON EACH OF THE READING SUBTESTS. STUDENTS IN THE LOWER ONE-FOURTH OF THE GROUP ON ANY SUBTEST WOULD SEEM TO BENEFIT FROM SPECIAL HELP. IN THESE TERMS, RITA NEEDS HELP IN LANGUAGE.

FIGURE 2-3. Test Analysis on Iowa Test of Basic Skills. Reprinted by permission.

fully and clearly. The teacher should not make up directions of his/ her own unless the test manual indicates that one is free to do this.

4. After administering the test the teacher should collect all materials, check them carefully, and package them as instructed by the principal or other school official. Sometimes the tests will be machine scored and sometimes the teacher will score them him- or herself. *Each* answer sheet should always be looked over to make sure it is completed properly. If the tests are to be machine scored it is important to follow the instructions for packing them and shipping them to the company.

5. When the tests are returned to the teacher, he/she should study the results and interpret them by using the items of information discussed earlier in this book. In examining the results, the types of errors students make should be analyzed to see if one can detect a pattern. Many companies are now providing a detailed written explanation of students' test scores and what they mean, like the one shown in Figure 2-3.

Preparing Students to Take Standardized Tests

Students at all levels need some preparation for taking any tests but especially standardized tests. Before students take the test the teacher should explain its purpose and put them at ease about it. They should know that it is important for them to do their best but also that they should not be threatened by it or be afraid of it.

For students who have never taken a standardized test it is a good idea to reproduce a sample answer sheet like the one to be used on the test and have students practice marking it. This is a good procedure to follow every time such a test is administered because it helps alleviate any problems that students might have in completing the answer sheet and marking their answers.

On the day one administers the test the teacher should be organized and help students do the same thing. A DO NOT DISTURB – TESTING sign should be hung on the door. The teacher should be sure that students have used the restrooms, gotten drinks, or whatever before the test begins. Desks should be cleared, pencils sharpened, and materials ready. It is important that the room for testing is as comfortable as possible. Preparation such as described here will make the testing go much more smoothly.

REPORTING TEST RESULTS AND READING INFORMATION TO PARENTS

Parents want to know how their children are doing in school and particularly in reading. They have the right to this information and teachers have the

responsibility of reporting test results to parents that are clear and accurate, and in no way confusing.

Information Parents Should Know

The type of information the teacher reports to parents will depend upon one's school's policies. These should be followed.

There are specific types of information that are particularly valuable to parents. These include the child's actual instructional reading level, some examples of specific needs in reading, and suggestions that parents could follow in helping their child at home.

Often schools give parents the results of standardized tests, which they should not do, if possible. These test scores reflect the child's frustration level and do not indicate exact performance (11). However, the law in many states requires that parents have this information. If standardized test scores are given to parents, they should be explained in terms of what they actually mean. Just giving out test scores without an appropriate explanation can lead to serious misunderstanding and misinterpretation on the part of the parents which, in turn, can lead to problems for the school.

Reporting the child's actual reading level as determined by an IRI or placement in the basal series is more appropriate information to give parents. This lets them know exactly how well their child is reading.

One good way to share with parents evidence about their child's reading is through tape recordings. Periodic tapes should be made of the child reading. These should be kept and used for parent conferences. They will help to show the child's actual reading performance and will also provide the teacher with the means to illustrate and explain any specific strengths and needs.

Another area that parents should be informed about is their child's specific needs. This does not mean sending home or handing out to the parents a list of twenty or thirty skills that a child needs. All the detailed listings of skills are for the classroom teacher's use and mean little or nothing to the parents. What parents need are specific examples of general reading progress such as "your child is having difficulty figuring out words of two or more syllables" or "your child is having difficulty understanding and remembering what he/she has read." These items can be easily illustrated to parents through the tapes mentioned above and work samples. They are much more valuable for parents than a lengthy list of skills that has no real meaning for them.

Finally, parents should be given suggestions as to how they can help or work with their child at home. These ideas should be simple and realistic. There are many good books that teachers can share with parents or use for ideas (5, 7, 16). The teacher should encourage his/her school to have a library of books, ideas, and materials for parents if it does not already have one.

Operating Within the Law

Since the laws of each state provide for certain rights of parents regarding knowledge of test results and access to records of a student's performance, the teacher should know what her/his state laws say and be sure to observe them.

During the past few years the legal rights of parents and students and the controversy over reading and various state laws have become significant issues for educators. Much of this concern may have arisen because some educators have followed a policy of keeping test information and records from parents. Therefore, the law provides protection for parents. Teachers should make certain to observe this law to avoid any possibility of lawsuits and court action (8, 14).

SUMMARY

A diagnostic reading teacher needs to understand the factors that influence reading growth and know how to use this information in planning an effective reading program. No single factor by itself can create the conditions conducive to effective reading. Reading growth is influenced by a combination of visual, auditory, language, health, environmental, and emotional factors interacting together.

Planning a diagnostically based reading program in the classroom depends upon the teacher having information about certain aspects of a child's reading. These include knowledge of reading levels, skill development, interests and attitudes, and reading capacity. Each is significant to the development of a child's reading program.

Tests play an important role in diagnostic teaching but are not the teacher's only source for gathering relevant information. Tests serve only as indicators of a student's performance. There is a variety of types of tests and test scores that the classroom teacher must understand to interpret and use tests effectively.

A major responsibility of the classroom reading teacher is to communicate with parents. The reporting of test scores and other information must be done within the laws of each state.

THOUGHT AND DISCUSSION QUESTIONS

1. What are the most significant areas of information needed by a classroom reading teacher to organize a diagnostic reading program? Which areas would be your first concern?

2. How should a teacher respond when told by a parent that his/her child (sixth grader) had failed to learn to read because of poor vision in the primary grades?
3. The newspaper of a small eastern community has printed the reading test scores by individual school. The results show that children in one school are reading three or more grade levels above those in other schools. Based on what you have learned about tests, how would you explain this report to the public?

APPLYING WHAT YOU HAVE LEARNED

1. Select a basal reading series used in your region of the country. Examine it to determine what resources it provides for gathering relevant information needed to organize and operate a diagnostic reading program.
2. Examine several different reading tests suggested by your instructor. Look through the examiner's manual to find out what types of reading scores are given and what types of information are presented to assist you with interpretation.
3. With other students in your class, construct an interest/attitude inventory that you might be able to use when you begin teaching.

BIBLIOGRAPHY

1. Balow, Irving H., et al. *Metropolitan Achievement Tests: Reading Survey Test.* New York, Psychological Corporation, 1978, 1979.
2. Block, J. H. *Schools, Society and Mastery Learning.* New York: Holt, Rinehart and Winston, 1974.
3. Bloom, B. S., et al. *Handbook on Formative and Summative Evaluation of Student Learning.* New York: McGraw-Hill Book Company, 1971.
4. Bond, Guy L.; Tinker, Miles A.; and Wasson, Barbara B. *Reading Difficulties: Their Diagnosis and Correction,* 4th ed. Englewood Cliffs, N. J.: Prentice-Hall, Inc. 1979, pp. 71-116.
5. Cole, Ann, et al. *I Saw a Purple Cow: 100 Other Recipes for Learning.* Boston: Little, Brown and Company, 1972.
6. Cooper, J. David, et al. *Decision Making for the Diagnostic Teachers.* New York: Holt, Rinehart and Winston, 1972.
7. DeFranco, Ellen B., and Pickarts, Evelyn M. *Parents, Help Your Child to Read: Ideas to Use at Home.* New York: Van Nostrand Reinhold Company, 1972.
8. Division of Pupil Personnel Services, Department of Public Instruction, State of Indiana, Indianapolis. "Family Educational Rights and Privacy Act of 1974, "memo interpreting P.L. 93-380.

9. Eames, T. H. "A Frequency Study of Physical Handicaps in Reading Disability and Unselected Groups." *Journal of Educational Research,* **29** (1935), 1–5.

10. Ekwall, Eldon. *Diagnosis and Remediation of the Disabled Reader.* Boston: Allyn & Bacon, Inc., 1976, pp. 1–21.

11. Farr, Roger. *Reading: What Can Be Measured?* Newark, Del.: International Reading Association, 1969.

12. Gates, Arthur I.; McKillop, Anne S.; and Horowitz, Elizabeth. (Gates-McKillop-Horowitz Reading Diagnostic Tests, 2nd ed. New York: Teachers College Press, 1981.

13. Guthrie, John T., et al. *A Study of the Locus and Nature of Reading Problems in the Elementary School.* Final Report, ED 127 568, 1976.

14. Harper, Robert J., and Kilarr, Gary. *Reading and the Law.* Newark, Del.: International Reading Association, 1978.

15. Harris, Albert J., and Sipay, Edward R. *How to Increase Reading Ability,* 7th ed. New York: Longman, Inc., 1980.

16. Jenkins, Jeanne Kohl, and MacDonald, Pam. *Growing Up Equal: Activities and Resources for Parents and Teachers of Young Children.* Englewood Cliffs, N. J.: Prentice-Hall, Inc., 1979.

17. Karlsen, Bjorn, et al. *Stanford Diagnostic Reading Test: (SDRT).* New York: Psychological Corporation, 1978.

18. Loban, Walter. *Language Development: Kindergarten Through Grade Twelve.* Urbana, Ill.: National Council of Teachers of English, 1976.

19. Madden, Richard, et al. *Stanford Achievement Test.* New York: Psychological Corporation, 1973.

20. MacGinitie, Walter H., ed. *Assessment Problems in Reading.* Newark, Del.: International Reading Association, 1973.

21. _____. *Gates-MacGinitie Reading Tests,* 2nd ed. Boston: Houghton Mifflin Company, 1978.

22. "Misuse of Grade Equivalents." Statement adopted by the Board of Directors of the International Reading Association, taken from *Reading Today* (June 1980).

23. Muehl, Sigmar, and King, Ethel. "Recent Research in Visual Discrimination: Significance for Beginning Reading," in *Teaching Word Recognition Skills,* compiled by Mildred A. Dawson, Newark, Del., I.R.A., 1971.

24. Potter, Thomas C., and Rae, Gwenneth. *Informal Reading Diagnosis,* 2nd ed. Englewood Cliffs, N. J.: Prentice-Hall, Inc., 1981.

25. Prescott, George A., et al. *Metropolitan Achievement Tests.* New York: Psychological Corporation, 1978.

26. Robinson, Helen M. *Why Pupils Fail in Reading.* Chicago: University of Chicago Press, 1946.

27. Ruddell, Robert B. *Reading-Language Instruction: Innovative Practices.* Englewood Cliffs, N. J.: Prentice-Hall, Inc., 1974.

28. Rupley, William H., and Blair, Timothy R. *Reading Diagnosis and Remediation.* Chicago: Rand McNally Publishing Company, 1979, pp. 43–63.

29. Spache, George D. *Investigating the Issues of Reading Disabilities.* Boston: Allyn & Bacon, Inc., 1976.

30. Strang, Ruth. *Reading Diagnosis and Remediation.* Newark, Del.: International Reading Association, 1968.

31. Thorndike, Robert L., and Hagen, Elizabeth. *Measurement and Evaluation in Psychology and Education,* 4th ed. New York: John Wiley & Sons, Inc., 1977.

32. Weintraub, Samuel. "Auditory Perception and Deafness." in *Reading Research Profiles.* Newark, Del.: International Reading Association, 1972.

33. _____. "Vision-Visual Discrimination," in *Reading Research Profiles,* Newark, Del.: International Reading Association, 1973.

FOR FURTHER READING

Burns, Paul C., and Betty D. Roe. *Teaching Reading in Today's Elementary School,* *2nd ed. Chicago: Rand McNally* College Publishing Company, 1980, Chapters 3, 4, and 5.

Cooper, J. David, et al. *The What and How of Reading Instruction.* Columbus, Ohio: Charles E. Merrill Publishing Company, 1979, Module CS, Comprehension Skills; Module WR, Word Recognition Skills; Module SS, Study Skills.

Heilman, Arthur. *Phonics in Proper Perspective,* 4th ed. Columbus, Ohio: Charles E. Merrill Publishing Company, 1981, entire book.

section II

assessment

Continuous assessment and diagnosis is an important component of the effective reading program. The two chapters in this section will help the teacher learn to place students in instructional materials for reading and will aid one in learning how to assess specific skill needs.

chapter 3

placing a student in basal materials

objectives

As a result of reading this chapter, one will

1. Understand the ideas and concepts related to placing students in instructional materials.
2. Know the criteria for determining a student's three reading levels.
3. Be able to administer an informal reading inventory.
4. Be aware of alternative procedures for placing students in instructional materials.

overview

Selecting appropriate materials for each student's reading instruction is a major component of a good diagnostic reading program. To accomplish this the classroom teacher must have a thorough understanding of a student's reading levels and know how to use a variety of techniques to determine these levels. This chapter will help the teacher develop the needed background and skills to accomplish this task. It is important that the teacher rely on his/her knowledge of reading skills and reading tests in going through this chapter. The knowledge and skills that one develops will help one carry out Step 1 of the diagnostic teaching process: Gather relevant background information.

A major concern of a diagnostic classroom reading teacher will be placing one's students in the material that will best help them learn to read. Since most teachers teach reading from some type of basal reader (25), it is logical to ask, "Which level of the basal reader will be best for each student?" Too many children are frequently placed in the wrong level of the basal series. This occurs because placement is done hurriedly or without sufficient thought. Perhaps the most important decision to be made by the teacher in planning a child's reading instruction is determining the correct level of the reading series in which to place him/her. This decision will require some subjective judgment but it can be made more validly if one learns to use certain tools and follow certain criteria.

Accurate placement of students in reading materials makes it easier to plan class instruction. With this information the teacher can form more manageable groups and get at the individual needs of all students more effectively. By having materials that he/she can read, a child's self-concept is greatly enhanced and he/she is able to be more successful in reading. Nothing tends to make people more successful in an activity than actually succeeding at it. For example, if one is a good piano player and feels that one has succeeded, there is a tendency to want to play more. The same holds true for a child learning to read. If a child is instructed with materials that she/he can read comfortably, she/he is likely to be more successful in learning to read.

Placing students in reading materials that they can read will reduce many classroom behavior problems. A student who is able to read his/her material and do his/her work is less likely to create disturbances or be disruptive. While having students in materials that they can read will not eliminate discipline problems, it will certainly help alleviate them or prevent them from occurring. Not only will this make learning more effective for the individual student, but it will also make learning easier for the other students and teaching more enjoyable for the teacher. The reading growth of all students will be affected.

Too often classroom teachers place students in instructional materials too quickly. The amount of time spent in more accurate placement of students pays off with many benefits for the teacher and the students involved.

PROCEDURES FOR PLACING STUDENTS IN INSTRUCTIONAL MATERIALS

There are many different procedures that can be used for placing students in instructional materials. Some of these were briefly referred to in Chapter 2. Each procedure has certain strengths and weaknesses that must be considered when deciding which to use in placing students for reading instruction. It should be remembered that not all procedures are to be used for all students.

The Informal Reading Inventory (IRI)

The Informal Reading Inventory or IRI, as it is commonly called, has been discussed by reading experts for more than sixty years (1). In general, it consists of a series of passages graded in difficulty from the primer or preprimer level to the eighth- and sometimes twelfth-grade levels. Each passage is accompanied by a series of questions that the teacher asks the student after a given passage is read. Figure 3-1 shows a sample IRI passage taken from the Analytical Reading Inventory (27). The IRI is simply a way of having a student take a sample of reading material from a specific level and "try it on to see how it fits." This is much like going into a store and trying on a certain piece of clothing for size. Just as certain sizes vary slightly, certain reading materials vary slightly. A second-grade-level reader in one series might not be exactly the same as a second-grade-level in another series.

The IRI can be used to accomplish several purposes in setting up the diagnostic reading program. These include

1. Determining each students three reading levels—independent, instructional, and frustration.
2. Measuring a student's use of decoding and comprehension skills in a contextual reading situation.
3. Using an IRI as a listening test to measure a student's capacity for reading.

There are different types of IRIs that can be used to accomplish these purposes. One is the IRI that accompanies a basal reading series. Most publishers provide an IRI, along with their materials, which is actually a set of passages taken from each reader. Reading authorities such as Farr (8) feel that this may be the best type of IRI because it actually allows the child the opportunity to try out the materials from those books that will be read. A disadvantage of this type is that children will sometimes remember the stories that have been taken from books in previous levels. While this should not be considered a major problem, it is a potential concern of which one needs to be aware. Figure 3-2 shows an example of an IRI that accompanies the Ginn 720 reading series.

Not all basal series have an IRI available, and a second type is the teacher-made version. In this case the teacher selects passages from 50 to 100 words from each of the levels of the reading series. Questions are then developed for each selection. This procedure requires more teacher time for preparation but does allow the teacher to have materials that actually match the reading series available. If a publishing company does not provide an IRI for its particular series, the teacher-made version is one of the better alternatives. A disadvantage of this procedure is that sometimes the passages selected are not really representative of the reading levels of the books from which they were taken.

Level 3 (138 words   12 sent.)

Examiner's Introduction
(Student Booklet page 66):   Joe wanted more than anything in the world to buy the electric train set in the trading post window. But should he do this? Please read the following story.

Joe sat down on the sidewalk in front of the trading post with his buckskin jacket thrown over his shoulder. He felt worried because it was difficult to know what to do.

"Grandfather told me never to sell these blue beads. He said they would bring me good fortune and good health. Grandfather is a wise and understanding man. He is proud to be an American Indian. He remembers when his grandfather gave him these same beads. He has often told me many interesting stories of how his grandfather rode horses and hunted buffalo on the plains."

Joe held the string of beads high into the air toward the sunlight. "These are perfectly beautiful beads," he said out loud. "I can't sell them because I too am proud of my great past. Yes, I will keep the beads!"

Comprehension Questions
and Possible Answers

(mi)   1. What is Joe's difficult decision?
(whether to sell the beads his grandfather had given him)

(f)   2. Where was Joe sitting?
(on the sidewalk in front of the trading post)

(f)   3. What did Joe's grandfather say the beads would do for Joe?
(bring him good fortune and good health)

(t)   4. What is meant by the word *remembers*?
(to recall from the past)

(f)   5. Who had given the beads to Joe's grandfather?
(Joe's great-great grandfather)

(t)   6. What is meant by the phrase "on the plains"?
(western great plains)

(ce)   7. Why did Joe finally decide he couldn't sell the beads?
(He was proud of his past.)

(con) 8. What is said in the story that makes you think Joe has respect for his grandfather?
(Stated: Grandfather is a wise and understanding man; he couldn't sell the beads.)

Miscue Count:

O___ I___ S___ A___ REP___ REV___

Scoring Guide	
Word Rec.	Comp.
IND 1–2	IND 0–1
INST 7	INST 2
FRUST 14 +	FRUST 4 +

FIGURE 3-1.   Sample IRI Passage (Form B, Level 3).

Source: Analytical Reading Inventory, p. 82. Reprinted by permission of Charles E. Merrill Publishing Co.

SILENT READING EVALUATION

Background   Have you ever wanted to do something for your mother or father? This is a story about what some children want to do for their mother on her birthday.

Purpose   Read the story to learn why Mom's birthday is important and what the children want to do.

COMPREHENSION QUESTIONS

1. How old will Mom be on her birthday? (Forty years old.)
2. Why is this birthday a milestone? (Mom wants to live to be eighty, and this birthday is halfway to eighty.)
3. What was Lucy's idea for a birthday present? (To give Mom a picture taken of all the children together.)
4. What were the children doing as they talked about Mom? (Eating, cleaning their plates, having dinner.)

SUCCESS CRITERION: COMPREHENSION

Success: 0 or 1 error (75%+)

Page 52 (page 46) - Level 11   123 words

ORAL READING EVALUATION

Background   The children go to Mr. Green's Studio to get the birthday picture made.

Purpose   Read the story to find out what happens in Mr. Green's Studio.

COMPREHENSION QUESTIONS

1. One word can describe Mr. Green's head, face, belly, shoes, and glasses. What is the word?   (Round.)
2. What did Lucy ask Mr. Green?   (If he took pictures on credit.)
3. What did Bonnie do for Mr. Green?   (She wiggled her front tooth.)
4. What kind of person do you think Mr. Green is? (Accept any answer suggesting kind, gentle, helpful, nice, and so forth.)

SUCCESS CRITERION: WORD RECOGNITION

Success: 11 or less errors (92%+)

SUCCESS CRITERION: COMPREHENSION

Success: 0 or 1 error (75%+)

Page 55 (page 49) - Level 11   141 words

"And this birthday is very important to Mom," Lucy continued. "She calls it a milestone. She says she plans to live until she's eighty and this birthday puts her halfway there. Forty! Right in the middle. A milestone!"

Mom forty! It seemed a great age. They thought about it in silence as they cleaned up their plates.

Finally Christopher said, "Are you planning something for Mom?"

Lucy nodded. "In a way," she said. "I have an idea, that's all." She looked around the table. "You want to come in on it?"

Dennis' eyes grew cautious. "What do you have in mind?"

"I want to have a picture taken of all of us together. I want it right now before Bonnie's tooth comes out."

FIGURE 3-2.   Sample IRI Passage.

Source: Pages 414-415 of Teacher's Edition of *Mountains Are for Climbing* of the READING 720 series by Theodore Clymer and others, © Copyright, 1976, by Ginn and Company (Xerox Corporation). Used with permission.

A third type of IRI is the one developed independent of any basal series. There are many of these now on the market and they will be reviewed at the conclusion of this chapter. These IRIs contain two or three forms and have had their difficulty levels checked using a readability formula. They provide the classroom teacher an excellent tool for evaluating a child's reading growth apart from the basal series. A problem that often exists with these IRIs is that the match between the levels on the tests and the basal materials is not always exact. For example, if the teacher finds that a child's instructional reading level is 2 on the IRI and that there are two or three second-grade books in the series, it may be difficult to tell which one should be used. This problem is usually overcome with experience as the teacher gets to know a particular series and a particular IRI.

A final variation of the IRI is the group IRI, which has been adapted for group administration. There is support in the literature for this procedure (12). However, the group IRI has certain drawbacks that make its use difficult but not impossible. Later in this chapter the development and use of a group IRI will be discussed.

The Group Placement Test

Another procedure for placing students in instructional material is the group placement test. This is a test that can be given to a large group at one time and has been developed by the publisher of the basal series. Figure 3-3 shows a sample group placement test designed to accompany the HBJ Bookmark Reading Program.

The group placement test is relatively easy to administer but it has numerous problems that lead one to question its value. These tests tend to place students in levels that are too difficult. Frequently, the tests are also too oriented to the measurement of isolated skills. While the concept seems sound, in reality it has not been found to be an effective way to place students in instructional materials. The group placement test appears to be the easiest way to place students, but in the long run it is probably more difficult because it only creates more work for the teacher and greater frustrations for the student because of errors made in placement. Such errors can result in wasted instructional time.

RATIONALE FOR USING AN IRI IN THE CLASSROOM

As already indicated, the IRI seems to be the most useful and accurate tool available for the classroom teacher to use in placing students for reading instruction. Its validity and reliability for determining a student's reading levels is well documented (8). Even though it is a test that must be individually administered to each student, the time spent in doing this individual testing gives

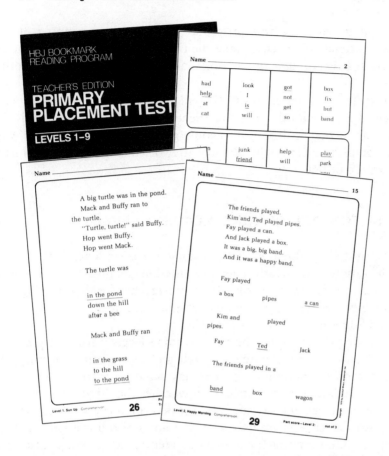

FIGURE 3-3. Group Placement Test from HBJ Bookmark Reading Program.

Source: From *Primary Placement Test, Teacher's Edition* by Maurine A. Fry and Jerry D. Harris in *HBJ Bookmark Reading Program,* copyright © 1979 by Harcourt Brace Jovanovich, Inc., and reproduced with their permission.

the teacher more valuable information about the student and leads to a more precise reading program.

Since the IRI is the only procedure that allows for accurate placement of students in reading materials, the classroom reading program must make use of this tool. The most effective use of the IRI in the elementary school reading program is to have every teacher in the school use it to determine initial placement of a new student and the movement of students from one level to the next in the basal series. Too often movement in the series is determined by completion of the book (to level 7 after level 6) or by the scores on an isolated skills test (mastery tests). The IRI allows the teacher to observe and measure each student's reading in a contextual setting where it is necessary for the student to use all of his/her reading skills together. If the teachers throughout a school systematically use the IRI, there would probably never be a time when a single teacher would have to individually test all members of a class. However,

if other teachers do not use this procedure, then at the beginning of each school year the teacher will need to take the time to give the IRI to all the students in the class. Even though this is time consuming, it will be of benefit in the long run.

The time factor in individually testing all the students in a class is viewed by many teachers as a major deterrent to the use of an IRI. However, this time can be spread out so that it does not become a problem for the teacher. Ways to do this will be given later in the chapter after discussing how to administer, score, and interpret an IRI.

CRITERIA FOR DETERMINING READING LEVELS

The concept of a student's three reading levels—independent, instructional, and frustration—has already been presented in Chapter 2. The IRI is the most appropriate tool available to the classroom teacher for determining these levels. By using given criteria one can observe and evaluate a student's oral and silent reading and determine these three levels.

The criteria for determining the three reading levels were first presented by Betts (2). Since that time much research and discussion concerning the levels and the criteria for determining them has taken place (6, 16, 17, 19, 20, 21). While there is conflicting evidence as to whether the original Betts criteria are too rigid, they still are one's best guides for determining a student's reading levels. As long as these criteria are used as guides and not followed as absolutes, they will serve as sound criteria for helping to identify a student's three reading levels. Table 3-1 summarizes these criteria.

Independent Level

For a student to be able to read a given level independently he/she must be able to orally call approximately 99 per cent of the words correctly and answer approximately 90 per cent of the questions. The student should be

TABLE 3-1. Criteria for Determining Reading Levels.

Level	Word Recognition (WR)	Comprehension (Comp)	Behavior
Independent	99 per cent	90 per cent or more	Reads with ease; no signs of tension
Instructional	95 per cent or more	75 per cent or more	Reads with ease; still no signs of tension but has more WR and Comp errors
Frustration	Less than 90 per cent	Less than 50 per cent	Reading breaks down; tension observed

comfortable reading at this level and show no signs of tension. In evaluating a student's silent reading, his/her independent level is determined by using the comprehension criterion of 90 per cent.

Instructional Level

The instructional level is the point at which the teacher wants to place a student in instructional materials. If a student is to be able to read a certain level instructionally he/she must be able to read orally at least 95 per cent of the words and answer at least 75 per cent of the comprehension questions. Again, no signs of tension should be apparent. The teacher will note that there is considerable distance between the cut-off points for the independent level and the instructional level. In word recognition, for example, the independent cut-off point is 99 per cent, the instructional, 95 per cent. For comprehension, the independent cut-off point is 90 per cent, the instructional, 75 per cent. One learns how to deal with this as one finds out more about administration and interpretation of the IRI. It is this range between levels that one must learn to use flexibly in order to avoid the criticisms about the rigidity of the Betts criteria and the reading-levels concept. When the teacher is evaluating a student's silent reading, only the comprehension criterion would be used in determining the instructional level.

Frustration Level

At the frustration level a student's reading breaks down completely. He/-she orally reads less than 90 per cent of the words and comprehends less than 50 per cent of the material (answers less than 50 per cent of the questions). This is the level that one should avoid in placing a student for instruction. Placing a student at his/her frustration level could be very detrimental to reading growth. If silent reading is being evaluated, only the comprehension criterion should be used.

READING CAPACITY

A student's reading capacity can also be determined using an IRI. To do this, the IRI is used as a listening test and the student's listening level is assessed. This is a measure of the student's reading capacity.

When the IRI is used as a listening test, the examiner reads the material aloud to the student and asks the questions orally. The listening or reading capacity level is defined as the highest-level passage where a student can listen to the material being read aloud and correctly answer 75 per cent of the questions asked. By comparing this level to the reading levels, the teacher will be able to tell whether or not a student has the ability to improve in reading.

FLEXIBLE USE OF CRITERIA
FOR DETERMINING LEVELS

The criteria presented for determining reading and listening levels should serve as guide points in helping one determine the students' reading levels and reading capacity. In demonstrating the use of the IRI continuous stress will be placed on the flexible use of these criteria. They are not rigid standards and must be used in conjunction with teacher observation and sound judgment.

PROCEDURES FOR ADMINISTERING AN IRI

Many authorities in the field of reading have expressed differing opinions about how an IRI should be administered (3, 7, 11, 13). Some research has been conducted on the procedures to be followed and the various problems related to them (4, 5, 9, 10, 14, 15, 18, 22, 23, 26). The guidelines presented here are derived from a synthesis of the body of literature and research on this subject. While some reading experts may have other opinions, these guidelines have been effective and are based on sound evidence and professional opinion.

Ways to Administer An IRI

An IRI may be administered in any one of three different ways:

1. *Orally*   When the IRI is administered as an oral test the student reads a story aloud without having read it silently first while the teacher records on a copy of the story the deviations from the text made by the reader. These deviations are called errors (12) or miscues (9). Observations of the student's general reading behavior are also recorded. This copy of the story is called a record form or protocol. After the student has read the story the teacher takes the copy away and asks the student the comprehension questions and records the responses. The oral IRI gives the teacher a picture of the student's decoding ability and oral comprehension.
2. *Silently.*   As a silent test the student is given a copy of the story to read to himself/herself. After the story has been read the teacher takes the copy from the student and asks the comprehension questions. This provides a measure of the student's silent comprehension.
3. *Listening.*   The IRI can also be used as a listening test. The teacher reads a story aloud to the student. After he/she is finished reading, the comprehension questions are asked. The teacher continues reading stories at higher levels until the student's listening comprehension drops below 75 per cent. This gives a measure of the student's listening comprehension which can be compared to the student's reading level to determine capacity for reading.

If a teacher wants to administer the IRI in all three ways, three different forms will be needed. To use the IRI effectively to determine accurate placement for reading instruction, the teacher should have at least an oral and a silent measure on a student.

Determining Starting Points

A major consideration in starting the administration of an IRI is determining the appropriate level on which to begin. The teacher should administer the oral test first and begin at a level where the student can read comfortably. One will also need to determine the appropriate starting point for the silent test and the listening test.

Determining Starting Point for the Oral Test

The starting point for the oral test may be determined in several ways depending on the particular IRI one is using.

Using a Word List. Many IRIs have a graded word list that accompanies them. Use of this word list can enable the teacher to estimate where the student should begin to read the oral passages. Figure 3-4 presents a sample graded word list.

Basic Reading Inventory, Form C

Graded Word Lists
Graded Passages

List C-C	List C	List C 1417	List C 8224
1. down	1. father	1. morning	1. through
2. work	2. saw	2. picture	2. parade
3. fast	3. now	3. sing	3. gray
4. no	4. word	4. does	4. silver
5. to	5. know	5. had	5. blew
6. dog	6. one	6. way	6. wave
7. big	7. around	7. coat	7. feed
8. who	8. goat	8. baby	8. ten
9. green	9. thank	9. fight	9. real
10. funny	10. too	10. ready	10. chase
11. said	11. man	11. or	11. track
12. this	12. house	12. pocket	12. winter
13. did	13. car	13. truck	13. joke
14. can	14. him	14. bee	14. star
15. are	15. bike	15. made	15. done
16. want	16. of	16. street	16. such
17. me	17. should	17. school	17. different
18. help	18. book	18. it's	18. splash
19. stop	19. pet	19. brown	19. shirt
20. ran	20. some	20. friend	20. meet

FIGURE 3-4. Sample Graded Word List from an IRI.

Source: Page 103, *Basic Reading Inventory*, Second Edition, by Jerry L. Johns. Reprinted by permission of Kendall/Hunt Publishing Co.

The teacher gives the student a copy of the word list and has him/her read the words aloud beginning with the lowest level. As the student reads, the teacher records the responses using the following coding:

Coding Procedure for Word Lists

1. Word Correct—leave space blank.

    horse _____

2. Does Not Know Word or Does Not Attempt

    put minus

    horse _____−_____

3. Miscalls Word

    Record response

    horse _____hay_____

4. Miscalls Word and Self-corrects

    Mark a C and do not count as an error

    horse _____hay^C_____

If the student asks the teacher to pronounce a word for him/her, the teacher should tell him to try it or to skip it and go on. The teacher should not pronounce the words for the student. One should avoid the temptation of teaching the unknown words while testing. The student continues to read the words aloud until he/she misses *5 or more* words in any one list. (This criterion may vary slightly depending on the IRI being used and the number of words in the list. Usually the list will contain 20 words and the teacher is looking for the place where the student misses *25 per cent or more* of them.) Once this point has been reached, the teacher should stop the reading of the word lists.

To determine the starting point for the oral paragraphs, the teacher should examine the word lists read by the student and look for the highest level where the student got 100 per cent of the words correct. This should be the student's independent level and the starting point for the oral paragraphs. In examining the marked word list in Figure 3-5, one learns that Charles read the word lists from primer through grade level 4 where he missed 6 words. The highest level where he got 100 per cent of the words correct was level 2. Therefore, the teacher would begin his oral paragraphs at level 2. If Charles had failed to obtain 100 per cent on any word list, the teacher should begin with the lowest level of the oral paragraphs.

Beginning with the First Story. Another way to determine the starting point for the oral paragraphs is to begin with the lowest-level story in the test.

(Primer) (1) (2)

1. not _____
2. funny _____
3. book _____
4. thank _____
5. good _____
6. into _____
7. know _____
8. your _____
9. come _____
10. help _____
11. man _____
12. now _____
13. show _____
14. want _____
15. did _____
16. have _____
17. little _____
18. cake _____
19. home _____
20. soon _____

1. kind _____
2. rocket _____
3. behind _____
4. our _____
5. men _____
6. met _____
7. wish _____
8. told _____
9. after _____
10. ready _____
11. barn _____
12. next _____
13. cat _____
14. hold _____
15. story _____
16. turtle _____
17. give _____
18. cry _____
19. fight _____
20. please _____

1. mile _____
2. fair _____
3. ago _____
4. need _____
5. fourth _____
6. lazy _____
7. field _____
8. taken _____
9. wolf _____
10. part _____
11. save _____
12. hide _____
13. high _____
14. bad _____
15. love _____
16. brave _____
17. reach _____
18. song _____
19. cup _____
20. trunk _____

(3) (4)

1. beginning _____
2. thankful _____
3. written _____
4. reason _raisin_
5. bent _____
6. patient _____
7. manage _____
8. arithmetic _____
9. burst _brush_
10. bush _____
11. gingerbread _____
12. tremble _tumble_
13. planet _____
14. struggle _____
15. museum _—_
16. grin _____
17. ill _____
18. alarm _____
19. cool _____
20. engine _____

1. worm _____
2. afford _after_
3. player _____
4. scientific _____
5. meek _____
6. rodeo _redo_
7. festival _—_
8. hillside _____
9. coward _____
10. boom _____
11. booth _____
12. freeze _____
13. protest _—_
14. nervous _—_
15. sparrow _____
16. level _____
17. underground _____
18. oxen _____
19. eighty _____
20. shouldn't _____

FIGURE 3-5. Sample Marked Word List for Charles.

Source: Woods and Moe, *Analytical Reading Inventory*, Second Edition, 1981. Pp. 40–41. Reprinted by permission of Charles E. Merrill Publishing Co.

By observing the student's oral reading, comprehension, and general reading mannerisms, the teacher can estimate where to go from that point. One can continue on to the next higher level story or skip stories. The main thing to remember is that the student should begin the test at an independent level. This procedure is appropriate to use when the particular IRI has no word lists. It is more time-consuming in many instances, but it may be the teacher's only choice. As the teacher becomes more proficient in noting certain tendencies about a student's reading, the use of this procedure becomes easier.

Using Standardized Test Scores. If the teacher has a standardized reading-test score on a student, it can be used to estimate where to begin the oral passages. Since the teacher already knows that the standardized test score most likely represents frustration level for the student, one can drop back two levels to begin the oral paragraphs. For example, Debbie has a standardized reading-test score of 4.1. Assuming that this is frustration level, the teacher can drop back to level two to begin the oral passages. This would provide one with an estimated starting point.

Consider Current Basal Placement. If the teacher knows the last level of the basal series that the student has read (this is why record keeping is so important—see Chapters 6 and 7) and feels that placement was fairly accurate, one could drop back one level to begin the oral paragraphs. For example, Ed is a new student in one's room. The records obtained from his previous teacher indicate that he was reading at grade level 5 in the basal series. It must be assumed that this was his instructional level and one should drop back to level 4 to begin the oral paragraphs. This will provide the teacher with an estimated starting point.

It must be remembered that none of these procedures is perfect for determining the starting point for the oral paragraphs. They provide only an estimated place to begin. If a teacher begins the first oral paragraph and finds that one has the student reading higher than his/her independent level, one should drop back until reaching the level where he/she is independent. For example, Larry's testing is begun at level 4 and it is found that this is his instructional level. The teacher should then give him level 3 which is also instructional. The teacher can then proceed to level 2, which has been determined to be his independent level. Then one would continue upward from level four until the frustration level is reached.

Determining Starting Point for the Silent Test

To determine the starting point for the silent test the results of the oral IRI must be examined. The student's word recognition and comprehension results should be looked over. The teacher will want to locate the level at which the student was independent in *both* word recognition and comprehension. Here are the results of Ann's oral paragraphs:

Ann R.	Oral IRI Results	
Level	*WR*	*Comp*
2	Ind.	Ind.
3	Ind.	Ind.
4	Inst.	Ind.
5	Inst.	Inst.
6	Frus.	Frus.

Ann was independent in word recognition and comprehension at both levels 2 and 3. Therefore, the starting point for her silent test should be level 3—the highest level where she was independent in both word recognition and comprehension.

Determining the Starting Point for the Listening Test

The starting point for the listening test is estimated by looking at the results of the oral and silent tests. The level where the student is instructional based on the results of these tests is likely to be the appropriate place to begin the listening test. For example, the teacher has determined that Sara is instructional at level 3. One should begin the listening test at this point. The teacher would administer the passages until reaching the level where Sara scores less than 75 per cent on the comprehension questions, since the listening level is determined as the highest level where the student is able to comprehend 75 per cent of the material. If in administering the first passage one finds that the level is too high (student scores less than 75 per cent), one should drop back to the next lower passage. If Sara scores less than 75 per cent, one should continue going back until the level where she can answer 75 per cent of the questions or more is reached.

Determining Stopping Points on the Oral and Silent IRI

The point at which one stops the testing of a student on the oral IRI is determined by her/his word recognition and comprehension responses. The *oral* test should be continuted until the student reaches his frustration level in both word recognition and comprehension. On the silent test one continues until the student reaches frustration in comprehension only. The following are the test-score patterns for Students A and B:

	Student A				**Student B**		
Oral		*Silent*	*IRI*		*Oral*		*Silent*
WR	*Comp.*	*Comp.*	*Level*		*WR*	*Comp.*	*Comp.*
Ind.	Ind.		3		Ind.	Ind.	Ind.
Ind.	Ind.	Ind.	4		Frus.	Inst.	Ind.
Inst.	Frus.	Ind.	5		Inst.	Inst.	Ind.
Inst.	Inst.	Inst.	6		Inst.	Frus.	Inst.
Frus.	Frus.	Frus.	7		Frus.	Frus.	Frus.

Both students were frustrated in one area (Student A, oral comprehension, level 3; Student B, oral word recognition, level 4) before they actually reached their true frustration levels. Therefore, the rule of thumb for the stop-

ping point on the oral test is to have the student reach his/her frustration level in both word recognition and comprehension before stopping the testing.

In some cases the teacher will need to stop the testing when a student shows signs of frustration other than those in word recognition and comprehension. These signs would include extreme nervousness, crying, or refusing to do the reading. The teacher must make the decision to stop the testing based on his/her observations. If these or other signs of extreme frustration occur one should discontinue the testing even though the word recognition and comprehension have not reached the frustration level.

Most published IRIs will have some type of scoring guide at the bottom of each passage that will help the teacher to quickly calculate the student's score and determine whether the performance of the student was at the independent, instructional, or frustration level. Figure 3-1 presented earlier in this chapter has a sample scoring guide from a published IRI. This guide enables a teacher to determine the student's score without doing the mathematical calculations.

Coding Oral Reading Errors

As a student reads orally from the passages of an IRI the teacher will need to record the word-call errors that are made. Some authorities refer to these errors as miscues (9). There are two categories of miscues to record—those that *are to be counted* in figuring the student's score and those that are recorded for observation purposes but *not to be counted* in the scoring. Table 3-2 presents a coding system to be used for the recording of these miscues.

The miscues that are counted in the scoring are the ones that reveal a student's decoding ability. The *misreading* is any error in which a student miscalls a word or any part of it. To record this miscue, one draws a line through the word or part of the word that is miscalled and writes in what was said. *Omissions* are words that have been left out or skipped as the student reads. These are circled. *Unknown words* are words that a student does not know or does not attempt. One should not tell the student the word because that would be giving him/her clues that might aid in working out other words in the passage and thus contribute to an inflated comprehension score. The teacher should mark UK above the unknown word and tell the student to skip it and go on with the reading.

The second category of miscues to look for while a student is reading orally is the one that provides information about the student's general reading behavior and reading mannerisms. These *are not* counted in figuring the student's score on the passage but are recorded and used for analysis purposes. The *hesitation* is a definite pause between words that may indicate that the student does not have an adequate sight vocabulary or is a word-by-word reader. This mannerism is recorded by putting a slash mark between each word where the pause occurs. *Insertions* take place when a student adds a word. This is recorded by inserting a caret where the word was added and writing in what was

TABLE 3-2.   Coding System for Oral Reading Miscues.

Category I
Miscues That Count in Scoring

Type of Miscue	Description	Symbol	Example
Misreading	Word called incorrectly	Draw line through word and write in what was said.	The boy sang ~~loudly.~~ *loud*
Omission	Word left out	Circle the omitted word.	The (boy) sang loudly.
Unknown word	Word not known; *do not pronounce word for student.*	Write UK above the word.	The boy sang *UK* loudly.

Category II
Miscues That Do Not Count in Scoring

Hesitation	Definite pause between words	Put slash marks at points of pause.	The / boy / sang loudly.
Insertion	Word or words added	Insert caret (∧) under word added.	*little* The ∧boy sang loudly.
Punctuation	Punctuation skipped	Circle.	The boy sang loudly⊙ He wanted to be heard.
Repetition	One or more words repeated	Draw wavy line under words repeated.	The boy sang loudly.

said. Insertions sometimes make the passage more meaningful to the reader. These errors could indicate the type of thinking the student is doing while he/she is reading or they could show carelessness on the reader's part.

Punctuation errors are those that occur when a student skips a punctuation mark. These are recorded by circling the punctuation skipped. Skipping punctuation can influence a student's comprehension ability.

A final error that is recorded and not counted in the student's oral reading is *repetition*, or the repeating of one or more words. A wavy line is drawn under the word repeated.

General observations of the student's oral reading behavior should be made while the student is reading aloud. The teacher should make notes in the margin for such items as finger pointing (FP) and word-by-word (WW) reading. The codes noted in the parentheses may be used for these behaviors.

TABLE 3-3.   Coding for Silent-Reading Behaviors

Behavior	Description	Code
Finger pointing	Uses finger to keep place	FP
Head movement	Moves head along line while reading	HM
Lip movement	Moves lips while reading	LM
Vocalization	Says words aloud while reading	VOC

The first category of errors or miscues coded during oral reading is used in scoring the student's reading to determine whether it is the independent, instructional, or frustration level. Both the first and second category of errors or miscues are used for analysis purposes, which will be discussed later.

Coding Silent-Reading Behaviors

As a student reads silently there are certain mannerisms that one should look for. These will help one in understanding the student's total reading performance. Table 3-3 summarizes the coding for the silent-reading mannerisms.

Finger pointing refers to the student's use of his/her finger to keep the place while reading. One can note this mannerism by recording an FP on the test record form. Finger pointing may indicate that the student is having difficulty visually keeping the place or it could be a sign of general frustration. *Head Movement*, the moving of the head along the line of print as the student reads, is noted by recording HM. *Head movement*, like finger pointing, may indicate general frustration with the material or visual difficulties. *Lip movement* is noted by recording an LM and *vocalization* by recording VOC. Both of these behaviors may also indicate frustration with the material or a bad habit that could interfere with the student's comprehension.

As with the oral-reading behaviors presented earlier, the silent-reading behaviors should be recorded and used at the time of analysis to determine a complete picture of the student's reading. Behaviors other than the ones indicated here might be observed in some students. Any specialized observations should be noted and recorded.

General Steps to Follow in Administering an IRI

Now that the basic procedures for determining the starting points for the IRI and the coding procedures for oral and silent reading have been presented, the teacher is ready to put them all together to administer the test. The following steps should serve as guides:

1. *Classroom space should be arranged for testing.* There should be a place in the classroom where the test can be administered. A table

and chairs will be needed but the location for testing need not be completely isolated from the other students. A place off to the side of the room where one will be relatively free from distractions will be sufficient.

2. *The materials should be organized.* The test protocols and booklets that the teacher will need should be ready and available. There should be several sharpened pencils. Any materials that might distract the student or get in one's way should be removed.

3. *General instructions should be given and rapport built with the student.* One should tell the student as the testing begins that the purpose of the test is to find out as much as possible about his/her reading and that certain things will be written down as he/she reads. One should put the student at ease and encourage him/her to read just as he/she normally does.

4. *The student should be appropriately seated for testing.* The student should be seated slightly in front of the teacher, and to one's right or left as shown in the photograph. This enables one to record responses in a less obvious manner and at the same time observe the student's behaviors.

This Teacher is Seated Slightly to Her Student's Right and Behind Him As She Administers an IRI.

5. *The starting point for the oral IRI should be determined.* Using one of the procedures suggested the teacher should determine the starting point for the oral IRI. The student should begin with a paragraph which she/he can read comfortably if possible.

6. *The oral paragraphs should be administered.* Each paragraph should be introduced by telling the student to read the story aloud and that some questions will be asked. (Some IRIs have a motivation section in which a purpose for reading is given. For testing purposes it is suggested that this be deleted. Some IRIs also use pictures. These should

be covered and not used in testing.) After each story has been read orally, the test copy should be removed from the student before asking the questions.

7. *The oral paragraphs should be continued until the student reaches frustration in both word recognition and comprehension.* The scoring guide at the bottom of the protocol page should be used to determine the student's performance on each passage. When the student reaches frustration in both word recognition and comprehension, the testing should be stopped.

Example of Scoring Guide

	Word Recognition	Comprehension
Ind.	0–1	0–1
Inst.	2–3	1 1/2–2
Frus.	6	3

8. *The Silent IRI should be administered.* Using the guidelines presented earlier, the appropriate starting point for the silent IRI should be determined and the test administered.

9. *The listening test should be administered.* For a listening measure, one should now use a third form of the IRI and administer it as a listening test following the criteria given earlier.

Once these nine steps have been completed, one has the information to help place the student in the appropriate level of the basal series. The next step is to learn to interpret the results.

INTERPRETING IRI RESULTS

The data the teacher has gathered on each student, using an IRI, must now be summarized, analyzed, and interpreted before one can make the decisions needed to develop a reading program. The results of the IRI will help one to make four important decisions about each student's reading:

1. In what level of the basal series should the student be placed for instruction?
2. What strengths and needs does the student have in word recognition?
3. What strengths and needs does the student have in comprehension?
4. What is the student's capacity for improving his/her reading?

After completing the administration of the IRI one's recording and scoring should be checked carefully. On the front covers of each test protocol one should summarize the information that has been obtained. Figures 3-6, 3-7, and 3-8 present the test protocols on Mike R., who will be discussed to illustrate

STUDENT RECORD SUMMARY SHEET — *Oral*

FORM A

Student __Mike R.__ Grade __4__ Sex __M__ Age __8-1__ yrs. mos.

School __Anthony__ Administered by __M. Sonders__ Date __9-8-81__

Grade	Word Lists	Graded Passages			Estimated Levels		
	% of words correct	WR	Comp.	Listen.			
Primer	100						
1	100	Ind	Ind				
2	95	Ind	Inst			Grade	
3	95	Inst	Frus		Independent	____	
4	90	Inst	Inst		Instructional	____	
5	80	Frus	Frus		Frustration	____	
6	70				Listening	____	
7							
8							
9							

Check consistent oral reading difficulties:

____ word-by-word reading
____ omissions
____ substitutions
____ corrections
____ repetitions
____ reversals
____ inattention to punctuation
____ word inserts
____ requests word help

Check consistent word recognition difficulties:

____ single consonants
____ consonant clusters
____ long vowels
____ short vowels
____ vowel diagraphs
____ diphthongs
____ syllabication
____ use of context
____ basic sight
____ grade level sight

Check consistent comprehension difficulties:

____ main idea
____ factual
____ terminology
____ cause and effect
____ inferential
____ drawing conclusions
____ independent recall

Identifying special reading strengths:

_____
_____
_____
_____

FIGURE 3-6.
Source: Analytical Reading Inventory, Second Edition, 1981. Reprinted by permission of Charles E. Merrill Publishing Co.

STUDENT RECORD SUMMARY SHEET *- silent*

FORM B

Student ___**Mike R.**___   Grade ___**4**___   Sex ___**M**___   Age ___**8-1**___
                                                                      yrs. mos.

School ___**Anthony**___   Administered by **M. Sanders** Date ___**9-8-81**___

Grade	Word Lists	Graded Passages			Estimated Levels		
	% of words correct	WR	Comp.	Listen.			
Primer							
1			*Ind*				
2			*Ind*		Independent		Grade ___
3			*Ind*		Instructional		___
4			*Inst*		Frustration		___
5			*Inst/Frus*		Listening		___
6			*Frus*				
7							
8							
9							

Check consistent oral reading difficulties:

____ word-by-word reading
____ omissions
____ substitutions
____ corrections
____ repetitions
____ reversals
____ inattention to punctuation
____ word inserts
____ requests word help

Check consistent word recognition difficulties:

____ single consonants
____ consonant clusters
____ long vowels
____ short vowels
____ vowel diagraphs
____ diphthongs
____ syllabication
____ use of context
____ basic sight
____ grade level sight

Check consistent comprehension difficulties:

____ main idea
____ factual
____ terminology
____ cause and effect
____ inferential
____ drawing conclusions
____ independent recall

Identifying special reading strengths:

_____
_____
_____
_____

FIGURE 3-7.

Source: Analytical Reading Inventory, Second Edition, 1981. Reprinted by permission of Charles E. Merrill Publishing Co.

STUDENT RECORD SUMMARY SHEET – *Listening*

FORM C

Student ___*Mike R.*___ Grade ___*4*___ Sex ___*M*___ Age ___*8-1*___

yrs. mos.

School ___*Anthony*___ Administered by *M. Sonders* Date ___*9-8-81*___

Grade	Word Lists	Graded Passages			Estimated Levels
	% of words correct	WR	Comp.	Listen.	
Primer					
1					
2					Grade
3					Independent _____
4			*100*		Instructional _____
5			*80*		Frustration _____
6			*80*		Listening _____
7			*80*		
8			*60*		
9					

Check consistent oral reading difficulties:

____ word-by-word reading
____ omissions
____ substitutions
____ corrections
____ repetitions
____ reversals
____ inattention to punctuation
____ word inserts
____ requests word help

Check consistent word recognition difficulties:

____ single consonants
____ consonant clusters
____ long vowels
____ short vowels
____ vowel diagraphs
____ diphthongs
____ syllabication
____ use of context
____ basic sight
____ grade level sight

Check consistent comprehension difficulties:

____ main idea
____ factual
____ terminology
____ cause and effect
____ inferential
____ drawing conclusions
____ independent recall

Identifying special reading strengths:

_____
_____
_____
_____

FIGURE 3-8.
Source: Analytical Reading Inventory, Second Edition, 1981. Reprinted by permission of Charles E. Merrill Publishing Co.

procedures for interpreting the IRI results and making the decisions needed to set up a diagnostically based reading program.

Determining Levels for Placement

To determine Mike's reading levels one must study the pattern of responses on his oral and silent reading tests. In trying to identify his independent, instructional, and frustration levels, there are two rules that should be kept in mind:

1. The oral and silent reading tests should be studied together but more weight should be given to the silent test because it most nearly reflects what a student must do on his own.
2. When deciding on levels, if in doubt one should always go to a lower level as opposed to a higher one. It is easier to move a student up than it is to lower his/her level.

Examining the results presented in Figures 3-6 and 3-7, one can see that Mike is reading independently on the oral test at level 1. His oral comprehension begins to drop at second level, reaches frustration at three, and comes back up to instructional at level 4. From the silent test results one can see that he is independent up through level 3. Since more weight will be given to the silent results, one would say that *Mike's independent reading level is from level 1 to 3.* He might encounter difficulty with some level 3 materials, but since his silent scores held up, he probably could handle most materials independently at this level.

Mike's instructional level is clearly level 4. On the silent test he is wavering between instructional and frustration at level 5. Because he is showing definite frustration on the oral test at level 5 and frustration is beginning to appear on the silent test at this level, he should definitely be placed for instruction at level 4. This means that the teacher should place Mike in the fourth-grade level of the basal series.

Now one has analyzed and interpreted the IRI results on Mike. His reading levels are

Independent	1–3
Instructional	4
Frustration	5

Mike can now be placed in the basal series of instruction. At the beginning of the school year or when a student has been unsuccessful in reading, it is good to start him/her slightly below his/her identified instructional level to build confidence. In Mike's case this is probably not necessary because he is reading at his grade level.

The reading levels that one identifies from the IRI will frequently come out as a range as Mike's did on his independent level. This is normal and can be expected. In cases where this occurs with the instructional level the teacher will need to consider this range in making a final decision about placement in the basal. For example, one has Mark, a fifth-grade student, who has an instructional range of from grade 4 to grade 6. He reads equally well at all levels. There are five other students in the class who also read instructionally at sixth-grade level. There is no reason why one should not try Mark at sixth-grade instructional level to see how he performs.

Determining Capacity Level

Mike's reading capacity level is determined by looking at his performance on the listening test. The results are presented in Figure 3-8. The criterion for determining a student's listening level is the highest level where he was able to answer 75 per cent of the questions over a passage. In Mike's case, this is level 7, the highest point where he got 80 per cent (the closest point to 75 per cent).

One can now compare Mike's listening and reading levels:

Reading		Listening
Ind	1-3	7
Inst	4	
Frus	5	

This comparison indicates that Mike should have the capacity to improve his reading since his listening score is three levels higher than his instructional level. If Mike's reading and listening had been equal or if his listening had been lower than his reading, this would have indicated a need for work on oral language development, especially listening, to increase his capacity for reading.

Analyzing Word-Recognition Responses

Much information can be obtained about a student's word recognition or decoding skills in reading by analyzing the errors or miscues that were made on the oral IRI. The following steps should be used to make this analysis:

1. Make a list of the oral word-recognition miscues that change the context. Those errors that do not change the context are not indicative of word-recognition problems. For example, if a student said "hill" for "mountain" this is not a change of context. One should record the errors on a sheet set up like the one in Figure 3-9. The stimulus

Stimulus	Response	Possible Problem
darker	dark	ending er
cave	cove	long a—final e
Mark's	Mark	ending 's
shaking	shaked	ending ing
have	had	sight word
broke	break	long a—final e
foul	—	—
racer	race	ending er
amaze	amos	long a—final e
staple	stapled	long a—final e
intense	—	—
clamps	clowns	medial error— possibly vowel

FIGURE 3-9. Oral Word Recognition Errors for Mike R.

word is the one that was printed in the test. The response is what the student said when he was reading aloud.

2. List the possible problem or problems indicated by the miscue. In some cases an error or miscue is just an error and does not really indicate any particular problem.

3. Study the list of miscues to identify strengths and weaknesses. For a mistake to indicate a problem it should reappear in the list several times as a pattern. In Figure 3-9 one can see that Mike has a pattern of problems with endings and long vowel, final *e*. Mike also rather consistently gets the initial and final consonants of the word correct. This is certainly a strength for him.

The word-recognition strengths and weaknesses that the teacher is able to identify from the IRI are probably more significant than those one would detect on an isolated skills test because they are in context. The oral IRI actually provides a sample of how the reader uses or applies his decoding skills in context.

Analyzing Comprehension Responses

The final part of the analysis on the IRI is identifying comprehension strengths and weaknesses. The teacher must now look at the type of question that the reader got correct and the type missed. Each IRI will categorize com-

prehension questions differently. Some will talk about fact or literal (F), inferential (I), and vocabulary (V) questions while others use the terms main idea (mi), conclusion (con), inferential (I), cause and effect (c/e), and so on. One should be familiar with the comprehension categories on the IRI one is using and then complete the following steps to analyze the results:

1. Count the number of each type of comprehension question asked for the stories read. Then count the number of each type of comprehension question the student missed. Total across the paragraphs read the number of each type of question attempted and the number missed. (See Figure 3-10.)

2. Using the following formula, calculate the percentage of *each type* of comprehension question missed:

$$\frac{\text{Number missed}}{\text{Number attempted}} \times 100$$

3. Study the pattern of percentages to determine the relative strengths and weaknesses. A student should generally have no more than 25 per cent error in any comprehension category.

4. Complete the same analysis for the silent comprehension. (See Figure 3-11.)

5. Compare the results of the oral and silent comprehension and look for consistent patterns. One will notice that Mike is consistently low in factual comprehension and cause-effect. His oral inferences seem low but he missed only one out of three questions. On the silent inferences he made no errors. Therefore one would conclude that making inferences is probably not a problem for Mike. The main idea seems to pose more problems orally than silently for Mike and should probably be reviewed in instruction. Conclusions and terminology seem to be Mike's strongest areas.

			Level				
	1	2	3	4	5	Total	%
mi	0/1	0/1	1/1	0/1	1/1	2/5	40
inf	0/1	0/1	1/1	–	–	1/3	33
f	0/2	1/2	1/3	1/3	2/2	5/12	42
term	0/1	0/1	0/2	0/1	0/2	0/7	0
c–e	0/1	0/1	1/1	1/2	1/2	3/7	43
con				0/1	0/1	0/2	0

FIGURE 3-10.   Oral Comprehension Error Summary for Mike R.

	Level							
	1	2	3	4	5	6	Total	%
mi	0/1	0/1	0/1	0/1	0/1	1/1	1/6	17
ce	0/2	0/1	1/1	0/1	1/2	1/2	3/9	33
t	0/1	0/1	0/2	0/2	1/1	0/2	1/9	11
f	0/1	0/2	0/3	2/3	2/3	2/2	6/14	43
	0/1	0/1	0/1	–	0/1	–	0/4	0
inf		0/1			0/1		0/2	0

FIGURE 3-11. Silent Comprehension Error Summary for Mike R.

In summary, the results of the oral and silent comprehension analysis lead one to conclude that Mike's strengths in comprehension are drawing conclusions, using terminology, and making inferences. His weaknesses are in main ideas, facts, and cause-effect.

Summarizing IRI Results

Once the teacher has completed the analysis and interpretation of the IRI results, they should be summarized and recorded on some record form for easy use (see Chapter 6, on "Record Keeping"). Having the information recorded in a systematic manner will assist one in organizing and operating a diagnostic reading program.

Verifying Basal Placement

The results of the IRI will help one decide on the level of the basal reader to be used for each student. The IRI, like any other test, is not perfect. Therefore, its results should be verified in actual classroom work. When the level of basal reader placement for each student has been determined, one should set up some temporary groups and have them "try the books on for fit". During this trial period, students should read one or two stories using a Directed Reading Lesson (DRL). One can check the comprehension of students through oral questions and written exercises. One should observe general working habits and behavior to detect any signs of frustration such as too many word-call errors during oral reading, boredom because books are too easy, or inability to learn because the vocabulary load is too great. If the levels of placement seem appropriate, one can proceed with the program. If there are any problems, one should re-evaluate the placement levels.

ORGANIZING TO ADMINISTER THE IRI IN THE CLASSROOM

A major concern for a classroom teacher in using the IRI will be finding the time to administer it to twenty-five or thirty individuals. With appropriate planning, it can be done.

At the beginning of the school year one should take two or three weeks to get to know the students' reading abilities. During this period one can administer IRIs to the students. If the task is spread out over several weeks, it will not seem so monumental. One can test two or three students per day over a two-week period.

If there is an available auxiliary such as a teacher's assistant or aide, one can have him/her supervise the class doing independent work while one tests. Some teachers find the use of volunteer parents helpful in this situation.

Most teachers will not have any type of assistance. Therefore, giving constructive and useful independent seatwork will keep the other students involved while one is testing. One can take the time to discuss the testing with the class. They should be told how important it is and encouraged to help out by not disturbing others. Students can help one plan the types of things they can do during the time one is testing. Some of the activities should be fun and not all work. Quiet, small group games and activities can also be used. The key to making things successful while testing is sufficient preplanning and discussion with the class in terms of how to behave and act during this time. The task of individually testing all of the students is not that difficult once some basic procedures have been worked out.

In working out plans for giving the IRI to the class, the following guidelines will help one decide who to test first and how to get the most information possible from this initial two- or three-week period.

1. Examine previous reading records (if available) to identify those students about whom the teacher has raised a question concerning placement level. These children should be tested first.

2. Look at standardized test scores to identify those students who are reading one or more years above or below their grade level. These children should be tested next.

3. While the above students are being tested, give the remainder of the class stories to read from grade level readers and provide comprehension exercises over the stories. Use two or three stories on different days. Check the exercises. Look for those students who score less than 75 per cent. Test them next.

4. Finally, test all remaining students. If for some reason one is unable to finish the testing and has reached this point, one should have some idea of the placement level for these students. Also, one will have checked the extreme cases.

DEVELOPING AND USING A GROUP IRI

A variation of the IRI is the group informal reading inventory, which will be referred to as the GIRI. This type of test attempts to determine a student's level for placement and provides some information about comprehension strengths and weaknesses. The major advantage of the GIRI is that it utilizes the concepts and criteria from the IRI but can be administered in a group situation. Because the test is group administered it is not as reliable in accurately predicting a student's reading levels as is the IRI. There are no GIRIs on the market but some are in the process of being developed (24). However, in most cases a teacher who selects this procedure for placing students will have to develop the test.

Guidelines for Developing a GIRI

Johnson and Kress (12) present guidelines for developing one version of a GIRI. The following steps are an adaptation of their ideas based on our experience in the classroom.

Step 1. Select a series of passages that cover a range from at least two levels below the grade one is teaching to at least two levels above the grade. For example, a third-grade teacher will want passages from first-grade level to at least fifth-grade level. Each passage should be between 50 and 100 words in length. Passages can be taken from an existing IRI, from the basal series, or from any other sources. It is best to select passages from materials that have been given grade-level designations because this will eliminate the need to check the readability of the selections. Also, if one chooses materials from the basal series from which one will actually be teaching, this will really be "trying the books on for fit."

Step 2 (optional). If the passages one has selected were taken from sources that were not carefully graded, one will need to check their readability levels. Use an appropriate readability formula to do this. One should have readabilities that fall in the mid-range of the grade levels one is testing, for example, 1.5, 2.5, and so on. If readabilities are not in these ranges, rewrite or select other stories as needed.

Step 3. Write multiple-choice questions for each passage. If one has used an existing IRI, turn the available questions into multiple-choice ones. Balance the questions to insure that one covers different types of comprehension—vocabulary, main idea, details, inference, and cause-effect. Write eight to ten questions for each passage. Keep in mind that ten is an easy number to use in figuring scores.

Name_____ Grade_____ Date_____

Ind Lv_____ Inst Lv_____ Frus Lv_____

	% ___	___	___	___	___
	Level 1	2	3	4	5
main idea	1	1	1	1	1
inference	8	3	2	4	7
vocabulary	2-7	4-8	3-8	5-6	2-3
facts	3-4-6	5-6-7	5-6-7	2-7-8	4-6
cause-effect	5	2	4	3	5-8

Comprehension

Strengths   Needs

FIGURE 3-12. Sample GIRI Scoring Sheet.

Step 4. Check the questions to make certain that it is necessary to read the passage in order to answer them. (This is referred to as passage dependency.) Do this by giving two or three students from another class (or use other teachers) the questions to answer without reading the stories. Any questions that are consistently gotten right by a majority of the persons answering them may not be dependent on the passage. Adjust the questions as needed.

Step 5. Type the test in a neat, readable format. Have each story on one page with the questions on another. *Do not have the story and questions on the same page.*

Step 6. Develop a scoring sheet like the sample in Figure 3-12 for easy scoring and analysis. The numbers in the boxes refer to the questions on the test. The numbers in one's own test will probably fall in a different pattern.

Once the teacher has completed these six steps he/she is ready to administer the test. In some schools, groups of teachers from several grade levels will work together to construct a GIRI. This makes the task of construction easier and also makes it more likely that one will have passages from a beginning reading level to a more mature level.

Administering and Interpreting a GIRI

Administration of the GIRI should take place when students will have sufficient time to complete the task without interruptions. One should prepare students by having them get two sharpened pencils on their desks and removing all other items. Then one may proceed as follows:

1. Tell students that they are going to take a test that will help show how well they read. Encourage them to do their best and try to answer all questions. If students are certain they do not know an answer, tell them *not to guess.* Instruct students to read each story and answer the questions *without* looking back at the story.

2. Have students begin reading two levels below actual grade placement and have them continue two levels above. For example, a third grader should read from level 1 through level 5. If this range seems incorrect for any student, adjust the range based on one's observations.

3. After students have completed the tests, grade them and mark one's scoring sheets. Using the comprehension criteria for the IRI presented earlier in this chapter, determine the reading levels for each student. Study the sample GIRI scoring sheet presented in Figure 3-13 for Tina. Using the criteria for the IRI comprehension levels (independent, 90%+; instructional, 75%, frustration, less than 50%) one can determine her independent level to be grade 3, her instructional level to be grade 4, and her frustration level to be beginning at grade 5 even though she did not completely frustrate at that point. In some instances one will not be able to determine all three levels for a student because the group test will not have sufficient range. In cases where this occurs, administer passages at other levels if there are any or give an IRI. Tina's comprehension is strong in all areas except inference and vocabulary.

4. Using the information obtained from the GIRI one can now place one's students in the basal series. "Try out" the placements just as suggested with the IRI.

Name_____ Grade_____ Date_____

Ind Lv_____ Inst Lv_____ Frus Lv_____

	% 100	100	100	75	62.5
	Level 1	2	3	4	5
main idea	1	I	1	1	1
inference	8	3	2	④	⑦
vocabulary	2-7	4-8	3-8	⑤6	②③
facts	3-4-6	5-6-7	5-6-7	2-7-8	4-6
cause effect	5	2	4	3	5-8

Comprehension

Strengths   Needs

FIGURE 3-13.   Sample GIRI Scoring Sheet.

The GIRI can also be administered as a listening test. However, when this is done one will need two forms of the test. The procedures for constructing a GIRI can also be followed for constructing a group listening test.

PUBLISHED IRIs

This section briefly presents the published IRIs that are currently available on the market. Those that accompany a particular basal series are not presented.

Analytical Reading Inventory, Second Edition
Mary Lynn Woods and Alden J. Moe
Charles E. Merrill Publishing Company, 1981
Number of Forms: three-protocols reproducible
Range of Levels: primer through grade nine
Content: general
Scoring: scoring guide provided; no calculations needed
Word Lists: yes

The Contemporary Classroom Inventory
Lee Ann Rinsky and Esta de Fossard
Gorsuch Scarisbrick, Publishers, 1980
Number of Forms: three in different content areas; protocols reproducible
Range of Levels: primer through grade nine
Content: fiction, social studies, science
Scoring: scoring guide provided; no calculations needed
Word Lists: yes

Basic Reading Inventory, Second Edition
Jerry L. Johns
Kendall/Hunt Publishing Company, 1981
Number of Forms: three—protocols reproducible
Range of Levels: preprimer through grade eight
Content: general
Scoring: scoring guide provided; some calculations needed
Word Lists: yes

Ekwall Reading Inventory
Eldon E. Ekwall
Allyn and Bacon, Inc., 1979
Number of Forms: four-protocols reproducible
Range of Levels: preprimer through grade nine
Content: general
Scoring: scoring guide provided; no calculations needed
Word Lists: yes

Informal Reading Assessments
Paul C. Burns and Betty D. Roe
Rand McNally College Publishing Company, 1980
Number of Forms: four-protocols reproducible
Range of Levels: preprimer through grade twelve
Content: general
Scoring: scoring aid provided; no calculations needed
Word Lists: yes

Diagnostic Reading Inventory, Second Edition
H. Donald Jacobs and Lyndon W. Searfoss
Kendall/Hunt Publishing Company, 1977
Number of Forms: three-protocols reproducible
Range of Levels: grades one through eight
Content: general; taken from high-interest, easy-vocabulary materials
Scoring: conversion tables provided; some calculations required
Word Lists: yes
Comments: prior experience with IRIs suggested

Classroom Reading Inventory, Third Edition
Nicholas J. Silvaroli
Wm. C. Brown Publishers, 1976
Number of Forms: three-protocols reproducible
Range of Levels: preprimer through grade eight
Content: general
Scoring: scoring guide provided; no calculations needed
Word Lists: yes
Comments: pictures with each story

SUMMARY

Placing a student in the appropriate level of the basal reader for instructional purposes is one of the most important decisions the diagnostic reading teacher will have to make in setting up a student's reading program. The most valid procedure available to the classroom teacher for doing this is the informal reading inventory or IRI.

Because the IRI is such a valid procedure for determining students' reading levels and provides the teacher much information about the students' decoding and comprehension abilities, it should be used regularly by all elementary teachers for all students. Even though it is a test that must be individually administered, the resulting benefits lead to more precise placement with the potential for a better reading program.

This chapter has presented a detailed discussion of procedures for administering and interpreting the various types of IRIs. A listing of available published IRIs has also been presented.

THOUGHT AND DISCUSSION QUESTIONS

1. What are the advantages and disadvantages of the various procedures presented in this chapter for placing students in instructional materials?

2. The Betts criteria for determining reading levels have been criticized as being too rigid or too high. What must the classroom teacher do in using these criteria to avoid these criticisms?

3. In planning to administer IRIs to all of the students in your class, what type of independent activities can you have students do that will keep them constructively involved while you are testing? List them.

APPLYING WHAT YOU HAVE LEARNED

1. Administer an IRI to one student. Tape record the oral reading so that you can listen to it after testing to check your coding. Analyze the results of your oral, silent, and listening tests to determine the students' reading levels and decoding and comprehension strengths and needs.

2. With a group of students from your class, construct a GIRI using one of the basal series most frequently used in your area. Arrange with your instructor to try out your test in a classroom.

BIBLIOGRAPHY

1. Beldin, H. O. "Informal Reading Testing: Historical Review and Review of the Research," in William K. Durr, ed., *Reading Difficulties: Diagnosis, Correction, and Remediation.* Newark, Del.: International Reading Association, 1970, pp. 67–84.

2. Betts, Emmett Albert. *Foundations of Reading Instruction.* New York: American Book Company, 1957.

3. Cheek, Martha Collins, and Check, Earl H., Jr. *Diagnostic-Prescriptive Reading Instruction.* Dubuque, Iowa: William C. Brown Company, Publishers, 1980, Chapter 4.

4. Christenson, Adolph. "Oral Reading Errors of Intermediate Grade Children at Their Independent, Instructional, and Frustration Reading Levels," in J. Allen Figurel, ed., *Reading and Realism*, 1968 Proceedings, Vol. 13, Part 1. Newark, Del.: International Reading Association, 1969, pp. 674–677.

5. Ekwall, Eldon E. "Should Repetitions Be Counted As Errors?" *Reading Teacher*, 27 (Jan. 1974), 365–367.

6. ____. "Informal Reading Inventories: The Instructional Level," *Reading Teacher*, 29 (Apr. 1976), 662–665.

7. ____. *Diagnosis and Remediation of the Disabled Reader.* Boston: Allyn & Bacon, Inc., 1976, Chapter 11.

8. Farr, Roger. *Reading: What Can Be Measured?* Newark, Del.: International Reading Association, 1969.

9. Goodman, Kenneth S. "A Linguistic Study of Cues and Miscues in Reading," *Elementary English*, 42 (Oct. 1965), 639–643.

10. ____. "Analysis of Oral Reading Miscues: Applied Psycholinguistics," in Frank Smith, ed., *Psycholinguistics and Reading.* New York: Holt, Rinehart and Winston, 1973, pp. 158–176.

11. Harris, Larry A., and Smith, Carl B. *Reading Instruction: Diagnostic Teaching in the Classroom,* 2nd ed. New York: Holt, Rinehart and Winston, 1976, pp. 119–121.

12. Johnson, Marjorie Seddon, and Kress, Roy A. *Informal Reading Inventories.* Newark, Del.: International Reading Association, 1965.

13. ____. "Individual Reading Inventories," in Leo M. Schell and Paul C. Burns, eds., *Remedial Reading: Classroom and Clinic,* 2nd ed. Boston: Allyn & Bacon, Inc., 1972, pp. 185–206.

14. Kender, Joseph P. "How Useful Are Informal Reading Tests?" *Journal of Reading,* 11 (Feb. 1968), 337–342.

15. McCracken, Robert A. "The Informal Reading Inventory as a Means of Improving Instruction," in Thomas C. Barrett, ed., *The Evaluation of Children's Reading Achievement.* Newark, Del.: International Reading Association, 1967, pp. 79–96.

16. McCracken, Robert A., and Mullen, Neill D. "The Validity of Certain Measures in an I.R.I.," in William K. Durr, ed., *Reading Difficulties: Diagnosis, Correction, and Remediation.* Newark, Del.: International Reading Association, 1970, pp. 104–110.

17. Pikulski, John. "A Critical Review: Informal Reading Inventories," *Reading Teacher,* 28 (Nov. 1974), 141–151.

18. Packman, Linda. "Selected Oral Reading Errors and Levels of Reading Comprehension," in Howard A. Klein, ed., *The Quest For Competency in Teaching Reading.* Newark, Del.: International Reading Association, 1972, pp. 203–208.

19. Powell, William R. "Reappraising the Criteria for Interpreting Informal Inventories," in Dorothy L. DeBoer, ed., *Reading Diagnosis and Evaluation.* Newark, Del.: International Reading Association, 1970, pp. 100–109.

20. ____. "Validity of the IRI Reading Levels." *Elementary English,* 48 (Oct. 1971), 637–642.

21. ____. "The Validity of the Instructional Reading Level," in Robert E. Leibert, ed., *Diagnostic Viewpoints in Reading.* Newark, Del.: International Reading Association, 1971, pp. 121–133.

22. Reed, Shirley Anne. "An Investigation into the Effect of Prestated Purposes on the Silent Reading Comprehension of Good and Poor Readers Using an Informal Reading Inventory." Unpublished doctoral dissertation, Ball State University, 1979.

23. Rupley, William H. "Informal Reading Diagnosis." *Reading Teacher,* 29 (Oct. 1975), 106–107, 109.

24. Shipman, Dorothy, and Warncke, Edna W. *Group Assessment in Reading: Classroom Teacher's Handbook,* Englewood Cliffs, N. J.: 1983 (in process at time of this printing).

25. "What Teachers Use to Teach Reading," research in progress, Center for the Study of Reading, Champaign, Ill., 1980.

26. Williamson, Leon W., and Young, Freda. "The IRI and RMI Diagnostic Concepts Should Be Synthesized." *Journal of Reading Behavior,* 6 (July 1974), 183–194.

27. Woods, Mary Lynn, and Moe, Alden J. *Analytical Reading Inventory,* 2nd ed. Columbus, Ohio: Charles E. Merrill Publishing Company, 1981.

FOR FURTHER READING

Select an IRI suggested by your instructor or one from the list presented in this chapter and review its manual.

Cheek, Martha Collins, and Cheek, Earl H., Jr. *Diagnostic Prescriptive Reading Instruction.* Dubuque, Iowa: William C. Brown Company, Publishers, 1980, Chapter 4.

Harris, Albert J., and Sipay, Edward R. *How to Increase Reading Ability*, 7th ed. New York: Longman, Inc., 1980, Chapter 8.

chapter 4

assessing specific skills

objectives

As a result of reading this chapter, one will

1. Know the importance of skills in the reading program.
2. Know the role of skills testing in diagnostic teaching.
3. Know how to select appropriate skills tests.
4. Have an overview of a variety of skills tests.

overview

It is essential for an elementary teacher to know and understand the importance of skills in the reading program. This chapter will develop the concept of skills testing as it relates to the diagnostic teaching of reading. Criteria for selecting appropriate skills tests will be provided. A variety of skill tests and their intended uses will be discussed. The information gained from this chapter will assist one in using steps 1, 2, and 3 of the diagnostic teaching model:

Step 1. Gather relevant information.
Step 2. Generate alternative actions.
Step 3. Evaluate alternatives and select ones to carry out.

There are essentially two basic philosophies about the teaching of reading: (1) a skill-oriented approach in which the teacher teaches specific skills such as vowels, blends, main ideas, inferences, and so on, and (2) a whole language-oriented approach in which the teacher has students reading and working in materials with emphasis on the use of grammatical and meaning cueing systems. The question that elementary reading teachers must answer is "Which of these philosophies is correct or best?" Current research on all aspects of reading instruction suggests that neither philosophy is best. *Both offer some significant insights into the teaching of reading that must be considered and used.* The question should really be, "What can we learn from both philosophies that will help us improve the teaching of reading?" When one examines the recommendations and suggestions for teaching reading given by such internationally known authorities as Harris (6), Heilman (9), Harris and Smith (7), Burns and Roe (2), and Spache (12), one sees that they, too, are attempting to take the best from both philosophies and meld them into *workable* procedures for *successfully* teaching children to read. The question is not really an either/or situation.

THE ROLE OF SKILLS IN A READING PROGRAM

The teaching of skills is important to the successful teaching of reading. Bond and Dykstra (1) concluded that reading programs that emphasized the systematic teaching of decoding skills tended to produce better readers up through third grade. This conclusion was also supported by Chall (3) in her re-analysis of existing research. Since that time, further studies such as Guthrie's (5) have added more support for the conclusion that the effective reading program is one that systematically emphasizes the teaching of skills—decoding, comprehension, and study skills. This conclusion *does not mean* that skills should be taught in isolation as separate entities. What one has learned from the language-oriented philosophy and research on the teaching of reading (4) offers some guidance in making decisions about how to approach skill teaching. In this way one attempts to take the best from both philosophies.

One of the first things that the diagnostic reading teacher must consider is how skills fit into the total reading process and reading instruction. While research may lead one to conclude that systematic skill teaching is important (5) it does not give absolute information on the exact skills to teach. Research does offer some guidance on the identification of which skills to teach in decoding and a possible sequence for that teaching in terms of some skills (8, 10, 11). In the area of comprehension, however the suggestions available from research as to which skills to teach and how to approach the teaching are less well defined. Fortunately, knowledge in this area is increasing rapidly (13).

Much of what is known and done about which reading skills to teach is based on past experience and trial and error in teaching. Only a little that is known is based on research evidence.

Knowing Which Skills to Teach

It is important for the diagnostic reading teacher to know which skills to teach and the order or sequence in which they should be taught. Very likely, the school in which one will be teaching will already have made this decision for the teacher. All teachers throughout the building will be following the same skill sequence. This decision in most elementary schools is made when the school selects the basal reader it will be using. The scope and sequence of the adopted basal series becomes the scope and sequence of the reading program. For example, if a school selects Basal Series X, the scope and sequence of Series X becomes the scope and sequence of skills for the program. The skills that are listed in the scope and sequence for Series X are the ones that are tested for mastery, are taught, and are expected to be learned by the students.

If there are several basals being used, the scope and sequence of skills for *one* of the series should comprise the skills for the reading program regardless of which other sets of materials (basals) a student is using. This helps to insure continuity of skill development. It discourages or helps to prevent the placement of students in one series of readers after another, thus changing the skill sequence as the student moves from series to series. If a student needs to move into another basal series, he/she would still be taught the skills from Series X because they comprise the skills of the reading program. There is no one right sequence of skills, and the scope and sequence being followed should be altered and updated as new information is learned from current research. The important point is that the school should decide on a scope and sequence of reading skills that is followed by every teacher in the building. More than one basal series will have to be used in instruction, but the scope and sequence of skills from *one* of those series should be used as the core of the program.

The Importance of Skills to the Reading Process

As we have already noted, research tends to indicate that reading programs that systematically emphasize skills produce more effective readers. This does not mean, however, that *every* student must learn *every* skill. Some students will already know certain skills and some may not need a given skill. Reading skills should not be taught just for the sake of students learning the skills. Any given reading skill is important only if it helps the student to read better. As any skill is taught to a student, opportunities must be made available to make certain that it is applied in context or an actual reading situation. For example, a teacher has just taught his/her students the initial consonant sounds *r*, *t*, and *m*. Unless the students are given reading materials in which they must read stories and apply or use these consonant sounds in figuring out new words, the learning of the skill is of no value.

Too often problems arise in the use of a skills approach that cause the critics of the approach to discount its value. One major problem is that of teaching and testing skills in isolation. Frequently a skill is taught for the sake of the skill, tested in isolation, and students are not given chances to apply or use the skill in a real reading situation. This *is not good teaching of skills*. What has been learned from the language-oriented research (4) suggests that students do not use a skill in isolation as they do in context. Therefore, the opportunity to apply the skill must be provided in order to make the teaching complete. Most basal series are not as systematic in applying the skills taught as they should be. It therefore becomes the responsibility of the teacher to see that this is done.

It must also be remembered that not all students need all skills. Some students learn to read by acquiring only a few skills, while others seem to need many more. A diagnostic reading teacher should know how to look at a student's skill performance to determine whether he/she really needs the skill.

SKILL TESTING IN DIAGNOSTIC TEACHING

Specific skill testing is an important part of diagnostic teaching but it must be considered in relation to the student's actual reading performance in a "real" reading situation. Decisions about a student's mastery of a particular skill must be made by looking at samples of his/her reading and comparing this to his/her skill test results. Too often teachers accept a student's performance on an isolated skill test as final evidence in making a decision about whether the skill should be taught. An effective diagnostic teacher of reading will want to understand the relationship between a student's level of reading and his/her skill performance and know how to make a decision about which skills to teach based on the evidence one collects.

Level of Placement and Skill Testing

In Chapter 3 the importance of determining a student's three reading levels through the use of an IRI was stressed. How the IRI could be analyzed to obtain information about the student's decoding and comprehension skills was illustrated. However, just knowing a student's independent, instructional, and frustration reading levels does not insure that he/she has or has not mastered any given set of skills. Some students perform better on isolated skill tests and some show better performance on a contextual reading test like the IRI. Therefore, when making a decision about a student's skill performance one must look at his/her actual reading such as the sample obtained from an IRI and compare that to skill test results. Whether or not he/she can use the skill in context is what is important.

This can be illustrated by comparing the performance of two students in a class. Susan, for example, is a first grader. She is reading at the primer level.

One gives her the skill test on initial consonants. She misses 50 per cent of the items on the test. According to the test manual, Susan must get 80 per cent of the items correct for the skill to be considered mastered. The consonants she missed were *r*, *b*, and *t*. One also has her read an IRI passage at the primer level and a page from her text. There were four places in the material where she had to use the initial consonants *r*, *b*, and *t*. *She did not make any mistakes* using those consonants. The teacher must now decide whether or not to reteach those consonants. The response to that is that since Susan is able to use or apply the consonant sounds when she reads, more weight should be placed on her actual reading performance than on the isolated skill testing. She can use the consonants when she is reading even though she misses them in isolation. Her reading performance shows that she can apply the skill, while her skill testing only shows isolated use of the skill. The reading performance is the more important behavior to consider. One can make this decision about Susan *only* if one is sure that the words in context are not already known as sight words.

It is not unusual to find students like Susan at all grade levels. These students may not do well on an isolated skill test but when they read they are able to use the skills without any difficulties. If their teachers used only the results of the skill test to make a decision about teaching, the students would waste valuable time going over skills that they already know. *Decisions about a student's skill mastery must be made by looking at both skill test results and actual reading performance as measured on an IRI or in reading materials.* One cannot assume that a student knows any given set of skills because he/she reads at a particular level, nor that mastery of a given set of skills insures that a student can read at a certain level.

Bob's performance will illustrate this point. Bob is a fifth grader. He always gets 100% on the skill tests. However, when he reads he makes many errors in using the skills tested. For example, Bob, is reading instructionally at the fourth-grade level. He has just been given the skill test for prefixes. He got 95 per cent on the test. However, when he read from the IRI he miscalled three of the four words requiring the use of the same prefixes tested. Obviously he needs to be taught to apply the skill of which he demonstrates mastery in isolation. Therefore, some reteaching is needed. Certainly this reteaching needs to be designed to insure that he learns to apply in context what he seems to have in isolation.

The Need for Specific Skill Testing

The diagnostic reading teacher needs to know how to administer and interpret specific skill tests even though some cautions must be exercised in their use. These types of tests allow one to examine, in depth, the student's knowledge of a given skill. They are helpful in determining mastery of a skill in an isolated situation, but again, this performance must be compared to actual reading. By using specific skill tests and comparing the results to actual reading

performance, one will be able to determine a pattern in the student's reading and make more accurate judgments about the skills that need to be taught or retaught.

SELECTING APPROPRIATE SKILL TESTS FOR CLASSROOM USE

A part of one's reading program should include making decisions about which skill tests to use in determining student skill mastery. The following guidelines will help one make the needed decisions:

1. Consider the Scope and Sequence of Skills for the Reading Program

There are three possible sources where one will find the scope and sequence of skills to be taught in one's school: the adopted basal reader, a school curriculum guide, or an external management system. (These will be discussed later in this chapter.)

If one's school has an adopted basal reader, looking at its scope and sequence of skills will help to determine which skills should be taught at the levels where one's students are reading. This listing of skills may be found in the teacher's guide or in a supplementary chart that has been provided by the publisher.

If the school has no adopted reader, perhaps there is a reading curriculum guide that lists skills to be taught at various levels. If this is available, one's decision can be based on this information.

Some schools use an external management system that has a scope and sequence of skills with correlated tests. If one's school has such a system in use, this material can be a guide in selecting the skill tests to be administered.

If one is teaching in a school where none of the above items are available, then each teacher essentially may proceed as she/he wishes. (This is not the best arrangement, but it could happen.) In this case one should locate a scope and sequence of reading skills from any source available, such as a basal reader, a college methods text or a curriculum guide.

2. Select Tests To Match the Skills To Be Taught

After determining the skills one needs for teaching, one must then select the tests that measure those skills. If an adopted basal series or external management system is used the teacher will want to use the accompanying tests. If one's school has a curriculum guide of reading skills with tests, those should be used.

If no tests are available for the skills that should be taught, one will need to examine other tests (samples will be discussed in the next section) or construct tests of one's own (guidelines will be given later in this chapter) to measure the skills. The important thing to keep in mind is that the skill test one selects must measure the same skill one is teaching. Look at the following information:

SKILL.   Auditory discrimination of beginning consonant sounds; the student must match pictures that have the same beginning sound.

TEST.   Look at the pictures below and write the letter that stands for the beginning sound.

_____   _____

Obviously, the test shown does not match the skill indicated. When selecting a skill test one needs to make certain that the skill as one is going to teach it or has taught it is measured in the same way on the test.

Another consideration is whether or not the test can be group administered. With a class of twenty to thirty students one needs to be able to assess skills in a group situation, if at all possible.

3. Review the Procedures for Adminstration

After one has decided on the tests to be used one needs to master the procedures to be followed. The teacher should review all the items on the test to make certain that any problems that might occur as the students take the test have been anticipated.

PUBLISHED SKILLS TESTS

There are two basic types of skills tests that are published for classroom teacher use: the tests that accompany basal reading series and those that are independent of basals. While there are many other individual diagnostic reading tests on the market we are concerned here only with those that seem most appropriate for classroom use.

Basal Series Tests

Each basal reading series publishes some type of skill-assessment program that accompanies its materials. These assessments are either published as separate tests or are included in the pupil's workbook, teacher's guide, or both. Figure 4-1 shows some sample tests for basal readers and the accompanying components.

The skill-assessment materials that accompany basal readers are designed to measure the skills that are to be taught in each level of the series. Usually included with the assessment materials is a test, some type of record-keeping system and suggestions for reteaching. In many instances there are two forms of the test so that one may be used as a pre-test and the other as a post-test. Most series refer to this assessment program as their management system.

If one teaches in a school where a basal series is used and the assessment materials are provided, one should use them. These tests are designed to correlate closely with the materials one will be using in teaching and will therefore make the process of teaching more efficient. There is no reason to ignore these supportive materials.

As with all tests, one will discover in using them that there are certain items that cause problems or don't seem to measure what they say they are measuring. Therefore, it is necessary to continuously evaluate the tests and watch for areas that need modification. When discovering changes that are needed in certain tests, one will want to talk with the principal or other appropriate person about them.

Nonbasal Tests

There are numerous nonbasal management systems available for skill assessment. These systems are designed to be used with any basal series. They generally include the same types of components as those systems that accompany basals: tests, record systems, and suggestions for teaching and reteaching. While these systems can be effectively used, they can also pose more problems for the classroom teacher in terms of correlating the skill teaching with the basal series. If a school intends to select and use a non-basal management system it will need to provide the teachers with the appropriate inservice and support. Following are descriptions of some of the more commonly used assessment and management systems. All tests included in these systems can be administered to large groups of students at one time.

Prescriptive Reading Inventory
CTB/McGraw Hill, 1972
Del Monte Research Park
Monterey, California

FIGURE 4-1. Sample Basal Reader Skill Tests.

Levels:, Six Levels grades K-6.5
Level 1 K-1.0
Level 11 K.5–2.0
Level A (Red) 1.5–2.5
Level B (Green) 2.0–3.5
Level C (Blue) 3.0–4.5
Level D (Orange) 4.0–6.5

Description: *Prescriptive Reading Inventory* (PRI) is a criterion referenced testing system that assesses student mastery of reading-skill objectives normally covered in grades K-6. All tests are group administered and untimed.

Components: Available components include test books, examiner's cassettes, interpretive handbooks, practice exercises, and pre-tests, individual diagnostic records, teacher's resource files and program reference guides correlated to the major basal readers.

Criterion Reading
Random House School Division, 1971
New York, New York

Levels: Five levels, grades K-adult basic education
Level 1 Kindergarden (sensorimotor)
Level 2 Grade 1 (listening/speaking)
Level 3 Grades 2–3 (reading)
Level 4 Grades 5–6 (reading)
Level 5 Grades junior high to adult basic education (reading and writing)

Description: *Criterion Reading* is an assessment system for diagnosing reading needs. It covers 450 skills in the areas listed above. The system helps identify the critical skills that have not been mastered.

Components: All levels include a wall chart of skills, teacher's guide, pupil profile booklet, and group record booklet.

The Wisconsin Design for Reading Skill Development
National Computer Systems, 1974
Minneapolis, Minnesota

Levels: Six skill areas covering grade K-6

Word Attack
Level A Grade K
Level B Grade 1
Level C Grade 2
Level D Grade 3

Comprehension
Level A Grade K
Level B Grade 1
Level C Grade 2
Level D Grade 3

Level E Grade 4
Level F Grade 5
Level G Grade 6

Study Skills
Level A Grade K
Level B Grade 1
Level C Grade 2
Level D Grade 3
Level E Grade 4
Level F Grade 5
Level G Grade 6

Self-directed Reading
Level A Grade K
Level B Grade 1
Level C Grade 2
Level D Grade 3
Level E Grades 4-5

Interpretive Reading
Level A Grade K
Level B Grade 1
Level C Grade 2
Level D Grade 3
Level E Grades 4-6

Creative Reading
Level A Grade K
Level B Grade 1
Level C Grade 2
Level D Grade 3
Level E Grades 4-6

Description: A series of behaviorally stated objectives for the six skill areas listed above. Criterion referenced tests are included for word attack, comprehension, and study skills. All tests are group adminstered.

Components: Tests, rationale and guidelines, teacher's planning guide, pupil profile cards, and teacher's resource files.

Reading Yardsticks
Riverside Publishing Co., 1981
Chicago, Illinois

Levels: Covers essential reading skills, grades K-8.

Description: Diagnostic tests for classroom use. Measures mastery of essential reading skills. Provides both criterion-referenced and norm-referenced information. Can be used with any basal series.

Components: Test booklets and manual of instructions. Provides class diagnostic reports and group diagnostic reports.

Fountain Valley Teaching Support System in Reading
Richard L. Zweig Associates, Inc., 1977.
Huntington Beach, California

Levels: Six achievement levels covering grades 1–6 in six skill areas phonetic analysis, structural analysis, vocabulary development, comprehension, study skills.

Description: A criterion referenced classroom management system covering 367 reading skills that are evaluated with 77 individual tests at achievement levels 1–6. Can be used with any basal series.

Components: Test booklets and manual.

TEACHER-DEVELOPED SKILLS TEST

Even though a teacher may be using the skill tests that accompany a basal reader or an alternative test selected to go with the scope and sequence of reading skills, she/he may find from time to time that some informal tests to check or recheck pupil progress in a particular skill area will also be needed. Sometimes it will be necessary for the teacher to construct these tests.

Teacher-developed skills tests can prove to be very useful in diagnostic teaching. Some teachers like to build a file of these tests to use or refer to as they are needed. It is important to keep in mind that such tests can cover the specific skill areas in which the students are having the most difficulty.

Guidelines for Constructing Skill Tests

The following guidelines can be used to construct one's own skill tests:

1. Identify the skill that one wants to test, such as

    -   auditory discrimination of beginning consonant blends.
    -   initial consonant substitution.
    -   inferring the main idea.
    -   recalling ideas in sequence.

2. Write an objective to pinpoint the behavior one is looking for in the students, to discern whether or not they have the skill for which they are being tested. For example,

    -   Students will match eight out of ten pictures to a key picture for the consonant blends *bl* and *tr*.
    -   Students will change the initial consonant on a given known word and draw a line to the picture for the new word.

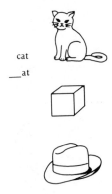

cat

___at

- Given five paragraphs to read, the student will be able to pick out the inferred main idea for four of the paragraphs.
- Given a paragraph to read the student will be able to arrange four events from the story in the order in which they happened.

3.   Write items to match the skills objectives identified.

Be sure that the items cover the skills one wants to test. The importance of this was illustrated earlier in this chapter in the discussion of selecting skill tests.

4.   Try the items out with selected students.

Have two or three students who will not be using the test try out the items. If any difficulties arise, change the items.

5.   Develop a usable format for the test.

Type or neatly write the test in a clear, readable format. Give clearly stated directions even for beginning readers or nonreaders so they will become accustomed to following them as one gives them aloud.

Many times as the teacher develops his/her own tests, he/she will want to refer to informal tests that have already been developed. It is also good to model the tests after the exercises in the readers that one has used for teaching the skills. One can save valuable time in constructing one's own tests by selecting informal tests from a variety of different sources. The following list of books contains tests for specific reading skills that will be useful in the classroom.

Reading Diagnosis Kit, Second Edition
Wilma H. Miller
The Center for Applied Research in Education
West Nyack, N.Y.,
1978

A Guide to Ecological Screening and Assessment
Veralee B. Hardin and Neila T. Petit
William C. Brown Company, Publishers
Dubuque, Iowa
1978

Teacher's Handbook for Diagnostic Inventories, Second Edition
Philip H. Mann, et al.
Allyn and Bacon
Boston, Mass.
1979

On the Spot Reading Diagnosis File
Margaret H. LaPray
The Center for Applied Research in Education, Inc.
West Nyack, N.Y.
1978

Informal Reading Diagnosis, Second Edition
Gwenneth Rae and Thomas C. Potter
Prentice-Hall, Inc.
Englewood Cliffs, N.J.
1981

Decision Making for the Diagnostic Teacher
J. David Cooper, et al.
Holt, Rinehart and Winston, Inc.
New York, N.Y.
1972

Teacher's Handbook on Diagnosis and Remediation in Reading
Eldon E. Ekwall
Allyn and Bacon, Inc.
Boston, Mass.
1977

Handbook in Corrective Reading: Basic Tasks, Second Edition
Ruth Gallant
Charles E. Merrill Publishing Company
Columbus, Ohio
1978

SUMMARY

Research evidence indicates that programs that systematically emphasize reading skills produce a better reader than those that do not. There is no one right set of skills to teach and not all skills are needed by all readers. For a skill to be important to the reader, he/she must have the opportunity to apply or use the skill in a real reading situation.

Specific skill test results must be compared to an actual sample of a student's reading to determine whether a certain skill really needs to be taught.

Skill tests used by the diagnostic classroom reading teacher can include those that accompany the basal series, other published tests, or teacher-developed tests.

THOUGHT AND DISCUSSION QUESTIONS

1. When you are selecting a specific skill test, why is it important to compare the skill test to the way the skill was taught?
2. Why is it probably more efficient to use the skill tests that accompany the basal series in your school?
3. Identify those times when teacher-developed tests might be needed by the diagnostic reading teacher.

APPLYING WHAT YOU HAVE LEARNED

1. Select a commonly used basal series in your area. Examine and study the skill-assessment materials that accompany it.
2. Review one of the published skill assessment systems discussed in this chapter.
3. Select one of the students you tested at the conclusion of Chapter 3 and administer a skills test recommended by your instructor. Compare the results and make your recommendations for the skills that need to be taught.
4. Select any reading skill and construct an informal skill test for it. Administer the test to a student and evaluate your results.

BIBLIOGRAPHY

1. Bond, Guy L., and Dykstra, Robert. "The Cooperative Research Program in First Grade Reading." *Reading Research Quarterly*, 2 (Summer 1967).

2. Burns, Paul C., and Roe, Betty D. *Teaching Reading in Today's Elementary Schools*, 2nd Ed. Chicago: Rand McNally College Publishing Company 1980.

3. Chall, Jeanne. *Learning to Read: The Great Debate*. New York: McGraw-Hill Book Company, 1967.

4. Goodman, Yetta M., and Burke, Carolyn. *Reading Strategies: Focus on Comprehension*. New York: Holt, Rinehart and Winston, 1980.

5. Guthrie, John T., et al. *A Study of the Locus and Nature of Reading Problems in the Elementary School*. Final Report, ED 127 568.

6. Harris, Albert J., and Sipay, Edward R. *How to Increase Reading Ability*, 7th ed. New York: Longman, Inc., 1980.

7. Harris, Larry A., and Smith Carl B. *Reading Instruction: Diagnostic Teaching in the Classroom*, 2nd ed. New York: Holt, Rinehart and Winston, 1976.

8. Heilman, Arthur W. *Phonics in Proper Perspective*, 4th ed. Columbus, Ohio: Charles E. Merrill Publishing Company, 1981.

9. Heilman, Arthur J., et al. *Principles and Practices of Teaching Reading*, 5th ed. Columbus, Ohio: Charles E. Merrill Publishing Company, 1981.

10. Levin, Harry, and Watson, J. "The Learning of Variable Grapheme-to-Phoneme Correspondences: Variations in the Initial Consonant Position," *in A Basic Program on Reading*, U.S.O.E., Project No. 639, Ithaca, New York: Cornell University, 1963.

11. Marchbanks, Gabrielle, and Levin, Harry. "Cues by Which Children Recognize Words." *Journal of Educational Psychology*, 56 (April 1965), 57–61.

12. Spache, George D., and Spache, Evelyn B. *Reading in the Elementary School*, 4th ed. Boston: Allyn & Bacon, Inc., 1977.

13. Spiro, Rand J., et al., ed. *Theoretical Issues in Reading Comprehension*. Hillsdale, New York: Lawrence Erlbaum Associates, Publishers, 1980.

FOR FURTHER READING

Refer to the books listed in this chapter on pages 21, 22, and 23.

section III

organization

Effective teaching of reading depends upon the teacher having his/her class organized in such a manner that he/she can get at the needs of all students efficiently. This section of the text will help one learn how to

- organize the students and continuously reorganize them as needs change.
- organize the material for easy use.
- keep records that assist in both organization and management.

chapter 5

organizing the class for instruction

objectives

As a result of reading this chapter one will

1. Know the purposes and procedures for organizing a class for reading instruction.
2. Be acquainted with a variety of organizational patterns.
3. Know the basic steps to follow in organizing a class for teaching reading.
4. Have the basic knowledges and skills needed to implement procedures for continual reorganization of a class as an ongoing part of reading instruction.

overview

This chapter is designed to provide classroom teachers with the basic background and procedures necessary to organize the class for reading instruction based on diagnostic information. Emphasis will be placed on identifying different types of organizational patterns that can be used and criteria for selecting those most suited to the individual teacher. An important aspect of classroom organization for effective reading instruction is the ongoing reorganization of groups and other instructional patterns. This chapter will provide the guidelines and procedures needed to prevent organization from becoming static. In working with this chapter the teacher will need to use his/her general knowledge about reading instruc-

tion and reading diagnosis. The information presented in this chapter will help one with Steps 2, 3, 4, and 5 of the diagnostic teaching model:

Step 2. Generate alternative actions.
Step 3. Evaluate alternatives and select ones to carry out.
Step 4. Teach.
Step 5. Evaluate results.

The most persistent problem faced by new teachers is the organizing and managing of the classroom program, especially the reading program (4). Often one hears beginning teachers and teachers who have been teaching for many years say, "I know how to teach reading. My problem is how to get things organized and keep everyone constructively involved all at the same time." Certainly this problem pertains to any classroom at any level, but it is even more important in the elementary classroom where the teacher always has several levels of reading instruction to organize and manage.

The more a student is involved in direct instruction or instructionally related tasks, the better his/her reading achievement is likely to be (1, 5, 8). Therefore, it becomes increasingly important for the classroom reading teacher to know how to organize for effective instruction and be able to manage the program to allow for maximum involvement of students. A teacher who knows how to teach reading but cannot organize properly to get the job done is of no value to the students or the program.

Most authorities in reading combine the topics of organization and management as they discuss them (6, 7). They are related, of course, but many teachers have problems in this area because they frequently confuse the two concepts and have not clearly defined the tasks relative to each. For this reason this text has a section on organization and one on management. The two sections support each other and should help one to clearly define the two concepts.

Before a teacher can manage his/her program, some organization must take place. An organizational plan helps a teacher to

1. Meet the individual needs of the students.
2. Motivate the students.
3. Lead into an effective management system.

A clearly defined organizational plan helps one meet the individual needs of the students in the class. No elementary classroom ever has students who are all the same. Even if some attempt has been made to cut the range of the reading levels of the students in one's class, there will still be individual differences that will need to be accounted for in instruction. Within any given reading level some students will be able to move faster than others and there will be differences in skill needs. Some students may respond better to one approach than another. Through effective organization the teacher can account for these differences. It is unlikely that there is an elementary classroom where a teacher could really have only one group or instructional unit. Some classroom teachers try to do this, but they are not considering realistically the needs of their students.

Effective organization also helps motivate students. A systematic approach to one's teaching will more likely take into account differing interests which will in turn lead to increased motivation. If students are more motivated this

will lead to a more positive attitude which will encourage them to want to learn.

Finally, a well-designed, clearly understood, organizational plan will lead to a more effective management system. As already noted, organization and management are definitely related but there are specific tasks relative to each that must be understood.

CLASSROOM ORGANIZATION DEFINED

Organizing one's classroom for reading instruction means that one must look at the students and determine the best way to go about teaching them to read. It also involves keeping appropriate records and having one's resources and materials together for easy access and use. The next two chapters will focus on these topics. This chapter is concerned only with organizing students for effective teaching.

Thus far, this text has concentrated on developing the background and skills needed to gather relevant information about each student's reading. Essentially, this is Step 1 in the diagnostic teaching process. Now one arrives at Step 2—generate alternative actions—and Step 3—evaluate alternatives and select ones to carry out. This is where the organizational process begins.

The first task related to organizing one's class for instruction is interpreting the information one has gathered on the students through testing, observations, and work samples. One must look at the information on each student and determine his/her reading levels, skill needs, and interests and attitudes. After making these decisions, the teacher is then ready to look at the students as a group and determine similarities and differences among them.

There is no way that a classroom teacher with twenty-five or thirty students can work with each one separately. Therefore, looking for similarities and differences provides one with the information that is needed to make the decisions about how to organize the students for teaching.

Finally, organization involves putting students together in the appropriate patterns that will make it possible to provide the needed instruction. The decisions relative to this are based on the similarities and differences one sees in the students' reading and the skills that one has as a teacher in using various organizational patterns. Some patterns are more appropriate for some teaching styles than others. A classroom teacher will have to learn which patterns are best in terms of being manageable as well as being effective in accomplishing the goals established for one's reading program.

In summary, classroom organization involves developing a plan for putting students together for reading instruction. This includes interpreting the relevant information one has gathered on the students, looking for similarities and differences in their reading needs, and finally selecting the appropriate patterns for carrying out the instruction.

TYPES OF ORGANIZATIONAL PATTERNS

An effectively organized classroom depends upon the use of a variety of organizational patterns designed to meet the different needs of students. Each pattern must be considered in terms of its basic strengths and weaknesses. No one pattern is appropriate all the time. As student needs change and program goals change the teacher will have to use different patterns of organization. Also, changing the organizational patterns that one uses for instruction will add variety to the classroom and make it more interesting for both the teacher and the students.

Individualized Instruction

When educators discuss individualized instruction they are frequently talking about teaching one student at a time. There are instances when this type of instruction is appropriate, but in most elementary classrooms it is unrealistic and impractical, especially when the teacher must deal with twenty-five or thirty students. This does not mean that the classroom teacher should ignore individualized instruction but rather suggests a need for a broader concept of individualization.

Individualized instruction is the type of teaching that takes place when the teacher puts together those students who have the same basic needs. For reading, each student is taught on his/her instructional level and with content that he/she needs to learn. There will always be times when the teacher will need to instruct an individual student, but the major portion of the instruction will take place in groups that are *constantly changing as the needs of students change.* Therefore, individualization of instruction really involves both grouping and one-to-one teaching. The major assumptions underlying diagnostic-prescriptive teaching are based on this concept of individualization. Even though it is impossible and inefficient to teach each student individually, there will be times in every reading program when one student will need instruction in a particular area and will have to be taught alone. But such times can be kept to a minimum if one organizes the class according to individual needs and keeps this organization flexible. Teachers sometimes are apologetic about using groups in their teaching. There is no reason to apologize for having groups if they are formed on the basis of student needs and are reorganized as needs change. As long as this occurs the teacher is individualizing instruction.

Grouping Patterns

There are many different types of grouping patterns that can and should be used in the reading program. Each has different purposes that must be considered in deciding when and where to use them. No single type of grouping

will adequately meet the needs of all students and all teachers. Certain types may be used more than others, but an effective reading teacher will always want to ask oneself the question, "Am I varying my organizational patterns enough to meet student needs and keep instruction interesting?"

Many educators have a negative reaction toward the use of groups. If this happens it is usually associated with the way some teachers have used groups. If, with groups, a teacher shows favoritism or expresses negative feelings, she/he can build up negative reactions on the part of students. Thus a negative stigma is often attached to grouping. If a teacher forms groups and leaves them exactly the same all year, students get the feeling that they are stuck and there is no way to get out or move on. Therefore, grouping must be approached in a positive manner and a teacher must make certain that her/his actions and attitudes do not give students negative feelings about its use.

Basic Instructional Groups. Basic instructional groups are probably the most common type of group in the reading program. These groups have been organized on the basis of the students' instructional reading levels and are used for the major portion of the basal-reader instruction. There is no "magic" or "right" number of basic instructional groups that a teacher should have. Obviously, the more groups a teacher has in the reading program the more complex is the management. To many educators, the "right" number of instructional groups to have is three, but this is not true *unless three just happens to be the number that allows one to meet the needs of the students involved.*

Basic instructional groups should not remain exactly the same throughout the year. This is a misuse of such groupings. Rather, they should be reorganized as the reading levels of students change. The number of groups that a teacher should have will depend on the various needs of the students. The number must not become so unrealistic that the program becomes unmanageable.

Skill Groups. Skill groups are those that are formed for the purpose of teaching a specific skill or set of skills. Such groups are usually organized within a given basic instructional group in order to have all students reading at the same instructional level. Many times one's basic instructional group will be the skill group because all students at that level will need the same skill instruction. As students advance more in their ability to read, each basic instructional group will probably have a greater number of skill groups within it.

If possible, skill groups should be kept a part of the basic instructional groups because this makes it easier to give students directed opportunities to apply the skills. By having all students at a given instructional level, the teacher can easily select materials that all students can read for the application of the skills being taught.

Multi-aged Groups. Multi-aged groups are formed by having students from different age/grade levels work together. These groups can be used for a variety of purposes including basic instruction, skill teaching, interest activities,

or any other appropriate activities. Some schools use multi-aged groups to form basic instructional groups. This allows for more efficiency in teaching because students who are reading at the same level can be put together for instruction, thus reducing the number of groups needed in the school for reading instruction.

There are a few precautions in using multi-aged groups. First, it is important that the student's interest and maturity level be considered. Students from different age levels should not be put together if their levels of maturity or interests are drastically different. This type of situation is not good for either the student or for teaching. For example, a third grader and a sixth grader reading at the seventh-grade level may have very different interests and levels of maturity even though their reading levels are the same. Therefore, they should not be reading the same selections.

Interest Groups.   Interest groups are formed when students of the same or similar interests get together to work on a project, share a book they have read, perform a play, or become involved in any number of creative activities. These groups are composed of students from a variety of reading levels because the activities drawing them together do not require that all students be at the same instructional level. By sometimes using this type of grouping pattern the teacher lets students know that it is possible for students from different reading levels to work together. It also helps to relieve any negative stigma that may be associated in students' minds with grouping.

Subject Groups.   Subject groups are formed around a particular subject— math, science, social studies, health, art, or whatever. The purpose of these groups is to have students work on a given task related to the subject. Perhaps the teacher wants students from a certain reading group to work on social-studies material to apply a reading skill that has been taught. Sometimes one may form subject groups by combining students from different reading levels and giving them different tasks as a part of a unit that requires different reading demands. Although subject groups may be used at other times during the day than those scheduled for reading, they should still be considered a part of the reading program because they will provide some of a teacher's best opportunities to see that students apply the reading skills they have been taught.

Activity Groups.   Activity groups and interest groups are very similar and in many instances are the same. The reasons for using activity groups vary slightly from those for using interest groups. Activity groups usually require little or no reading tasks. Instead, they focus on a game, construction activity, or some other enrichment activity. Periodic use of activity groups adds variety to the reading program and provides good motivation for the students. However, the activities used should be related to reading in some way. For example, a group might be working on the construction of a model of a locomotive as the result of having listened to a story or a record about it.

Total Group. There are times in the reading program when total group instruction is appropriate, but these times are limited. Activities such as listening comprehension and reading stories to the class are examples of when one might work with the total group. If there are skills and concepts that are needed by all the students and can be properly taught to the entire class, then total group instruction can be used. Many times, however, it is used when it really is not appropriate. One will teach a skill—for example, blends—to the whole class whether they need it or not, with the assumption that "It doesn't hurt anything." One really cannot draw this conclusion.

Team Learning

Sometimes it is easier for students to learn together or to learn from each other. This type of learning can be called team learning. It involves putting two or three students together to work on the same task or so that one can help the other(s) learn a particular skill or concept. There is nothing wrong with this type of learning. Some teachers feel that it is "cheating," but in reality for some students it is a very effective way of learning. It may be possible, for example, to give two students a task in a workbook or at a learning center and have them work on it together and learn from each other. This may be a more effective way for them to learn and may help them overcome some of their learning frustrations.

Language-Arts Block

Another organizational pattern to consider in planning a reading program is the language-arts block. This is really a scheduling pattern that allows the teacher much more flexibility in working with all the language arts.

In the language-arts block, reading, spelling, writing, English, and all other aspects of the language arts are scheduled for a given block of time—for example, two hours. During this period the teacher is free to work in all of the language arts as he/she regards it appropriate. On some days one may want to spend more time on reading and less time on English. This also makes it possible to do a better job of integrating all the language arts and correlating reading, writing, and so on. The language-arts block concept lends itself to better individualization of reading and all the other language arts. Specific examples related to the implementation of the language-arts block will be presented in Chapter 9.

Finally, it should be kept in mind that an effective reading program may use many combinations of these organizational patterns. No one pattern will work all the time. As one becomes more effective in organizing and managing a reading program, one should attempt to incorporate many of these patterns in teaching.

DEVELOPING A BEGINNING ORGANIZATIONAL PLAN

Any organizational plan that is developed for a reading program is always tentative. As the needs of the students change a teacher will want to change his/her basic plan. The steps and procedures for the initial organization will be different from those one considers in reorganizing throughout the year. The steps suggested here for initial organization have worked for many teachers. It is important to remember that these steps must be used flexibly.

Steps to Follow

Step 1. Obtain the Appropriate Diagnostic Information.   This is the first step in the diagnostic teaching process: gather relevant background information. Previous chapters have discussed how to determine a student's reading levels, specific skill needs, and interests and attitudes. This information can be obtained by testing, using work samples, observing students, or referring to the student's permanent reading record. Even if one has a student's reading record that provides complete information, some type of confirming activities should be carried out to verify the student's reading levels, skill needs, and/or interests. This can be done by "trying on reading" as suggested in Chapter 3—using exercises designed to check specific skills—and by talking with students. Confirming activities should be kept simple and to a minimum.

If complete reading records are not available, the teacher may need to do some testing. One of the most important things to determine in testing is the student's reading levels. Therefore, some IRI should be given. This will not only provide reading-level information but will also provide some indication of skill strengths and needs. Table 5-1 summarizes some of the relevant background information on a third-grade class which will illustrate the steps to follow in initially organizing a class for instruction. This table has information on the students' reading levels and some limited comments on their skills which was taken from the reading record cards. Some activities were carried out in class to confirm these levels and it is assumed that all of them are accurate except for Sandy, Jeff, Sue, Joe, and Betty. The records indicate that they should be able to read at level 4 but that appears to be too difficult. The teacher is now ready to proceed to Step 2 in developing a beginning organizational plan.

Step 2. Decide on the Type of Organizational Patterns to Use.   The teacher should examine the background information obtained on the class to determine the type of organizational patterns that will be needed to teach reading. Obviously, some basic instructional groups will be needed in almost every case. From that point one must decide if one needs specific skill groups, interest groups, or whatever. The decisions that one makes about skill groups will depend on the range of skill needs within a basic instructional group. If there are many different needs, it may be that some short-term specific skill groups

TABLE 5-1. Relevant Background Information on a Third-Grade Class at the Beginning of the School Year.

Name	Level of Reader Completed*	Skills Mastery
Larry	5	Mastered all skills except prefixes dis, un
Ed	7	Mastered all skills through level
Mary	8	Mastered all skills through level
Ann	7	Mastered all skills through level
Sid	2	Mastered *no* skills at level
Mark	8	Mastered all skills except inferring sequence
Sandy	3	Mastered all skills except vce
Jeff	3	Mastered all skills through level
Kay	5	Mastered all skills through level
Tim	7	Mastered all skills through level
Mike	8	Mastered all skills except cause-effect and inferring sequence
Sue	3	Mastered all skills except vce, main-idea inferences
Jackie	5	Mastered all skills through level
Joan	7	Mastered all skills through level
Ted	8	Mastered all skills through level
Jane	7	Mastered all skills through level
Dorothy	5	Mastered all skills through level
Bruce	7	Failed to master syllabication, schwa, details inference, cause-effect
Frank	8	Mastered all skills through level
Peggy	2	Mastered no skills at level
Joe	3	Mastered all skills except vce and inference
Betty	3	Mastered all skills through level

*Key to reader levels
1	Readiness
2-3	Preprimer
4-5	Primer
6	First
7-8	Second
9-10	Third
11	Fourth
12	Fifth
13	Sixth

should be formed. As for interest and other types of groups, these may be used throughout the year as the need requires.

From the data in Table 5-1 one can see that several basic instructional groups will be needed because there are several different reading levels. Skill needs will be discussed in a later step.

Step 3. Organize Basic Instructional Groups. Begin this step by examining the reading levels of the students. Table 5-1 has information from the last book that the students completed. One's confirming activities have verified that the levels indicated by the next book in the series are appropriate places to be-

gin instruction for all the students except Sandy, Jeff, Sue, Joe, and Betty. The next thing to do is to cluster the students together by the reading levels *to which they should be assigned* for instruction.

Level 6	Level 8	Level 9	Level 3	Level 4
Larry	Ed	Mary	Sid	Sandy
Kay	Ann	Mark	Peggy	Jeff
Jackie	Tim	Mike		Sue
Dorothy	Joan	Ted		Joe
	Jane	Frank		Betty
	Bruce			

The three groups that would read in levels 6, 8, and 9 are placed appropriately according to confirming activities. Therefore one can begin their instruction at the level of the basal reader as indicated. As already noted, the students who should read at level 4 are not able to do so. From the confirming activities one knows that these five students probably need more work at level 3. One can now combine the two students who need level 3 (Sid and Peggy) with the five who need more work at level 3. One now has four groups to manage in the reading program—one each at level 3, level 6, level 8, and level 9.

Sometimes it will be necessary to consider combining two levels of students in order to have a more manageable number of groups. When this need arises, one should review the instructional levels of the groups to see if any can be combined and at the same time still provide the instruction that the students need. For example, one may have a group that needs to be instructed at level 5 of the basal series. Another group is in level 6 but would seem to profit from more instruction and practice at level 5 in order to help them develop their reading skills more adequately. It would be appropriate to combine these two groups, which would still give the students the opportunity for needed instruction and at the same time will help the teacher develop a more manageable organizational plan. In forming the basic instructional groups and reorganizing them throughout the year, the teacher will have to make similar decisions, always keeping in mind the needs of the students and the manageability of the organizational plan.

Step 4. Select the Instructional Materials for Each Group.   Once the basic instructional groups are formed the teacher is ready to select the level of the basal series to be used for instruction. In most cases it will simply be the next level in the series. In the example that has been used, the three groups in levels 6, 8, and 9 are ready to begin instruction in those levels. The group of five students who have been in level 4 and will now read at level 3 presents a different set of circumstances. The teacher should select a book for them that they have not read. This means that the two students who are ready for level 3 and have not had it will be placed with the other five in a reading text comparable to level 3. One can make this choice only after knowing what other basal

readers are available in the school and selecting one that is comparable to level 3 in the core series being used. Finding one that perfectly matches the level and skills of the core reader is not very likely, but one should come as close as possible in making a selection.

Step 5. Identify the Skills One Will Teach and Organize Skill Groups if Needed. Begin by examining the skill needs of each basic instructional group. If all or most of the students have mastered the skills in the level of the reader they have completed, the teacher should follow the sequence of the basal series and teach the skills as indicated by the teacher's guide.

In the basic instructional groups that have been organized in the example, the four students reading at level 6—Larry, Kay, Jackie and Dorothy—have mastered all the skills through level 5. They are ready to proceed with the instruction in level 6. No special skill groups or reteaching of skills not mastered will be needed for this basic instructional group. The group that has been identified as reading at level 8 is a little different. All the students except Bruce have mastered the skills up through level 7. Bruce failed to master syllabication, schwa, details, inferences, and cause-effect but can still read at level 7 and appears to be ready for level 8 as we have determined through our confirming activities. A special skill group probably is not needed for Bruce but as other groups are taught the skills that Bruce has not mastered from level 7, he should be worked in for reteaching.

In some cases basic instructional groups will be organized around specific skill groups for the reteaching of skills not mastered or skills whose mastery has not been retained. These are formed by selecting the skill that needs to be retaught for the largest number of students and starting a group for it. Those students who do not need the skill selected for teaching can work on another skill, be given enrichment activities, have opportunities to read a book of their choice, work on a special project, or use their time reading in a content area while the specific skill is being taught to those who need it.

Following these five steps should help one develop a beginning organizational plan for the class. But keep in mind that it is only a beginning plan and will be changed as the needs of the students change.

MAKING ORGANIZATIONAL CHANGES THROUGHOUT THE SCHOOL YEAR

As already noted, the initial organizational plan for reading instruction is very tentative. As one begins teaching reading to the class, events will take place that will create the need for change. One now employs Steps 4 and 5 of diagnostic teaching:

Step 4 Teach.
Step 5 Evaluate results.

In carrying out these steps the need will arise to change one's organization to more effectively meet the individual differences of the students and improve one's own teaching. An effective organizational plan is one that is not rigid but changes as the students change. Throughout the year, many organizational changes may be required.

Conditions That Make Change Necessary

As reading is taught, the students' reading levels will change. Most students will improve their reading level but sometimes one finds that a few students have regressed or that one has misjudged their level. Students do not change as rapidly in their reading levels as they do in their specific skill areas, but it is reasonable to expect some growth in reading level throughout the year. In a few instances there may even be very sudden changes whereby a student will grow two or more levels in a short period of time. An effective diagnostic reading teacher should be constantly looking for these changes. It is not necessary to wait until a student finishes a book to consider moving him/her to a different reading level.

Changes in a student's skill needs also create conditions that will necessitate changes in one's organizational structure. Skill changes can and do occur very rapidly. Most students will master a skill in a few days. But there may be one or two who do not achieve mastery. In working with the students, the teacher will observe new skill strengths and needs that will have to be taken into consideration as she/he teaches.

Other factors in a class will also influence the decision to make organizational changes. Behavior problems may occur in the groups. Some personalities may not function well together or discipline problems may arise that interfere with learning. Some students may lose interest in their work or in the materials being used. And parental concerns may provide a need to make organizational changes. While these factors do not fall into the category of reading, they must be considered as part of any classroom organization.

Criteria for Making Changes

There are three basic types of conditions that create the need for organizational changes:

1. Reading-level changes.
2. Skill-need changes.
3. Other behavioral and/or learning changes.

To make decisions about these areas one needs to have some criteria to follow. While there are no absolute guidelines, some can be helpful in directing one's decisions.

Reading-Level Changes. As a rule children move from one level of the reading series to the next with little variation in the sequence. Most children probably read at level 8 because they have just finished level 7 and level 8 comes next. As previously mentioned, changes in reading level are likely to take place more slowly than changes in skill needs.

To determine whether students should have their reading level changed the teacher should rely on the criteria for the three reading levels that were presented in Chapter 3. Evidence as to whether students are in need of a change of level can come from IRI results, work samples, or general observations by the teacher.

As one observes students in a reading group, it will become apparent how they are performing. By the way they answer questions, one can observe their comprehension. Through oral reading, one can judge their decoding abilities. Samples of student work from workbooks and other written exercises can also give some insights and indications as to whether a student's reading-level placement needs to be changed.

If a teacher decides that a student's reading-level placement should be changed, some concrete evidence will be needed to make this change. One of the better ways to acquire it is through using passages from the IRI or passages from the readers themselves. For example, Bob is reading level 10 of the basal reader. Through observations and work samples the teacher has decided that he should move to a higher level. From the IRI one takes the oral and silent passages from level 10 and level 11 and has him read them. Based on the criteria for determining levels, the teacher decides that he should be placed at level 11. Bob has not completed his book at level 10 but that should be no concern. Through observations the teacher has determined that he has the skills needed to complete level 10. There will be more comment on this later.

Another way to determine Bob's need to change levels is to select passages from the level-10 and level-11 books for him to read orally and silently and then to apply the criteria for determining levels. This procedure is more informal than the IRI procedure but seems simpler to some teachers. It is recommended, however, that one use the passages from the IRI. It is more structured, can be administered in a short period of time, and provides a better indication of whether or not a student's reading placement should be changed.

As already indicated, most students move from one level of the reader to the next based on the completion of the book. This is not satisfactory evidence on which to base this decision. When all the students in a group complete the book, the IRI procedure described above should be followed. Since the IRI is the most valid procedure for determining a student's reading level, its use in the manner described should lead to more accurate placement of students throughout the reading program. This is especially true if all teachers in a school follow this procedure.

Skill Changes. Skill changes for students are more easily determined than reading-level changes. The results of the skills-mastery tests that accom-

pany the basal reader will provide much of the information one will need about specific reading skills. Many times, however, teachers depend on the skill tests to determine reading-level changes, which are really not appropriate for this purpose.

If one's school does not use skills-mastery tests, some formal or informal skill tests should be used to check mastery of the skills that have been taught. The suggestions given in Chapter 4 can be followed. Work samples can also provide the information needed about skills.

One important point to remember is that the skills-mastery tests tend to measure a student's use of a skill in isolation. Therefore, one should always compare the results of any skill test to an actual sample of a student's reading to know whether or not she/he applies the skill in context. This information can be gained by using the IRI passages or by having a student read a portion from his/her text. Some students will be able to read and apply the skills but will do poorly on skills tests. In such cases, it is the reading that should be given the greater consideration. Any decisions made about skill needs should be made by comparing the skill tests and the actual ability of the students to use the skill in reading.

Other Changes.   Sometimes students will change in terms of their general behavior and/or learning style. Decisions related to these areas will usually be made by the teacher on the basis of observations of the student's work. Factors such as how well a student works with others or gets along with them, how a student functions in a particular size group, or how a student is able to handle the pace of instruction in a given group must all be considered by the teacher in making organizational changes. These factors along with the reading level and skill information must all be considered as the teacher decides about changes to be made in the classroom organization for the reading program.

ORGANIZING THE FIRST-GRADE CLASSROOM FOR READING INSTRUCTION

Organizing the first-grade classroom for reading instruction is somewhat different from organizing at other grade levels. The basic principles and procedures for organizing are the same but the information needed and the focus on beginning reading instruction are different. There are three basic sources of information for the first-grade teacher to use in organizing the class:

1. The kindergarten teacher's judgment.
2. Results of tests, formal and informal.
3. The first-grade teacher's observations.

Each of these sources will provide valuable information about the prereading and reading abilities of the students.

Reading authorities (3) suggest that there are numerous prereading skills and abilities that should be considered as a part of the readers' prereading development. These can be divided into four areas:

1. Oral language.
2. Visual discrimination.
3. Auditory discrimination.
4. Left-to-right orientation.

The significance of each of these to reading has been discussed in an earlier chapter. In organizing the reading program in the first grade the teacher should have as much information as possible about these areas. In some instances the kindergarten teacher will have a checklist like the one presented in Figure 5-1 to provide information about each child's prereading or reading. When this type of information is not available or the child has not attended kindergarten, the first-grade teacher must obtain this information through informal activities and observations and/or tests. Standardized reading-readiness tests such as the following ones can be used to gather information about some of these areas.

Comprehensive Test of Basic Skills Readiness Test, CTB/McGraw-Hill, 1977
Skills Tested: Letter forms, letter names, listening for information, letter sounds, visual discrimination, sound matching, language, mathematics.

Clymer-Barrett Prereading Battery
Personnel Press, 1968
Skills Tested: Recognition of letters, matching words, discrimination of beginning sounds in words, discrimination of ending sounds in words, shape completion, copying a sentence.

Metropolitan Readiness Tests
Harcourt, Brace, Jovanovich, Inc., 1976
Skills Tested: Level 1   auditory memory, rhyming, letter recognition, visual matching, school language and listening, quantitative language.
    Level II   beginning consonants, sound-letter correspondences, visual matching, finding patterns, school language, listening, quantitative concepts, quantitative operations.

All basal readers have some type of prereading and/or readiness component. Many of these include diagnostic tests that can be used to determine a student's ability to use the various prereading skills. Figure 5-2 shows such diagnostic tests of prereading skills from Harcourt Brace and Houghton Mifflin. From these tests, information can be obtained for organizing the first-grade class for instruction.

Deciding to Begin Reading Instruction

A major concern in the kindergarten and/or first-grade classroom is when to begin reading instruction. Much controversy has existed for years over this

I. Vocabulary
   A. Word Recognition
      1. Interested in words _____
      2. Recognizes own name in print _____
      3. Knows names of letters _____
      4. Knows names of numbers _____
      5. Can match letters _____
      6. Can match numbers _____
      7. Can match capital-small letters _____

   B. Word Meaning
      1. Speaking vocabulary adequate
         to convey ideas _____
      2. Associates Pictures to words _____
      3. Identifies new words by
         picture clues _____

II. Perceptive Skills
   A. Auditory
      1. Can reproduce pronounced two
         and three syllable words _____
      2. Knows number of sounds in
         spoken words _____
      3. Can hear differences in words _____
      4. Able to hear length of word
         (which is shorter? Boy-
         Elephant) _____
      5. Able to hear sound:
         At beginning of word-end
         of word-in middle of word _____
      6. Hears rhyming words _____
      7. Aware of unusual words _____

   B. Visual
      1. Uses picture clues _____
      2. Recognizes:
         Colors-Sizes (big, little-
         tall, short) _____
      3. Observes likenesses and
         differences in words _____
                         in letters _____
      4. Left-right eye movements _____

III. Comprehension
   A. Interest
      1. Wants to learn to read _____
      2. Likes to be read to _____
      3. Attention span sufficiently
         long _____

   B. Ability
      1. Remembers from stories read
         aloud: Names of character _____
                   Main ideas _____
                   Conclusions _____
      2. Can keep events in proper
         sequence _____
      3. Uses complete sentences _____
      4. Can work independently for
         short periods _____
      5. Begins at front of book _____
      6. Begins on left hand page _____
      7. Knows sentence begins at left _____

IV. Oral Expression
   A. Expresses self spontaneously _____
   B. Able to remember five word
      sentences _____
   C. Able to make up simple endings
      for stories _____
   D. Able to use new words _____

FIGURE 5-1. Kindergarten Checklist

Source: Dr. June Spooner, Dean Road Elementary School, Auburn, Alabama.

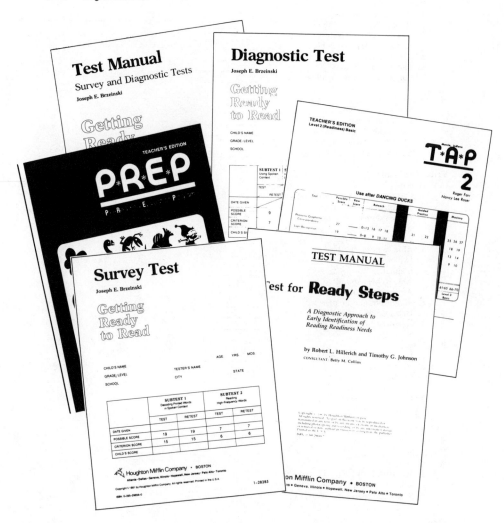

FIGURE 5-2. Prereading Tests from Harcourt Brace and Laidlaw Basal Reading Series.

issue (2,3). While tests and observations will help a teacher make this decision, there is a very simple approach that can be followed. This is having the children "try on" reading to see how it "fits," just as someone would try on some new clothes to see how they fit.

One way to begin the "trying on" of reading is through the use of language experience (see Chapter 8 for details on the use of language experience). This can be done by having a small group of students develop a language-experience story. The teacher should select five words from the story and teach them. The next day the words should be on cards. Each child should be tested separately to see if he/she knows the words. One should repeat the procedure with a new story at least one more time. The next day after this story the teacher

A Group Doing a Language Experience Story.

should check the retention of the words. Any child who is remembering three out of the five words is probably ready to begin reading.

This procedure of "trying on" reading can also be followed using a basal reader. One picks a story, selects some words to teach, and follows the same procedures as suggested above with language experience. The same procedure can be repeated with the book and the same criterion followed for determining whether students are ready to begin reading.

Organizing Instructional Groups

The task of organizing the first-grade classroom for instruction will follow the same basic procedures as outlined earlier in this chapter. However, one will need to use the type of information that has been discussed about prereading and "trying on" reading. The teacher will first need to decide which students need prereading development and which are ready to begin reading instruction. Once this decision has been made one can begin to organize the groups.

For those students who need prereading development, the groups should be organized according to the areas where instruction is needed. For those

whom the teacher has determined that reading instruction is appropriate, she/he may want to group them according to the number of words they were able to retain during the "try on" period.

LIMITATIONS TO BE CONSIDERED BY THE BEGINNING TEACHER

A beginning teacher will have many pressures and excitements to face. In developing one's organizational plan for reading, one will need to start out on a small scale. It is best not to use too many groups or too many complex organizational patterns. As one becomes more comfortable in using certain patterns new ones can be added. The teacher should constantly evaluate his/her organization with the following questions:

1. Am I too dependent on one organizational pattern?
2. Do the organizational patterns which I am using meet the needs of my students?
3. Do my organizational procedures coordinate with and enhance the school's philosophy of reading instruction?

On-going evaluation of one's own organizational skills will help one become a better teacher of reading. With an effective organizational plan one should be able to develop more efficient management skills.

SUMMARY

Organizing a class for reading instruction means that one must look at the needs of the students and group them together in patterns that will allow their individual needs to be met. Careful organization is a prerequisite to effective management. Any organizational plan that one develops is tentative and must continuously be reorganized as one teaches. Changes made in the organizational structure of a reading program should be based on criteria other than just completion of a book.

The principles governing the organization of the first-grade classroom are the same as those governing any classroom. However, the decisions concerning organization at this level should be based on information about the students' prereading abilities. This information can be obtained through the records from the kindergarten teacher, tests, and classroom observations.

A beginning teacher will want to continuously evaluate her/his organizational plans and try to add new procedures and techniques. One should not expect to be able to do everything at once.

THOUGHT AND DISCUSSION QUESTIONS

1. What source of relevant background information would be most beneficial to you in organizing your class for reading instruction?
2. Identify the times when the various types of grouping patterns discussed in this chapter would be useful in the reading program.
3. Making certain that one's organizational plan does not become rigid and static is of prime concern in teaching reading. Discuss ways that you can insure that this does not happen.

APPLYING WHAT YOU HAVE LEARNED

1. Visit with a classroom teacher at the primary level and the intermediate level to discuss their organization for reading instruction.
2. Using simulated data provided by your instructor, develop a beginning organizational plan for reading instruction.

BIBLIOGRAPHY

1. Burns, Paul C., and Roe, Betty D. *Teaching Reading in Today's Elementary Schools*, 2nd ed. Chicago: Rand McNally College Publishing Company, 1980.

2. Coltheart, Max. "When Can Children Learn to Read—and When Should They Be Taught," in T. Gary Waller and G. E. Mackinnon, eds., *Reading Research: Advances in Theory and Practice*, New York: Academic Press, Inc., 1979, pp. 1–30.

3. Durkin, Dolores. *Teaching Young Children To Read*, 3rd ed. Boston: Allyn & Bacon, Inc., 1980.

4. *First Year Teacher Evaluations*, Muncie, Indiana. Teachers College, Ball State University, 1977, 1978, 1979, and 1980.

5. Huitt, William G., and Segars, John K. "Characteristics of Effective Classrooms." Research for Better Schools, Inc., Philadelphia, Oct. 1980.

6. Lapp, Diane, ed. *Making Reading Possible Through Effective Classroom Management*. Newark, Del.: International Reading Association, 1980.

7. Lapp, Diane, and Flood, James. *Teaching Reading to Every Child*. New York: Macmillan Publishing Company, Inc., 1978, Chapter 3.

8. Stallings, June. "Allocated Academic Learning Time Revisited or Beyond Time on Task." *Educational Researcher*, Vol. 9, No. 11, (Dec. 1980), 11–16.

FOR FURTHER READING

Burns, Paul C., and Roe, Betty D. *Teaching Reading in the Elementary School*, 2nd ed. Chicago: Rand McNally College Publishing Co., 1980, Chapter 10.

Cooper, J. David, et al. *The What and How of Reading Instruction*. Columbus, Ohio: Charles E. Merrill Publishing Co., 1979. Module COM, p. 335.

chapter 6

record keeping

objectives

Upon completion of this chapter one will be able to

1. Understand the concept of a record-keeping system.
2. Understand how a record-keeping system relates to diagnostic teaching.
3. Understand the components of an effective record-keeping system.
4. Know several different record-keeping systems that can be used in the classroom reading program.

overview

This chapter will discuss the importance of record keeping as it relates to the reading program. How a record keeping system can be employed within the diagnostic teaching model will be stressed. The components of an effective record-keeping system will be identified and explained with practical examples presented. The information gained from this chapter will help one to employ Steps 2, 3, 4, and 5 of the diagnostic teaching model:

Step 2. Generate alternative actions.
Step 3. Evaluate alternatives and select ones to carry out.
Step 4. Teach.
Step 5. Evaluate results.

In Chapter 5 organizing a classroom for effective reading instruction was discussed along with patterns for this organization and some useful ways to implement those patterns. This chapter will explore the important part played by record keeping in the organization of a reading program. A sound record-keeping system is essential to effective organization and management in the classroom.

Record keeping becomes important as soon as one completes Step 1 of the diagnostic teaching model—Gather Relevant Information About Each Student. Effective record keeping allows the teacher to organize the information needed to make important decisions about the needs of his/her students. Without some type of record keeping, the teacher would have a difficult time utilizing diagnostic teaching.

THE IMPORTANCE OF A RECORD-KEEPING SYSTEM

Record keeping can be defined as the system selected by the teacher that is used to organize the information obtained about each student's reading abilities. Records that are formulated in schools for purposes of reading instruction contain a wide variety of information. Facts about skill development, reading levels, interests of the learner, or specific results from diagnostic measures are types of information that can be placed in a child's classroom record. An effective record-keeping system can be referred to by the teacher in determining skill strengths and weaknesses, deciding which reading skills should be taught and when, and keeping abreast of the general academic growth of the learner (5, 6).

Some teachers have a tendency to merely follow the teacher's guide of the basal series and do *all* the skills presented in that sequence. By implementing an effective record-keeping system, the teacher can keep individual skill-development data organized so that the records serve as an important resource in planning instruction. The teacher can then refer to the records of each child, decide what the child or group of children need, and formulate those needs into a workable plan. The records provide the teacher with the information needed to make the decisions about what the individual or group needs, and the teacher's guide provides the resources for teaching.

Today one often hears that children cannot read and write as well as children did in the past (3). Even though this attitude might stem in part from misinformation, teachers themselves may be partly responsible in not being more accountable to the public. With school funding becoming a crucial issue in all parts of the country, teachers need to demonstrate more than ever that schools are improving student achievement. The implementation of an effective record-

keeping system in the elementary reading program is one means by which schools can concretely demonstrate their accountability to the public.

Record keeping provides a method of assuring continuity in teaching reading and also communicating with parents. Parent-teacher conferences become much more meaningful when the parents view the records kept by the teacher, take part in a discussion about the content of the records, and ask any questions that would further clarify the teacher's instructional direction. As other conferences occur during a school year, parents can have the opportunity to reexamine their children's records and note additional skill development or growth in reading.

Record keeping and organization of a classroom for reading instruction go hand in hand. Once the diagnosing is completed it is imperative that written records be kept. These records will not only assist the teacher in getting a classroom organized but also in keeping the organizational plan running smoothly (2).

THE RECORD-KEEPING SYSTEM AND DIAGNOSTIC TEACHING

As already discussed, diagnostic teaching is an ongoing process of making decisions about each student's reading program. The decisions the teacher must make are based on the information that has been gathered about the student's reading. In order to be able to utilize this information, the teacher must have it organized in some manner for easy access. Thus an effective record-keeping system is essential. By having records of each student's reading progress, the teacher will be able to study the information and use it to make the decisions necessary for a successful diagnostic reading program.

An effective record-keeping system also helps the teacher increase his/her instructional efficiency. By having all information about a student's reading readily available in one location, the teacher can consult the records to decide what to teach and see what materials have been used in previous instruction. In examining the completed sample record in Figure 6-1, one can readily see this student's reading level, which skills have been taught and mastered, which skills have been taught and not mastered, which skills have not been taught, and which books in the basal series have been used. With this information the teacher can more efficiently make the decisions needed in planning the reading program for this student.

As pointed out, research indicates that an effective reading program has an instructional component of continuous diagnosis and mastery. For this to be implemented in any reading program, and especially the diagnostic reading program, records of progress must be kept by all teachers and passed along from year to year.

Houghton Mifflin Reading Program

DIRECTIONS

The Cumulative Individual Reading Record Folder provides space for recording an individual student's scores on the tests for each level—A through O—of the Houghton Mifflin Reading Program. In addition, it may be used to record the test results of the *Informal Reading Inventory* and the *Vocabulary and Skills Inventory*.

Level A: Space is provided on the front of the folder to record the scores for *Checkpoints: Getting Ready to Read* and the *Survey and Diagnostic Tests for Getting Ready to Read*. The small number in each box shows the Criterion Score (CS) for the particular skill tested. Record the student's score for each test beside the Criterion Score. Starting with *Checkpoints*, each skill description is identified with a skill reference number that corresponds to the Houghton Mifflin Reading Program Scope and Sequence of Skills.

Levels B–O: Starting at Level B, the skill descriptions for the tests are preceded by a lesson number to correspond with the order of the Basic Reading Skill Instruction Lessons in the Teacher's Guide at that level. The tests assess virtually all the skills presented in the Basic Reading Skill Instruction Lessons. A small number of skills, designated by asterisks, do not lend themselves to a testing format. For these skills that should be evaluated by the teacher, no Criterion Score is given. However, space is provided for checking teacher-evaluated skills.

ASSESSMENT TESTS: Enter a check mark for each Assessment Test for which the result was at the Criterion Score. Enter a plus (+) for each test for which the score was above the Criterion Score. Enter a minus (−) for each test for which the score was below the Criterion Score. The Criterion Scores for equivalent forms of Assessment Tests are shown in small numbers in the score boxes for the Form A tests.

TESTS OF BASIC READING SKILLS (TBRS): Transfer to this folder the scores from the Class Record Form or from the score boxes in the student's booklet for the *Tests of Basic Reading Skills*. Circle or write in color those scores that are below the Criterion Score (CS).

A: GETTING READY TO READ   Date 12/4/81

	SURVEY	DIAGNOSTIC				
	Decoding Printed Words in Spoken Context	Reading High-Frequency Words	Using Spoken Context	Identifying Letters	Listening for Beginning Sounds	Letter-Sound Associations	Identifying High-Frequency Words
	CS 15	CS 6	CS 7 7	CS 23 24	CS 15 (13)	CS 15 15	CS 7 8

A: GETTING READY TO READ (K–1)

	CS
Checkpoint 1 Date 9-25-81	
Identifying Letters D1-3	8 8
Listening for Beginning Sounds D1-4	8 8
Letter-Sound Associations D1-4-5	8 9
Decoding Printed Words D1-6	4 (3)
Checkpoint 2 Date 10-5-81	
Identifying Letters D1-3	8 8
Listening for Beginning Sounds D1-4	8 (5)
Letter-Sound Associations D1-4-5	8 9
Decoding Printed Words D1-6	4 4
Checkpoint 3 Date 10-13-81	
Identifying Letters D1-3	8 8
Listening for Beginning Sounds D1-4	8 (6)
Letter-Sound Associations D1-4-5	8 8
Decoding Printed Words D1-6	4 5
Checkpoint 4 Date 10-20-81	
Listening for Beginning Sounds D1-4	8 (7)
Letter-Sound Associations D1-4-5	8 8
Decoding Printed Words D1-6	4 4
High-Frequency Words D1-6	4 4
Checkpoint 5 Date 10-28-81	
Identifying Letters D1-3	8 9
Listening for Beginning Sounds D1-4	8 8
Letter-Sound Associations D1-4-5	8 8
Decoding Printed Words D1-6	4 5
Checkpoint 6 Date 11-11-81	
Listening for Beginning Sounds D1-4	8 (7)
Letter-Sound Associations D1-4-5	8 8
Decoding Printed Words D1-6	4 5
High-Frequency Words D1-6	4 5
Checkpoint 7 Date 11-20-81	
Identifying Letters D1-3	8 8
Listening for Beginning Sounds D1-4	8 8
Letter-Sound Associations D1-4-5	8 8
Decoding Printed Words D1-6	4 5
Checkpoint 8 Date 12-2-81	
Listening for Beginning Sounds D1-4	8 (7)
Letter-Sound Associations D1-4-5	8 8
Decoding Printed Words D1-6	4 5
High-Frequency Words D1-6	4 4

VOCABULARY AND SKILLS INVENTORY

Date of Testing _____   Instructional Reading Level _____

INFORMAL READING INVENTORY

Date of Testing _____   Instructional Reading Level _____

Houghton Mifflin Company • BOSTON

Atlanta • Dallas • Geneva, Illinois • Hopewell, New Jersey • Palo Alto • Toronto

Copyright © 1981 by Houghton Mifflin Company. All rights reserved.
Printed in the U.S.A.

FIGURE 6-1. Completed Reading Record.

B: BEARS (PP) Date 12-16-81

	Word Recognition	FORM A CS	A	FORM B B	TBRS CS
	Word Recognition				12 14
1.	Digraph th D1·7b	4			4 4
2.	Following Directions CA1·1	4			4 4
* 3.	Comma of Address C4·2a				
4.	End Sounds l, t D1·7c	4			4 4
5.	End Sounds n, p D1·7c	4			4 4
6.	Letter Sounds & Context D1·7	3			4 4
7.	Digraph sh D1·7b	4			4 5
8.	Word Referents C3·1a	3			4 5
9.	Cluster fr D1·7d	3 3			4 (3)
* 10.	Exclamation Mark C4·1c				
11.	Drawing Conclusions CA5·2	3			4 4
* 12.	Clusters lp, mp D1·7e				
* 13.	Intonation				
14.	Predicting Outcomes CA6·2	2 (1)	2		4 (3)
15.	Cluster st D1·7d, e	3			4 4
16.	Noting Details CA2·1	2			4 4
17.	Categorizing CA10·2	3			4 4
18.	End Sounds m, d, g D1·7c	4			4 4

C: BALLOONS Date 1-25-82

	Word Recognition	FORM A CS	A	FORM B B	TBRS CS
	Word Recognition				12 13
1.	Noting Correct Sequence CA3·3	2			4 4
* 2.	Contractions with 's D1·7f				
* 3.	Sound Association for x D1·7c				
4.	Plurals D1·7h	4			4 4
* 5.	Verbs Ending with s D1·7g				
6.	Clusters sw, fl D1·7d	2			4 4
7.	Letter Sounds & Context D1·7	3			4 4
8.	Cause-Effect Relationships CA7·2	2 2			4 (3)
9.	Word Referents C3·1a	3			4 4
10.	Main Idea CA4·2	2 (1)	3		4 (2)
11.	Digraph ch D1·7b	4			4 4

D: BOATS Date

	Word Recognition	FORM A CS	A	FORM B B	TBRS CS
	Word Recognition				12 12
1.	Following Directions CA1·1	3			4 4
* 2.	End Sounds nt, nk D1·7e				
* 3.	Ending ing D1·7g				
4.	Digraphs th, sh, ch D1·7b	4			4 4
5.	Predicting Outcomes CA6·2	2			4 4
6.	Sound Association c/s/ D1·7n	3			4 4
* 7.	Ending ed D1·7g				
8.	Noting Important Details CA2·1	3 3			4 (3)
9.	Clusters fl, sw, fr, pl D1·7d	2			4 4
10.	Multi-meaning Words C1·1c	2			4 4
11.	Categorizing CA10·2	2			4 4
* 12.	Reviewing Endings s, ed, ing D1·7g				
* 13.	Consonants and Vowel Recognition D1·2c				
14.	Word Referents C3·1a	3			4 4
15.	Drawing Conclusions CA5·3	3			4 4

E: SUNSHINE Magazine 1 Date 3-25-82

	Recognizing High-Frequency Words	FORM A CS	A	FORM B B	TBRS CS
	Recognizing High-Frequency Words				12 12
1.	Cause-Effect Relationships CA7·1	2			4 4
2.	Short a Sound D1·7l	4			4 4
3.	Long a Sound D1·7l	4			4 4
* 4.	Quotation Marks, Comma C4·8a				
5.	Correct Sequence CA3·3	2 2			4 (2)
6.	Doubling Consonants Before Endings D1·7j	4			4 4
7.	Sound Associations for y D1·7l	2			4 4
8.	Dropping Final e Before Endings D1·7j	4			4 4

Magazine 2 Date

	Recognizing High-Frequency Words	FORM A CS	A	FORM B B	TBRS CS
	Recognizing High-Frequency Words				12
* 9.	Contractions with 's, n't, 'll D1·7f				
10.	Sound Associations for oo D1·7m	2			4
11.	Compound Words D1·7o	2			4
12.	Ending er D1·7g	2			4
13.	Predicting Outcomes CA6·2	2			4
14.	Short e Sound D1·7l	3			4
15.	Long e Sound D1·7l	3			4
* 16.	Intonation				
17.	Sound Association for ai/ay/ D1·7m	3			4
18.	Drawing Conclusions CA5·2	2			4

Magazine 3 Date

	Recognizing High-Frequency Words	FORM A CS	A	FORM B B	TBRS CS
	Recognizing High-Frequency Words				12
19.	Short i Sound D1·7l	3			4
20.	Long i Sound D1·7l	3			4
* 21.	Sound Association for kn/n/ D1·7b				
22.	Multi-meaning Words C1·1c	3			4
23.	Main Idea CA4·2	2			4
24.	Short and Long a, e, and i D1·7l	4			4

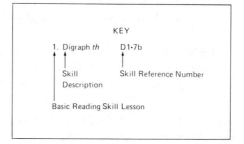

KEY

1. Digraph th   D1·7b
   ↑ Skill Description   ↑ Skill Reference Number

Basic Reading Skill Lesson

COMPONENTS OF EFFECTIVE RECORD-KEEPING SYSTEMS

There are four basic components that need to be present in any record-keeping system:

1. Identification of skills taught.
2. Record of reading levels.
3. Indication of instructional materials used.
4. Comments from the teacher.

Each of these will be discussed in the sections that follow.

Identification of Skills Taught and Mastered

In order to have a record-keeping system that can be used for planning, a complete listing of reading skills must be included. The skills to be listed are determined from the overall scope and sequence from a specific basal reading series or from the school's own scope and sequence. This allows the teacher to systematically record the student's progress in skill development.

The record-keeping form should contain spaces to indicate whether a skill has been taught, mastered, not mastered, or retaught. Figure 6-2 presents an example of a form from the Scott, Foresman reading series. Note the marking system for skill development in the upper-left corner.

Many schools have their own system for recording skill development, such as this one:

   –   skill taught but not mastered.
  +   skill mastered.
  ⊕   skill retaught or practiced after mastery.

If the space is left blank the teacher examining the record will know the skill has not been taught. Whatever system is followed, it is strongly suggested that all teachers in a building use the same markings.

The skills listing will comprise a major portion of any record-keeping system. This will provide an up-to-date picture of each student's skill development and should be very helpful to the teacher in planning instruction.

Record of Reading Levels

Another important component of an effective record-keeping system is a record of each student's reading level, as presented in Figure 6-3. In the upper-right-hand corner is a space to record the student's instructional reading level at

Effective Record Keeping Is Essential to an Elementary Reading Program.

the beginning and the end of the year. By having this information available each teacher will be able to tell whether or not a student's growth pattern in reading has been continuous or whether there have been periods of no growth or sporadic growth. This will be very helpful to the teacher in making decisions about each student's reading program.

Indicates Instructional Materials Used

Another important component of a record-keeping system is a place to keep track of the instructional materials that have been used in reading. Some children require more instructional materials than others. The most obvious type of material to record would be the books for the basal reading series. It is important to record the exact name of the reading text that is used. Figure

Scott, Foresman
Basics in Reading

SF

Scott, Foresman and Company

Directions

Record your evaluation of the pupil's progress in each skill. Suggested codings:
  − Needs help
  + Satisfactory

Skills listings are divided into four major categories. They are:

W—Word Identification
C—Comprehension
S—Study and Research
L—Literary Understanding and Appreciation

Numbers indicate the page in the Teachers Edition on which page references for teaching, practice, and testing of specific skills can be found. Symbols indicate the level of instruction, as follows:

○ Exposure prior to major instruction
★ First level of major instruction
△ Subsequent instruction prior to expected mastery
▲ Level during which mastery is expected
□ Maintenance expansion

Record test scores for Section Pretests, Section Checkpoints, and End-of-Book Tests on the back of this folder.

PUPPY PAWS	Preprimer 1	
W 28	□ Recognizes letters	
W 28	△ Context—pictures	
W 28-29	△ Context—meaning and syntax	
W 29, 30	△ Phonics—initial consonants b, d, f, g/g/, l, m, n, p, r, s, t	
W 29, 30	★ Phonics—initial consonants h, w, y	
W 31	★ Phonics—initial consonant blends	
W 32	○ Endings—s, 's	
W 32	△ Utility Words	
C 33	△ Punctuation—capital letters, period, question mark	
C 33	★ Punctuation—comma, exclamation mark, quotation marks	
C 33	△ Details	
C 33	○ Main idea	
C 33	★ Relationships—class	
C 34	○ Relationships—sequence, cause-effect	
C 34	○ Realism/fantasy	
C 34	△ Oral Reading	
S 34	○ Page numbers	
S 34	○ Table of contents	

JUMPING JAMBOREE	Preprimer 2	
W 28	△ Context—pictures	
W 28-29	△ Context—meaning and syntax	
W 29, 30	△ Phonics—initial consonants b, c/k/, d, f, g/g/, k, l, m, n, p, r, s, t	
W 29, 30	★ Phonics—initial consonants j, v, z	
W 30, 31	★ Phonics—final consonants b, d, f, g, k, l, m, n, p, r, s, t	
W 31	○ Phonics—internal consonants	
W 31	★ Phonics—initial consonant blends	
W 31	★ Phonics—consonant digraphs ch, sh, th; initial, final	
W 31	○ Phonics—vowels	
W 31	△ Phonics—variability: sound is represented by different letters	
W 31	○ Root word, no spelling change	
W 32	○ Endings—ed, 's	
W 32	★ Endings—es, s	
W 32	△ Utility Words	
C 33	○ Punctuation—apostrophe	
C 33	△ Punctuation—capital letters, period, question mark	
C 33	★ Punctuation—comma, exclamation mark, quotation marks	
C 33	△ Details	
C 33	○ Main idea	
C 33	★ Relationships—class	
C 34	○ Relationships—opposites, part-whole, cause-effect, sequence	
C 34	○ Realism/fantasy	
C 34	△ Oral Reading	
S 34	○ Page numbers	
S 34	○ Table of contents	

NO CAGES, PLEASE	Preprimer 3	
W 28	△ Context—pictures	
W 28-29	△ Context—meaning and syntax	
W 29	△ Phonics—initial consonants c/k/, g/g/	
W 29, 30	★ Phonics—initial consonants c/s/, g/j/, qu	
W 31	★ Phonics—final consonants x, ck, ll, nn, rr, ss, zz	
W 31	★ Phonics—internal consonants	
W 31	★ Phonics—initial consonant blends	
W 31	★ Phonics—consonant digraphs ch, sh, th; initial, final	
W 31	○ Phonics—vowels	
W 31	△ Phonics—variability: sound is represented by different letters	
W 31	★ Phonics—variability: letter represents different sounds	
W 31	★ Root word, no spelling change	
W 32	★ Endings—ed, es, s, 's	
W 32	○ Contractions	
W 32	○ Compounds	
W 32	△ Utility Words	
C 33	○ Appropriate word meaning	
C 33	○ Punctuation—apostrophe	
C 33	△ Punctuation—capital letters, period, question mark	
C 33	★ Punctuation—comma, exclamation mark, quotation marks	
C 33	△ Details	
C 33	○ Main idea	
C 33, 34	★ Relationships—class, opposites	
C 34	○ Relationships—part-whole, sequence, cause-effect, size	
C 34	○ Realism/fantasy	
C 34	△ Oral Reading	
S 34	○ Page numbers	
S 34	○ Table of contents	

FIRST FEATHERS	Readiness 1	
Skills without symbols and page numbers are taught and used throughout First Feathers.		
	Discriminates nonverbal sounds	
	Discriminates numbers	
	Discriminates rhyme	
	Discriminates shapes	
C 32	○ Distinguishes between realism and fantasy	
	Follows oral directions	
	Increases concepts and vocabulary	
	Marks responses	
C 32	○ Recognizes class relationships	
W 31	★ Recognizes details	
W 28	▲ Recognizes letters: capital and small a, b, c, d, e, f, g, h, i, j, k, l, m, n, o, p, q, r, s, t, u, v, w, x, y, z	
	Recognizes likenesses and differences	
C 32	○ Recognizes opposites	
C 32	○ Recognizes sequence relationships	
W 31	★ Recognizes utility words—18 high-frequency words, 8 color words	
W 28	★ Uses context	
C 31	★ Uses punctuation—capital letters, period, question mark	
	Uses left-to-right progression	
	Uses top-to-bottom progression	
	Uses numbered items on a page	
W 30	Uses phonics: initial consonants b, c, d, f, g, k, l, m, n, p, r, s, t	
	Works independently	

Scott, Foresman and Company

Editorial Offices: Glenview, Illinois

Regional Sales Offices: Palo Alto, California ● Tucker, Georgia ● Glenview, Illinois ● Oakland, New Jersey ● Dallas, Texas

ISBN 0-673-11805-3

FIGURE 6-2. Sample Reading Record from Scott, Foresman.

DRAGON WINGS Primer

W 28	△ Context—pictures, meaning and syntax	
W 28	△ Phonics—consonants: initial, final, internal	
W 28	△ Phonics—consonant blends: initial	
W 28	★ Phonics—consonant blends: final	
W 28	△ Phonics—consonant digraphs: initial, final	
W 29	★ Phonics—vowels: short *a, e, i, o, u;* long *a, e, i, o, u*	
W 29	○ Phonics—vowels controlled by *r*	
W 29	△ Phonics—variability	
W 29	△ Root word, no spelling change	
W 30	△ Endings—*ed, es, s, 's*	
W 30	★ Endings—*ing*	
W 30	○ Endings—*er, est*	
W 30	★ Contractions	
W 30	★ Compounds	
W 30	▲ Utility Words	
C 31	○ Pronouns	
C 31	○ Appropriate word meaning	
C 31	▲ Punctuation	
C 31	▲ Details	
C 31	○ Main idea	
C 31	△ Relationships—class, opposites	
C 31	★ Relationships—part-whole, sequence	
C 31	○ Relationships—cause-effect, size, place	
C 31	○ Realism/fantasy	
C 32	○ Conclusions	
C 32	△ Oral Reading	
C 32	○ Vocabulary	
S 32	★ Page numbers	
S 32	★ Table of contents	

CALICO CAPER Book 1

W 28	▲ Context—pictures	
W 28	△ Context—meaning and syntax	
W 28	△ Phonics—consonants: initial, final, internal	
W 28	△ Phonics—consonant blends: initial, final	
W 28	△ Phonics—consonant digraphs: initial, final	
W 28, 29	△ Phonics—vowels: short *a, e, i, o, u;* long *a, e, i, o, u*	
W 29	★ Phonics—vowels: long *e* (ea, ee); controlled by *r—a, e, i, o, u*	
W 30	△ Phonics—variability	
W 30	△ Root word, no spelling change	
W 30	○ Root word with spelling change: final consonant doubled, final *e* dropped, final *y* changed to *i*	
W 30	△ Endings—*s, es, ed, ing, 's*	
W 30	★ Endings—*er, est*	
W 30	▲ Contractions	
W 30	▲ Compounds	
W 31	□ Utility Words	
C 31	★ Pronouns	
C 31	○ Appropriate word meaning	
C 31	□ Punctuation	
C 31	△ Details	
C 31	★ Main idea	
C 32	△ Relationships—class, sequence	
C 32	▲ Relationships—opposites, part-whole	
C 32	★ Relationships—cause-effect, size	
C 32	○ Relationships—place, time	
C 32	○ Story problem/solution	
C 32	○ Realism/fantasy	
C 32	○ Conclusions	
C 32	○ Character feelings, actions, traits, motives	
C 33	△ Oral Reading	
C 33	★ Vocabulary	
S 33	△ Location Aids—pages, contents	
S 33	○ Location Aids—alphabetical order	
S 33	○ Graphic aids—maps; charts/tables/schedules	
S 33	○ Dictionary/glossary—guide words, entry, entry word, definitions, picture	

DAISY DAYS Book 2/1

W 28	□ Context—pictures	
W 28	△ Context—meaning and syntax	
W 28	△ Phonics—consonants: initial, final, internal	
W 28	△ Phonics—consonant blends: initial	
W 28	△ Phonics—consonant digraphs: initial, final	
W 28–30	△ Phonics—vowels: short *a, e, i, o, u;* long *a, e, i, o, u;* long *e* (ea, ee); controlled by *r—a, e, i, o, u*	
W 29	★ Phonics—vowels: long *e* (me), *y*(my), *o*(go)	
W 30	△ Phonics—variability	
W 30	▲ Root word, no spelling change	
W 30–31	★ Root word with spelling change: final consonant doubled, final *e* dropped, final *y* changed to *i*	
W 31	△ Endings—*s, es, ed, ing, 's, er, est*	
W 31	★ Endings—*en*	
W 31	□ Contractions; Compounds	
W 31	○ Suffix—*ly*	
W 31	○ Syllables	
W 32	□ Utility Words	
C 32	△ Pronouns	
C 32	○ Appropriate word meaning	
C 32	□ Punctuation	
C 32	▲ Details	
C 32	▲ Main idea	
C 32	○ Main idea/supporting details	
C 33	▲ Relationships—class, size	
C 33	□ Relationships—opposites, part-whole	
C 33	△ Relationships—sequence, cause-effect	
C 33	○ Relationships—place, time, analogous	
C 33	★ Story problem/solution	
C 33	★ Realism/fantasy	
C 33	○ Conclusions	
C 33	○ Evaluates solution to problem	
C 33	★ Character feelings, actions, traits, motives	
C 34	△ Oral Reading	
C 34	△ Vocabulary	
S 34	△ Location Aids—pages, contents	
S 34	★ Location Aids—alphabetical order	
S 34	○ Graphic aids—maps, schedules	
S 34	★ Dictionary/glossary—guide words, entry, entry word, definitions, picture	
S 34	○ Dictionary/glossary—illustrative sentence/phrase, root word, inflected form	
S 34	○ Reading Technique/Rate—rereads	

HOOTENANNY Book 2/2

W 28	□ Context—pictures	
W 28	△ Context—meaning and syntax	
W 28	▲ Phonics—consonants: initial	
W 28	△ Phonics—consonants: final, internal	
W 28	△ Phonics—consonant blends: initial, final	
W 28	△ Phonics—consonant digraphs: initial, final	
W 28–30	△ Phonics—vowels: short *a, e, i, o, u;* long *a, e, i, o, u;* long *e*(ea, ee), *e*(she), *y*(by), *o*(go); controlled by *r—a, e, i, o, u*	
W 29	★ Phonics—vowels: long *a*(ai, ay), *i*(ie), *o*(oa), *o*(oe), *u*(ue)	
W 30	★ Phonics—vowels: less common, *oi, oy*	
W 30	△ Phonics—variability	
W 30	□ Root word, no spelling change	
W 30	△ Root word with spelling change: final consonant doubled, final *e* dropped, final *y* changed to *i*	
W 31	○ Root word with spelling change: final *f* or *fe* changed to *v*	
W 31	△ Endings—*s, es, ed, ing, 's, er, est, en*	
W 31	□ Contractions; Compounds	
W 31	★ Suffixes—*ful, ly*	
W 31	○ Prefixes—*un*	
W 31	○ Syllables	
W 31	□ Utility Words	
C 31	△ Pronouns	
C 32	★ Appropriate word meaning	
C 32	○ Figures of speech	
C 32	□ Punctuation	
C 32	□ Details	
C 32	□ Main idea	
C 32	★ Main idea/supporting details	
C 32	□ Relationships—class, opposites, part-whole, size	
C 32	△ Relationships—sequence, cause-effect	
C 32	★ Relationships—place	
C 32	○ Relationships—time, analogous	
C 33	△ Story problem/solution	
C 33	△ Realism/fantasy	
C 33	★ Conclusions	
C 33	○ Fiction/nonfiction	

FIGURE 6-2. (*Continued*)

READING SKILLS PROFILE

M.S.D. Washington Township

Student's Name

Date of Birth

School

	K	1	2	3	4	5	6
Instructional Reading Level: 11, 12, 21, etc. (Beginning and end of school year) *Beg.							
End							

Preferred Learning Modes (Check one or more)

Visual

Auditory

Kinesthetic

I. WORD ATTACK

I-A   Left-Right Sequence
I-B   Likenesses and Differences
  1   Sounds
  2   Shapes
  3   Letters
  4   Words
I-C   Configuration Clues
I-D   Positional Words
I-E   Alphabet
  1   Upper case
  2   Lower case
I-F- Consonants
  1   Beginning
  2   Ending
  3   Medial
  4   Blends: 2, l, r, 3-letter.
  5   Digraphs
  6   hard/soft c
  6   hard/soft g
  6   voiced/unvoiced s
  7   Silent consonants
I-G- Vowels
  1   Short sound
  2   Long sound
  3   Short vowel: CVC
  3   Silent e: CVC(E)
  3   Two vowels together: CVVC
  3   Final long vowel: CV
  4   y as vowel
  4   w as vowel
  5   Diphthongs
  5   Schwa
  6   Vowel + r
  6   a + l, ll, w, u
  6   oo sounds
  6   ow sounds
  6   ea sounds
  6   ie sounds
  6   ei sounds
I-H- Structural Analysis
  1   Word families
  2   Plurals
  3   Unchanged roots and endings
  3   Changed roots and endings
  4   Possessives
  5   Compound words
  6   Contractions
  7   Prefixes
  8   Suffixes
  9   Syllabication
  10 (Accent -- refer to IV-B-1)

II. VOCABULARY DEVELOPMENT

II-A   Basal Sight Vocabulary
II-B   Dolch Sight Words (220)
II-C- Rhyming Elements
  1   Rhyming words
  2   Rhyming phrases
II-D- Word Meaning
  1   Synonyms (big--large)
  2   Antonyms (big--small)
  3   Homonyms (rode--road)
  4   Homographs(multiple meanings)
  5   Heteronyms (bass--bass)
  6   Usage
  7   Colloquial speech

III. COMPREHENSION

III-A   Listening Skills
III-B   Experience Charts
III-C   Classifying
III-D   Picture Clues
III-E- Following Directions
  1   Oral
  2   Written
III-F   Using the Context
III-G   Getting the Main Idea
III-H   Getting the Facts
III-I   Locating the Answer
III-J   Detecting the Sequence
III-K   Drawing Conclusions
III-L   Summarizing
III-M- Interp. and Creative Reading
  1   Fact or fiction
  2   Form of story
  3   Mood
  4   Author's intent
  5   Character analysis
  6   Creative activities
III-N- Critical Reading
  1   Fact vs. opinion
  2   Valid sources
  3   Comparison of viewpoints
  4   Propaganda
III-O   Punctuation (as guide to meaning)

IV. STUDY SKILLS

IV-A- Organizational Skills
  1   Alphabetizing
  2   Table of contents
  3   Index
  4   Note-taking
  5   Outlining
  6   Bibliography and footnotes
  7   Organizing and reporting information
  8   Skimming
  9   Reading rate
IV-B- Reference Skills
  1   Dictionary and glossaries
  2   Encyclopedia
  3   Atlas
  4   Reader's Guide
  5   Thesaurus
  6   Almanac
  7   Periodicals
  8   Newspaper
  9   Telephone directory
  10 Library skills
IV-C- Informational Skills
  1   Pictures for information
  2   Graphs, charts
  3   Tables
  4   Maps, globes
  5   Diagrams
  6   Time lines

KEY:

-			
+			

Not applicable at this time

Skill need

Skill mastery

Grade level emphasis

FIGURE 6-3.   Sample Record Showing Reading Levels.

158

6-4 shows a form that could be used for this purpose. This form is the back of the reading-skills profile card shown in Figure 6-3. By having this information available the teacher will be able to guard against the possibility of a child being placed in material that he/she has already read. An effective diagnostic reading teacher should always refer to available records to see what instructional materials have been used in previous instruction before deciding what to use in the current program.

In some schools other instructional materials used are recorded on this form. These would include supplementary materials used in the classroom as well as materials that might be used in a special reading program. The more complete the record of materials used, the easier it is for teachers to make decisions about what should be used in the future.

Comments From Teachers

A final component of an effective record-keeping system is a place for teacher comments. The record form presented in Figure 6-4 provides space for this purpose.

Comments made by the teacher will help clarify items in the record and help explain why certain decisions have been made. All comments should be specifically related to reading and should be professional in tone and style. Comments like the following are of little value to the next teacher and are considered unprofessional:

"It was a pleasure to have Susan in class."

"George was a lazy student."

"Mark never shut his mouth."

Professionally written comments of the following type will be much more useful to future teachers:

"Sara did not master auditory discrimination on the tests given but she could do the work in class with 100% accuracy; therefore I marked this skill as mastered."

"Jim enjoys reading most when he works in a group of 6 or 7 students; large groups make him shy."

"Larry's problem in completing his work in class is best handled by giving him only two things to do at a time; more than two at one time seems to overload him."

Teachers should give serious consideration to all comments that they put on any student records. Comments on reading records should be *only those* that

Major Reading Materials Used
(e.g.: Macmillan, Lippincott, Scholastic Individualized
Reading Kit, etc.)

K (Reading Readiness) _____

Gr. 1 _____

Gr. 2 _____

Gr. 3 _____

Gr. 4 _____

Gr. 5 _____

Gr. 6 _____

Motivational Interests

K _____

Gr. 1 _____

Gr. 2 _____

Gr. 3 _____

Gr. 4 _____

Gr. 5 _____

Gr. 6 _____

- -

Please complete the lower portion of this card as it applies to certain students.

TEACHER COMMENTS:

Special Needs
Related to Reading
(Check those which apply)

	Speech	Vision	Motor Coord.	Emotional	Remedial Rdg.
K					
Gr. 1					
Gr. 2					
Gr. 3					
Gr. 4					
Gr. 5					
Gr. 6					

FIGURE 6-4. Sample Reading Record Form Showing Materials Used.

160

will assist future teachers in making decisions about the student's reading program.

USING RECORDS THAT ACCOMPANY BASAL SERIES

Nearly all basal readers currently on the market have some type of record-keeping system that accompanies their materials. Some of the samples presented earlier in this chapter were taken from these sources. If one is in a school that has such a record, it should be used. There is nothing wrong with using a record of progress that goes along with a basal series. The records are designed to correlate with the readers, workbooks, and tests. This should help to make the teacher's job more efficient and easier to accomplish.

It is important that the same record of progress be used throughout the school. This helps to insure continuity in the reading program and prevents each teacher from having to come up with his/her own form.

Keeping Records Up-to-Date

A major concern of many teachers about record keeping is that it is very time-consuming. This is often true for teachers who let records pile up and do not complete them until the end of the term or year. Then the task is overwhelming.

One of the major reasons for having a record of a student's reading progress is to help the teacher make decisions about the reading program. If the records are not kept up to date, it is impossible for the teacher to use them in making decisions. Obviously, the teacher who lets the items that should be recorded pile up until the end of the year is not using the information available in them to make decisions. A physician cannot postpone recording all the details about a patient's health until the end of the year or even until the next time the patient is in the office. He/she records them immediately. A good diagnostician studies the patterns of a patient's records to make decisions about his/her health in the future. An effective classroom reading teacher must do the same thing in teaching reading. Therefore, records should be kept current. If records are kept up to date the amount of time to complete them will be minimal.

OTHER TYPES OF RECORD-KEEPING SYSTEMS

The information provided in previous sections of this chapter should help the teacher organize a basic record-keeping system and procedure. It is recommended that one system be used by all teachers in a building.

Class List	Book Report Nov. 10–15	Used Listening Center	Read book orally to class	Completed research project	
Anderson, Betty					
Allanson, Ollie					
Beach, Mildred					
Couch, Ted					

FIGURE 6-5. Duplicated Master Sheet.

Some teachers want and need to keep more records than others. Therefore, this section presents a variety of ideas for record keeping that could be used by the classroom reading teacher for different purposes. All the forms presented, of course, will not be appropriate for all teaching styles and situations. Some of them might be useful at a future time.

Duplicated Master Sheets

A sheet listing the names of all students on the left-hand side with many blank columns going across the page is a useful, all-purpose record form that can always be used by the diagnostic teacher. Figure 6-5 shows an example of such a form with a few of the columns completed. As new areas arise and need to be checked by the teacher, columns can be filled in. One can have an extra supply of these duplicated and can store them for ready use. The form can then

Name Lois Quinn	Rdg. Level 4	
Name of Book	Date Completed	Student Comments
The Boxcar Children	10/81	
Little House in the Big Woods	10/81	Very exciting
Horses are Fun	11/81	learned lots about caring for horses
Cats at Home	12/81	

FIGURE 6-6. Library Books Read.

```
┌─────────────────────────────────────────────────────────────────┐
│                                                                   │
│   I, _____   _____   promise to     │
│                                                                   │
│   read _____ books during the month of _____.       │
│                                                                   │
│   I will prepare a report about the book or have a conference with my teacher. │
│                                                                   │
│                                                                   │
│   Signed                                                          │
│                                                                   │
│                                                                   │
│                                                                   │
│   _____   _____   _____  │
│        Student                  Teacher          Parent (optional)│
│                                                                   │
│   Date _____                                          │
│                                                                   │
└─────────────────────────────────────────────────────────────────┘
```

FIGURE 6-7. Independent Reading Contract.

be used for checking specific skill areas, recording learning centers completed, or many other items.

Independent Reading Forms

Included in this section are two examples of record-keeping forms that can be used to keep track of a student's independent reading activities. Books that are read independently by the student may need to be recorded on a form for easy referral. Students can record their own books read. Figure 6-6 is an example of a form that could contain completed library books organized to include also comments by the student.

Another way to keep track of the independent reading students are doing is through the individual reading contract as in Figure 6-7. This form can be completed by students, signed by all those involved in the contract agreement, and kept filed by the teacher (1, 4). This is a very useful form for record keeping and can also motivate children to do more independent reading.

SUMMARY

Record keeping can be defined as the system selected by the teacher to organize the information gathered on a student's reading abilities. By implementing an effective record-keeping system, the teacher can keep individual skill-development data organized so that it can serve as an important resource in planning instruction. Teachers in turn become more accountable for their teaching. A record-keeping system also provides an important source of information for teachers when reporting to parents. The same record-keeping system should be used consistently from grade to grade throughout a school.

The components of an effective record-keeping system include (1) a listing of reading skills, (2) a place to record the student's reading levels, (3) a listing of the major instructional materials used, and (4) a place for teacher comments.

THOUGHT AND DISCUSSION QUESTIONS

1. How does a record-keeping system relate to classroom organization?
2. How does a record-keeping system help the teacher in diagnostic teaching?
3. What are the advantages of a record-keeping system in an elementary classroom?
4. Why should all teachers in a school use the same record-keeping system?
5. How can a teacher evaluate her/his record-keeping system for its efficiency?

APPLYING WHAT YOU HAVE LEARNED

1. Examine the record-keeping systems of several teachers. Evaluate them in terms of the criteria presented in this chapter.
2. Interview several teachers to obtain their feelings about what information should be kept in a classroom record system.
3. Examine the record-keeping systems of several basal series and compare them.

BIBLIOGRAPHY

1. Burns, Paul C., and Roe, Betty D. *Teaching Reading in Today's Elementary Schools.* Chicago: Rand McNally College Publishing Company, 1976.
2. Duffy, Gerald G.; Sherman, George B.; and Roehler, Laura R. *How to Teach Reading Systematically.* New York: Harper & Row, Publishers, 1977.
3. Farr, Roger; Tuinman, Jaap; and Rowls, Michael. *Reading Achievement in the United States: Then and Now.* Bloomington, Ind.: Indiana University, 1974.
4. Hall, Mary Anne; Ribovich, Jerilyn K.; and Ramig, Christopher J. *Reading and the Elementary School Child.* New York: D. Van Nostrand Company, 1979.
5. Spache, George D., and Spache, Evelyn B. *Reading in the Elementary School,* 4th ed. Boston: Allyn & Bacon, Inc., 1977.
6. Tinker, Miles A., and McCullough, Constance M. *Teaching Elementary Reading,* 4th ed. Englewood Cliffs, N. J.: Prentice-Hall, Inc., 1975.

FOR FURTHER READING

Burns, Paul C., and Roe, Betty D. *Teaching Reading in Today's Elementary Schools*, 2nd ed. Chicago: Rand McNally College Publishing Company, 1980.

Duffy, Gerald G., and Sherman George B. *Systematic Reading Instruction*, 2nd ed. New York: Harper & Row, Publishers, 1977.

Guszak, Frank J. *Diagnostic Reading Instruction in the Elementary School*, 2nd ed. New York: Harper & Row, Publishers, 1978.

Heilman, Arthur W.; Blair, Timothy R.; and Rupley, William H. *Principles and Practices of Teaching Reading*, 5th ed. Columbus, Ohio: Charles E. Merrill Publishing Company, 1981.

Hoover, Sharon, "All the Records You'll Ever Need to Keep." *Instructor*, (Aug. 1979), 86–91.

Spache, George D., and Spache, Evelyn B. *Reading in the Elementary School*, 4th ed. Boston: Allyn & Bacon, Inc., 1977.

Tinker, Miles A., and McCullough, Constance M. *Teaching Elementary Reading*, 4th ed. Englewood Cliffs, N. J.: Prentice-Hall, Inc., 1975.

Wallen, Carl J. *Competency in Teaching Reading*, 2nd ed. Chicago: Science Research Associates, Inc., 1981.

chapter 7

organizing materials and resources

objectives

Upon completion of this chapter one will be able to

1. Understand the importance of organizing materials and resources.
2. Understand how teacher performance is related to organizing materials.
3. Know and understand the concept of a resource file.
4. Utilize a variety of procedures for organizing materials and resources.

overview

The importance of organizing materials and resources for the reading program will be presented in this chapter. Also stressed will be the relationship between material organization and improved teacher performance. Guidelines and suggestions will be given for organizing materials on both the classroom and building levels, and practical tips will be offered and illustrated. The material in this chapter will be related to Steps 3, 4, and 5 of the diagnostic teaching model:

Step 3. Evaluate alternatives.
Step 4. Teach.
Step 5. Evaluate results.

Effective organization will help one carry out these steps in a classroom.

The proper organization of materials significantly improves teacher performance in the classroom. By organizing materials a teacher can

1. Know what is available for instructional purposes.
2. Become more efficient in all aspects of teaching.
3. Help eliminate unnecessary waste of material.
4. Improve student efficiency.

THE IMPORTANCE OF ORGANIZING MATERIALS FOR THE DIAGNOSTIC READING PROGRAM

An elementary teacher who is employing diagnostic/prescriptive teaching will have a reservoir of teaching materials in the classroom. These materials will include basal reading texts, extra workbooks, tape players, worksheets, learning centers, reference books, library materials, games, filmstrips, bulletin board ideas, and other items. The list is really endless, for a classroom reading teacher continues to collect and create new and different teaching materials all the time. Smith and Robinson state that "each classroom should house material to be read, listened to, and viewed" (4, p. 368). These materials must relate to both the teaching strategies employed by the teacher and the instructional needs of the learners.

As the teacher goes through the process of diagnosing the students to determine reading levels and skill strengths and weaknesses, he/she will begin to think about the instructional materials that one has and how they can be used with specific children or groups of children. Some of this material can be used when teaching skills and other material will be more appropriate for practicing and reinforcing skills. All these materials can be used to some extent in developing lesson plans and carrying them out.

By having instructional materials stored and organized effectively in the individual classroom or in an appropriate place in the elementary building, a teacher has the opportunity to continually peruse them to select the ones that best fit the needs of all students. Appropriate materials must be available for the child who may have no reading ability as well as for the advanced reader. Other resources will be needed for those students who are reading at grade level. In other words, teachers must gather the appropriate material and resources to meet the needs of all learners. One can attempt to meet these needs only if one has the kind of instructional material and resources that would provide the basis for profitable learning activities.

By organizing materials and supplies according to some systematic plan, the teacher can become more efficient in getting to the materials and preparing for teaching. If the available materials are stored in specific places or organized for easy accessibility they will be more readily located when they are needed. If a teacher has to spend an extensive amount of time looking for something, that

"something" will probably never be used. Misplacing a necessity in the classroom is not a rare occurrence. It happens to everyone at times. If materials are constructively organized, however, they will be located more easily and therefore used more frequently. Teachers have little time in their daily schedules for useless searching!

Instructional materials can also refer to such items as scissors, construction paper, answer keys to skills tests, and so on. If such materials and supplies are left anywhere around the room or carelessly stacked in a corner or hallway, they will become temptations to more wasteful persons. By properly organizing materials the teacher will help eliminate unnecessary waste. The child who sees carelessly stacked construction paper or the answer keys to skills tests thrown on a shelf will possibly be inclined to "snatch" any of those items when they are not really needed for the learning task at hand. By keeping materials organized and by having only the *necessary* materials available for students, the temptations for being wasteful will be greatly reduced and the students will pay more attention to the task at hand.

Organized materials and resources also improve student efficiency. If students can be sure that certain materials will be located in the same area consistently they will spend less time searching for them. The activities requiring special materials that one has designed to be completed independently by students will be much more effective if students can easily locate everything they need. There is nothing more distracting for students as well as for teachers than to

By Properly Organizing Materials Teachers Can Create a Better Atmosphere for Effective Teaching.

have to stop in the middle of an activity to locate a ruler, tape, writing paper, or other necessity that is crucial at the moment. Students will be more encouraged to embark on activities again if they meet success with them the first time. By properly organizing materials, a teacher is making that success more possible to attain.

Organizing Materials for Reading Instruction

Materials for reading instruction must be well organized in order to make them useful for the teacher and/or students. For this reason a two-level system of organization—a classroom-level organization and a building-level organization—is suggested.

Classroom-level organization is the keeping together in some systematic way the material *most* frequently used for reading instruction. Teachers rely on a variety of materials on a day-to-day basis. Such materials as basal reading texts, accompanying workbooks, writing paper, instructional bulletin-board supplies, and so on would fit into this category of materials.

Even though certain materials will be needed in the classroom on a day-to-day basis, others should be organized and stored at the building level. There are some materials that can be used by *many* teachers in the same building for their reading instruction. A teacher teaching initial consonant blends, for example, might need such materials as a pre-test and post-test related to that skill, an outline of the teaching steps related to the skill, several examples of worksheets that could be used for teaching and practicing purposes, and learning centers employing the use of the blends. More than likely, several teachers in the same building will also be teaching this skill at one time or another, so they too will need this material. By keeping it organized at a central place in the building, all teachers can use the material when they need it.

Building-level organization allows teachers to share their materials and ideas with other teachers. If certain materials are placed in a central area, the duplication of the same materials for each teacher is greatly reduced, thus saving funds for the instructional program. Building-level organization also allows an opportunity for teachers to have access to and implement a wider variety of materials than is available on the classroom level.

ORGANIZING MATERIALS AND RESOURCES WITHIN THE CLASSROOM

In order to begin the process of organizing materials in the classroom, the teacher must complete two basic steps: inventory current materials and organize the materials according to use. Teachers should inventory materials currently in their rooms. Textbooks—current editions as well as older ones—should

Name of Text	Author/Publisher	Level	Number of Copies		Condition
			Text	Workbook	
Raintrees	Scott-Foresman	2^1	9	10	fair
Eagles	Harper & Row	3^2	12	12	new
Moonglows	Macmillan	4^1	8	11	new
Hot Dogs	Doubleday	6^1	2	3	poor
Weathervanes	Ginn	1	3	5	fair

FIGURE 7-1. Textbook Inventory List—Classroom.

be sorted and classified according to use. The inventory listing should be complete. Inventories should contain the title of the material and how many or how much of the material is in the classroom. Figure 7-1 shows a sample inventory form that can be used to keep textbooks listed.

Supplementary materials such as instructional games might reinforce reading skills that have been taught. These games appear in different sizes of containers, from envelopes to boxes, and it is difficult to store them all in one place when not in use. Therefore, they should be stored according to size or durability, or both. Figure 7-2 shows an organizational inventory list that can assist a teacher in the efficient location of such games. The accuracy of this listing depends upon the careful return of the games to their proper places.

Audio-visual aids are quite expensive and can be seriously damaged by improper treatment. Audio-visual devices such as tape players, cassettes, filmstrip projectors, filmstrip viewers, record players, audio flashcard readers, and spellbinders can be easily used by students of all ages if they are given necessary handling instructions. These devices can be used in learning-center activities as well as in large-group activities. When not in use, audio-visual devices should be

Name of Game	Location of Storage
Consonant Lotto	Word Recognition Drawer
Scrabble	Top shelf of closet
Sight word bingo	Top shelf of closet
Comprehension Cosmo	Comprehension Box—file folder
Initial Consonant Cut-up	Word Recognition Drawer—file folder

FIGURE 7-2. Classroom Game Inventory.

Name of Equipment	Inventory Number	How Many
Movie Projector	AB 6072	1
Filmstrip Projector	IC 423	1
Filmstrip Viewer	IF 23, IF 24, IF 25	3
Phonograph	PH 102	1
Listening Center (Earphones)	AC 1298	1
Overhead Projector	IC 487	1

FIGURE 7-3. Audio-Visual Inventory.

stored safely under a cover or in their carrying containers to protect them from accidental harm or dust and dirt. Figure 7-3 illustrates a suggested inventory for audio-visual equipment. Recording the numbers from the machines will make it easier to locate them if they are removed from the room for any reason.

Once the inventory listings of the material in one's classroom have been completed, the material should be organized. Some textbooks, such as basal readers, are used almost every day and should be located within easy reach of the students. The textbooks that are used only for special research projects could be stored in a less convenient spot and then relocated for the students' use when needed.

Teachers also use extra textbooks as supplementary teaching materials. Whatever use they provide, these books need to be organized either by reading-level or by subject-matter classification.

Some teachers keep this material on shelves in the order the material is listed on their inventory lists. This makes the variety of books easier to locate. The books listed first on the list would be first on the shelf and the others would follow accordingly. Another method of organizing material on shelves is to classify it by reading level. All the books at the third reading level, for instance, would be grouped together with a label of "3rd level" written below the books on the shelf.

Whatever method the teacher decides to use must be adhered to to allow for easy and systematic location of the material. As more materials are added to the collection and others are deleted, the inventory list must be altered and updated to keep this information as accurate as possible.

There are many tradebooks that can be very useful and enhancing to a reading program. They can be organized into classroom libraries and arranged on shelves so that students can use the material easily. Books within a classroom collection can be arranged by reading level or by topic. Any books that students can select and read independently can be considered trade books and should be made available for them. High-interest/easy-vocabulary books can be added to a classroom library for less able readers.

Magazines, brochures, and pamphlets should also be organized in a class-

room. This type of material is valuable not only for the subject matter contained in them but also for "cutting-up" use in other projects. Teachers can designate the materials available for "cutting up" and locate them in a box or a drawer that is conveniently available to the students. Other material, especially brochures or pamphlets that can be used in reading instruction or activities within the content areas, should be filed according to subject. Information about the history of a state—wild flowers, trees, birds, and famous people—or about health-related subjects such as care of the eyes, the digestive system, and so on is often in a pamphlet or brochure. If this material is filed by subject in a drawer, then in leafing through them one can see at a glance the topics available for instructional use.

Professional magazines such as *Instructor*, *Learning*, or *Language Arts* are also useful for teachers. The magazines themselves are usually not stored in a classroom, but many teachers find it helpful to remove particularly worthwhile ideas from them to be filed. For instance, a creative-writing idea might prove interesting to a teacher, so it could be cut out and filed in a folder labeled "creative writing." When the teacher desires a new and/or creative activity related to creative writing, the file folder can serve as a reference.

DETERMINING WHERE MATERIALS CAN BE LOCATED

A room organized so that most people using the facility can locate materials will increase operational efficiency. Students who know where things are can be much more independent in performing their daily activities. Younger students might have to learn the names of some items—such as cassette tape player, reading games, or scissors—and how to recognize their names before they can learn where they are located in the classroom. Continual development of sight words with a concrete example of an item labeled and stored on a shelf is a very worthwhile reading activity for any developing reader.

In determining where materials should be located teachers can use their inventory lists (refer to Figures 7-1, 7-2, and 7-3) to decide which materials need to be used more frequently than others. Such material should be placed on nearby shelves in the classroom, in the most accessible file drawers, or somewhere else within the students' reach. Material that will be used less often should be placed in less accessible places such as covered boxes in a corner, higher shelves less easy to reach, or a storage area outside the classroom. As the year progresses this material should probably be relocated as the instructional and students' needs change (2). Some less accessible items that were not previously used could be exchanged with material at hand that is no longer used frequently.

The material that has been selected for immediate classroom use should be organized according to topic, interest, use, size, durability, or any other sensible way a teacher sees fit. The furniture in the classroom—tables, cabinets, open shelving, windowsills, doored shelving—should be evaluated for the size and

Labels Help Keep Materials Organized and Teach New Vocabulary.

quantity of material it can hold. Once this is done, the teacher can begin placing the instructional material and resources in the most logical location.

Games and other resource activities are also teaching devices and the teacher should organize them for their optimal use. Some games can be filed in boxes neatly labeled according to the skill they reinforce and then stacked on shelving. Made-up games can be noted or drawn right on file folders which can be labeled by skills (initial consonants, medial vowels, or whatever) and simply filed in a drawer or box. Some teachers like to label and file their games and folders according to the level and basal series that is used.

Labels can also direct students to specific places in the room where art supplies, reading games, audio-visual machines, and so on are stored. These labels can help students remain organized if they contain the words that the students recognize and find useful for their purposes.

Organizing Basals and Basal Materials

Basal materials must be organized in such a way as to make them as useful as possible. Shelving these basals together by levels seems to be the most help-

ful method. By placing the levels together, a teacher can always locate them quickly for instructional purposes. When basals are left in student desks, they are often misplaced or taken home and left there by mistake. If students know where the books are kept and also know that the teacher expects them to be there, then such problems can be eliminated.

Unused reading workbooks can be kept with the shelved basals also. These workbooks are then available for new students who are entering one's reading groups. Workbooks that the students are currently using should be left *with* the student. Providing a language-arts folder with pockets will give the students a place to keep their workbooks as well as other related language-arts material. By encouraging the students to replace the workbook in the folder pocket, the teacher can help train them to be organized in their own procedures.

There are many other instructional materials that a teacher uses frequently, including such items as supplemental reading textbooks, English/language texts, and spelling materials. These supplies should be shelved according to levels for easy accessibility. Often teachers obtain English/language texts that are the same grade level as the students' reading levels, providing as many levels of language texts as one has of basal readers. Like the basal readers, these books should be stored in a sequential order and recorded on an inventory sheet similar to the ones shown previously.

Instructional spelling materials also should be kept in some organized system. If spelling books are used, they can be shelved by level. Some teachers use spelling books that are equivalent to the child's reading level (correlating with the language-arts block concept to be presented later). In this case several levels of spellers must be shelved in the classroom. Sometimes the spelling books are paperbacks that resemble reading workbooks and can also fit into a pocket of the language-arts folder, thus giving the student more materials at his/her fingertips rather than on a shelf or desk across the room.

Basal-reading companies also provide practice sheets to reinforce reading skills as well as testing materials that accompany each basal. These testing materials can be pre- and post-tests for individual skills or they can be unit and/or whole-book tests. These materials usually arrive from the companies prepacked in small boxes. The material inside the boxes is packaged in the order of its presentation in the basal itself. Some teachers use the material (often reproduced sheets) right out of the box and in the order they occur. Teachers who teach from a predetermined skills sequence or school checklist remove these sheets from the boxes and file them in a file drawer or box according to skill. Sometimes this material is organized at the building level for all teachers to use. The files might look something like the illustration in Figure 7-4.

The files could be color coded according to skill or by basals. By having the practice sheets individually filed the teacher can locate them with little difficulty and then return them immediately. Sometimes the practice sheets and tests are reproduced for the entire basal set and then filed for immediate use as the skills are presented, taught, and mastered.

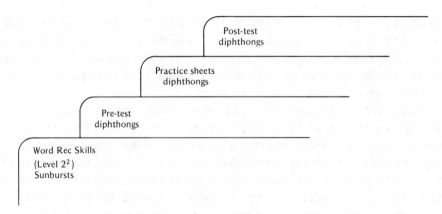

Post-test
diphthongs

Practice sheets
diphthongs

Pre-test
diphthongs

Word Rec Skills
(Level 2^2)
Sunbursts

FIGURE 7-4. Sample File Headings.

THE RESOURCE-FILE CONCEPT

A resource file is a central place where instructional materials can be stored. This file can contain individual skill exercises, activities related to specific basal stories read by the students, or a variety of professional ideas used to enhance the teaching of reading.

Teachers cannot teach effectively by merely using the basal suggestions and activities provided in the teacher's guide. Although the skill practices and assorted activities in a basal are usually of high quality, a teacher must still supplement instruction. As a teacher attends professional meetings, peruses professional magazines, and shares ideas with other teachers, he/she begins to collect a wide assortment of material and ideas—articles are clipped out, handouts from meetings are gathered, sample student work is accumulated, specific worksheets used, and so on. The filing of these is the beginning of a resource file.

Types of Resource Files

There are two types of resource files that teachers should have access to in their teaching. One type is the classroom-level resource file and the other type is the building-level resource center. It is called a center because it is usually larger than just one file.

Selecting the appropriate activities or materials is important in making one's classroom resource file as helpful as possible. This file should contain only the material that will complement and enhance the instructional reading program in the classroom. Teachers should continually refer to it as a source for developing their instructional plans. Some teachers file activities according to skills such as initial consonants, medial vowels, or literal comprehension. By doing this they can easily locate activities to accompany basal stories. Also in-

cluded in this file can be English/language arts sheets related to nouns, verbs, noun markers, and so forth. Anything placed in the classroom resource file must be organized and labeled so that it can be immediately located.

A building resource center extends, expands, or adds to the classroom resource file. The resource center is ultimately a collection of instructional, practice, and application activities correlated with all reading levels represented in the building (2).

The school principal is the key to the success of a building resource center. As the instructional leader, the principal is responsible for seeing to it that this center is organized properly and beneficially implemented for all concerned. The principal must help teachers realize the importance of the resource center and encourage its use.

There are many reasons for the creation of a building resource center. One reason is that it offers a teacher access to a full range of instructional materials. Even though teachers attempt to broaden and expand their own classroom resource file, they cannot possibly include a complete assortment of activities from prereading levels to the more advanced reading levels. A teacher may have difficulty locating skill lessons at the proper reading level for every child. The wide variety of material available in the resource center enables the teacher to use the most appropriate material, thus adding considerable quality to their reading instruction.

Another reason for the creation of a resource center is that it saves time and thus improves teacher effectiveness. A teacher will find it much easier and faster to use the resource-center activities for teaching, practicing, or application than having to originate his/her own instructional materials. Teacher effectiveness can continue to be improved with each new development or addition to the resource center.

A third reason for a resource center is to make more efficient use of materials. Rather than every teacher having the same game/activity that is used perhaps only four weeks out of a year, a few of these games can be available for all in the resource center. And instead of every teacher in the building spending time and the school's money in constructing learning centers that practice all the skills of reading, a few of the skill-related learning centers can be on file in the resource center. By using the resource-center concept effectively, a much wider assortment of materials can be provided and implemented.

Steps in Developing a Building Resource Center

Identifying Persons Responsible. The success of the building resource center depends on it being implemented or supported by key individuals from the educational staff. These people must be identified so that organization can begin. They are needed to make major decisions involving the center as well as to keep communications open with other faculty members. The quality of the resource center depends on the input of these key persons.

Some buildings have designated curriculum committees composed of a teacher from each grade level. For smaller schools, it might be more appropriate to designate teachers from the primary and intermediate levels rather than from each grade level. It is hoped that these teachers will volunteer for these positions since the organization of a resource center is so crucial to the effective operations of an elementary reading program. In addition, for these teachers to be truly motivated and work toward completing a goal, the building principal must be directly involved in the development of the center.

Locating Appropriate Space. Finding available space is often a problem. A typical school building is nearly filled to the limit without the additional materials collected by teachers. But with proper organization and condensation of the existing instructional materials, a surprising amount of room can be found in most buildings. Resource centers have been set up in empty classrooms, in closets off the main office, in old teacher's lounges that are centrally located, in out-of-the-way areas in hallways, or even in a portion of a media center. The location of the resource center should be determined by the building staff to be the most practical, useful, and accessible.

Taking a Materials Inventory in the Classroom. One of the most important things to do is to take a thorough inventory of material that is presently in each classroom (refer to earlier discussion of inventory listings). Individual inventory lists as discussed earlier can be made and then a large composite list can be developed from the classroom lists. On these inventory lists should be recorded *all* instructional material that is stored in each classroom. This making of such a list may be time-consuming for teachers, but it will be worthwhile if it contributes to the effective organization of the building resource center. Even materials that have been "collecting dust" for years in a classroom should be recorded on the inventory list because they might prove very helpful to another teacher.

Identifying Additional Materials That Will Be Needed. As the steering committee or curriculum committee evaluates the inventory lists, it might find gaps or inadequacies in some present material. The committee also may find some areas of instruction that have no corresponding material at all. In any case, it must be decided what additional published material should be purchased for the resource center to be as complete as possible. Sometimes the desired material creates such a long list that not all of it can be purchased immediately because of budget limitations. If this should happen, a priority listing is suggested. The purchases can then be worked into the school budget over several years.

Teacher-developed materials should also be added to make the center complete. Often teacher-developed materials are in the form of learning centers that can be used to practice and apply reading skills. A gap in this area can be

determined by comparing the already existing teacher-made materials to the reading-skills checklist. If there are skills that have no matching activities, then it indicates that new material should be developed.

Encouraging All Teachers to Participate in the Development of the Center. If teachers want to use a resource center, they all should play an active part in the actual development of the center. Teachers should be willing to continue to contribute materials to the center. Some schools use a contribution-box system to encourage teacher participation. This box can be placed next to the ditto or mimeograph machine and each teacher is encouraged to run one extra copy of every activity they make copies of and place it in the box. This enables the collection to include a wide variety of materials at many different levels. As teachers contribute to the box they can attach a description of the skill being developed and the appropriate grade level intended for each activity included.

Teachers also must be encouraged to develop new games and learning-center activities for the resource center. By assigning several games to each teacher to construct, the central committee can expand the amount of materials quite quickly. One school-building committee asked teachers to make two specific games (correlated with an identified skill) during the summer months while school was not in session. Then in the fall the teachers explained their games, shared their ideas, and merged the activities into the resource center. These teachers were proud of their creations and eager to have other people use them.

Developing a Plan for Organizing the Materials. Each set of materials within the file must be labeled according to the skill to which it is related. Sometimes the skills are labeled by codes such as A-1, A-2, and so on, with A representing readiness level, B representing first reading level, and so on. Some skills are labeled by name and level, such as color words (readiness), or main idea (3^1). Whatever labeling system is used, the same system should be implemented in the skill files as well as the learning-center file area. With corresponding coding, the file folder containing the instructional activities and practice sheets can be matched with the game or learning center that reinforces the skill. This allows the teacher to obtain both sets of material for use in the classroom.

Most of the material filed within a resource center can be stored in filing cabinets with each drawer containing certain skills or certain levels. The faculty must decide which filing system would be most appropriate. Learning centers and games can be stored in slotted mini-shelved cabinets so the title of the game or at least the skill and level can be easily seen. Another convenient storage system for games is to use large folders or envelopes the size of 20-by-24 pieces of tag board. These folders can be labeled by skill or level and make it possible for the games to be slipped in and out with relative ease. The filing system and organization of the resource center decided upon will depend largely

Organizing and Filing Learning Centers Within the Resource Center Will Make Them Readily Available for Classroom Use.

The Principal Is the Key to the Success of the Resource Center.

on the facilities available in the building and the creativity of the center developers.

Developing a System for Classroom Use and Implementation of Center Materials.   If all the teachers are going to use the resource center in their classrooms, then some type of check-out system needs to be implemented. The check-out system should be as simple as possible so that it requires little time to use. A clip board on the top of the filing cabinets seems to be a convenient system. The clip board contains sign-out sheets on which the teachers can record the material they remove, the level of the material, and the current date. With this information a teacher inspecting the check-out forms can quickly locate any material that is not in the file. This check-out system can be effective only with everyone's cooperation.

Periodically, the resource center should be checked for possible file folders being out of sequence, missing file folders, or certain activities missing from within a file folder. Also important here is the continual development of the center and the inclusion of new material. A committee of staff members including the principal should be responsible for the maintaining of the resource center. The committee membership could be on a revolving basis so that all personnel in the school have an opportunity to serve.

One final word about the building resource center is appropriate. This center will never serve its many purposes and be an effective addition to an elementary reading program unless *teachers use the instructional activities contained in the center.* The material will do a child no good if it is left lying on the shelves or filed neatly in the drawers. Teachers should be encouraged to use the material and in some cases need to have the activities demonstrated with a class. If teachers are helped to become more informed and comfortable with the resource-center concept then these centers will enhance and strengthen the diagnostic/prescriptive reading program.

SUMMARY

A diagnostic/prescriptive teacher, with a variety of supplementary teaching materials collected, must strive to organize these materials in the most effective method possible. By organizing these resources and supplies in some systematic plan, the teacher can become more efficient in all aspects of teaching, eliminate unnecessary waste, and improve student efficiency. There are two kinds of organization: a classroom level and a building level. Each contributes to the effective operation of a classroom reading program.

It is profitable for teachers to survey the abundant materials and resources that they presently have in their own classroom. Preparing inventory lists of this material will contribute to the overall organizational plan. Learning games and center activities should be shelved and/or filed for their optimal use.

Some points to remember about effective organization are to make good use of furniture and storage areas, label these areas for easy identification, file or shelve basal material by level or skill, and create a filing system for storing skill-teaching material. A classroom resource file also contributes to a teacher's efficiency and should contain only material that will complement and enhance the instructional reading program in the classroom.

A building resource center allows for all school personnel to share in the instructional materials used in the building. The school principal is the key to the success of a building resource center. The steps in developing a resource center are (1) identifying persons responsible, (2) locating appropriate space, (3) taking a materials inventory in the classroom, (4) identifying additional materials that will be needed, (5) encouraging all teachers to participate in the development of the center, (6) developing a plan for organizing the material, and (7) developing a system for classroom use and implementation of the center materials. The center will never serve its many purposes and be an effective addition to an elementary reading program unless teachers *use* the instructional activities contained in the center. If teachers are helped to become more informed and comfortable with the resource-center concept then the centers will serve to enhance and strengthen the diagnostic/prescriptive reading program.

THOUGHT AND DISCUSSION QUESTIONS

1. How does the idea of organizing instructional materials relate to diagnostic/prescriptive teaching?
2. What does teacher performance have to do with organizing materials?
3. Explain how a classroom resource file can enhance your teaching.
4. What advantages and disadvantages does a building resource center create?
5. How does the principal contribute to the success or failure of the organization of material and resources within a building?
6. How does organization relate to assessment?

APPLYING WHAT YOU HAVE LEARNED

1. Define organization as it relates to your classroom.
2. Visit a classroom teacher's room and describe on paper the organizational techniques you observe.
3. Interview a principal concerning his/her role in encouraging the development of an effective organizational plan for the building.
4. Evaluate, with a self-made checklist, a building resource center in the areas of skill filing, activities provided, check-out system, and classroom implementation.

5.   If there is no committee in your building established for the purpose of creating a building resource center, discuss the formation of it with your fellow teachers and principal.

6.   Evaluate your own classroom organizational abilities. You may want to do such things as inspect current inventory lists, make new inventory lists, check shelving organization of materials, or evaluate your filing system for skill teaching materials.

7.   Write down three concrete suggestions that you could make for improving your classroom organizational strategies.

BIBLIOGRAPHY

1. Aukerman, Robert C., and Aukerman, Louise R. *How Do I Teach Reading?* New York: John Wiley & Sons, Inc., 1981.

2. Cheek, Martha Collins, and Cheek, Earl H., Jr. *Diagnostic Prescriptive Reading Instruction.* Dubuque, Iowa: William C. Brown Company, Publishers, 1980.

3. Otto, Wayne, and Askov, Eunice. *The Wisconsin Design for Reading Skill Development: Rationale and Guidelines.* Minneapolis: National Computer Systems, Inc., 1970.

4. Smith, Nila B., and Robinson, H. Alan. *Reading Instruction for Today's Children*, 2nd ed. Englewood Cliffs, N. J.: Prentice-Hall, Inc., 1980.

FOR FURTHER READING

Good, T. L., and Brophy, J. E. *Looking in Classrooms.* New York: Harper and Row, 1973.

Lapp, Diane. "Individualized Reading Made Easy for Teachers." *Early Years*, **73**, (Feb. 1977), 63–67.

_____. ed. *Making Reading Possible Through Effective Classroom Management.* Newark, Del.: International Reading Association, 1980.

Wheeler, Alan. "A Systematic Design for Individualizing Reading." *Elementary English*, **50**, (Mar. 1973), 445–49.

Wood, R. Kent, and Stephens, Kent G. "An Educator's Guide to Videodisc Technology." *Phi Delta Kappan*, **58**, (Feb. 1977), 466–67.

section IV

management

Effective management is essential to the elementary reading program. The remainder of this text will explain to the teacher how classroom management relates to reading instruction. By reading these chapters, teachers will learn how to

- implement instructional strategies in the classroom.
- develop and implement appropriate lesson plans.
- implement a management plan.
- correlate reading instruction to the content areas.

chapter 8

instructional strategies
for the classroom

objectives

As a result of reading this chapter one will be able to

1. Understand the value of instructional strategies as they relate to reading instruction.
2. Understand and carry out more effective implementation of a basal reading series in a reading program.
3. Further use the basic parts of a Directed Reading/Thinking Activity (DRTA).
4. Identify and implement the basic parts of an instructional skills model.
5. Identify several alternative approaches to the basal reader.
6. Begin to know when and how alternative strategies and approaches to reading instruction should be used.

overview

The diagnostically based reading program must involve careful selection of the appropriate instructional strategies that will enable all students to improve their reading ability. To make this selection the classroom teacher must be able to implement a basic instructional skills model and the Directed Reading/Thinking Activity within the confines of the given school curriculum (often a predetermined basal series). In addition, the teacher must know when and how to use alternative teaching strategies and ap-

proaches that will enhance and strengthen the total reading program. The material in this chapter, a review of much of the material covered in other reading courses, relates to the following steps of the Diagnostic-Prescriptive Teaching Model:

Step 3. Evaluate alternatives and select ones to carry out.
Step 4. Teach.
Step 5. Evaluate results.

Thus far in this text ideas have been presented concerning diagnosis and organization in relation to an elementary reading program. It has been pointed out that diagnostic-prescriptive teaching is essential in dealing with the needs of students. Without the implementation of proper formal and informal diagnostic measures to guide a teacher in making decisions, the instruction could be meaningless and not based on student needs.

Organization is the next logical step following diagnosis. It is during this phase in a reading program that the teacher begins to plan instruction. The process of organizing a class for reading offers structure to a teacher so that he/she knows where to begin. However, selecting the appropriate instructional strategies for teaching reading crosses the boundaries of organization and moves into management. Selecting the appropriate instructional reading strategies helps the teacher manage the program and keep things running smoothly.

INSTRUCTIONAL STRATEGIES DEFINED

Instructional strategies are the overall plan of attack (13). These strategies are the recurring sets of interactions between teacher and student that are intended to achieve objectives and goals of learning. (16). Any one strategy can be used with a variety of reading methods and instructional materials, either published or prepared by the teacher. Instructional strategies are the systematic procedures that a teacher employs to teach and develop the skills and abilities needed to lead each learner to mature reading.

Strategies are used in arranging the learning experiences that will enable students to master those specific objectives that they have not previously mastered (16, p. 16). The teaching/learning activities that are utilized in the overall reading development of a child are called *instructional strategies.* Understanding of the learner, clear and concise objectives, and high-quality teaching situations with well-selected materials and methods are all absolutely necessary for the implementation of instructional strategies (8). The crucial factor is that the teacher be an effective facilitator of learning, empathetic with children, and informed about the nature of the reading process and effective instructional practices to accomplish the desired outcomes regardless of approach (8).

A classroom reading teacher will implement certain instructional strategies according to the philosophy she/he possesses about how a child learns to read. For instance, a teacher who believes that reading and learning to read are derived solely from a student's language will draw heavily from those instructional strategies related to language development and reading rather than a more skills-oriented approach. On the other hand, the teacher who believes that the reading development of a child is a systematic sequencing of skills and activities leading to the total act of reading might select a more eclectic set of instructional strategies like those suggested by many basal readers. Once it is determined which materials the children could read and which they couldn't, a teacher can design the instructional strategies accordingly.

The instructional strategies selected by a teacher should not only follow his/her philosophy but must also coincide with the policy and beliefs about reading instruction maintained by the school system. The important thing to keep in mind is that an effective reading teacher needs a variety of instructional strategies to draw from in order to teach children to read. As we have indicated earlier, the amount of direct, systematic teaching of reading for a student is related to his/her growth in reading. In order for a child to learn to read, he/she must be taught to read. Teaching is the instructional step that allows the teacher to assist the child in developing a specific skill (7). Instructional strategies provide the structure under which a body of skills can be formed.

Selecting Instructional Strategies

An effective classroom reading teacher should not utilize just one instructional strategy but should rely on a combination of different strategies. The selection of the strategies to be used for each individual student will depend heavily on three factors:

1. Reading levels.
2. Skill levels.
3. Interests.

These three factors must be given primary consideration as teachers develop and/or select the specific instructional strategies they will utilize in teaching reading.

First a teacher must consider the reading level of each learner. As already indicated, for a student to successfully learn to read he/she must be provided with materials that can be read at his/her independent or instructional level. Therefore, the teacher should select the level of the basal series or supplementary story material that coincides with each student's instructional reading level. In a few instances one may want to select material that will be on the student's independent level. This would be especially true for students who had been consistently unsuccessful in reading. Dropping to the student's independent level for instructional material could build his/her morale and provide a more successful reading experience. It is essential that each student or group of students be placed in reading materials where they can be successful.

Next the teacher must consider each student's skill needs. Which skills have been mastered? Which ones need to be retaught? Which skills come next in the scope and sequence of what is to be taught? Having examined diagnostic data and/or previous records, one should be able to make this decision, thus determining the *starting point* for skill instruction. In working with each student the teacher will learn new information that may alter decisions about which skills need to be taught or what methods should be used.

Finally, a teacher will want to consider the interests of the individual or group being taught. While it is not always possible to use only those materials which students like or are interested in, the teacher will want to try to account for different interests of students when selecting materials for instructional strategies.

Having considered these three factors—reading levels, skill needs, and interests—of each student or group, the teacher has made the initial, major decisions in developing instructional strategies for reading. Now comes the process of developing the specific teaching strategies to be used.

BASIC READING LESSON PLANNING

The major purpose of a basic reading lesson format is to help teachers systematically organize their reading instruction, include activities from a variety of sources, and provide the best learning experience possible for students. The classroom resource file and the building resource center (Chapter 7) are important sources for activities to be used within the basic reading plan.

A Directed Reading Lesson Outline

A directed reading lesson outline provides structure for the teacher in preparing day-to-day lessons. It helps the teacher balance activities in reading instruction to insure that students are exposed to all areas of skill development. This plan is frequently referred to in reading instruction as the Directed Reading Activity (DRA) or the Directed Reading/Thinking Activity (DRTA) (4, 3, 10, 14). We will refer to it as the DRTA for the remainder of this text.

The DRTA consists of four basic segments:

1. Skill building.
2. Readiness for guided silent reading.
3. Guided silent reading.
4. Follow-up (5).

Each of these enhances and adds to the other part, making all essential components of an effective reading lesson.

Skill Building. The part of the lesson entitled Skill Building presents and develops a specific reading skill. A child should be taught only one new skill at a time. In some instances this will be a comprehension skill or a decoding skill. The skill is taught and practiced with the child. Sometimes an opportunity is given to apply the skill in a real reading situation, or this may be delayed until you get to guided silent reading. The skill presented to the student in this part

is determined from his/her needs as indicated from diagnostic data or from the developmental scope and sequence of the reading program. One has already learned much about the specific teaching strategies to be employed in teaching reading.

Readiness for Guided Silent Reading. The part of the lesson called Readiness for Guided Silent Reading provides the structure for preparing the student or group of students to comprehend and enjoy the guided silent reading that is to follow. Included in readiness is the presentation of new vocabulary that will be used in the reading. The vocabulary should be presented in written context. As new words are taught students should be encouraged to use the decoding skills that have been previously learned to help them analyze new words. The teacher should not just tell the students the words. The vocabulary can be applied in the guided silent reading part of the lesson.

Another component of the readiness phase of the lesson is motivating and background building. The purpose of this section is to get the child interested in reading the selection and to make certain that he/she has the right concepts and background in order to understand the ideas presented. The motivation section may include showing pictures about the subject, discussing the topic, or many other activities. Theorists are saying that what takes place *before* children are asked to read may be the most important step. Teachers need to find out what children already know about a topic, provide a way to bridge the gap between what they know and the material to be read, and teach children the different organizational patterns that authors employ.

Guided Silent Reading. The guided silent reading is the "heart" of the Directed Reading/Thinking Activity. It is in this part where the skills of reading are applied. This is an opportunity for the students to *use* the skills presented in the skill-building phase of the reading lesson. In answering questions about the story, proving answers by orally rereading, or comparing events throughout the story, the child can demonstrate his/her ability to use the new skill in reading.

Guided silent reading procedures will help develop a child's thinking strategies. All levels of comprehension are developed within this portion of the lesson. Purpose-setting questions are asked prior to students' silent reading of the story or section of a story. These direct the children's thinking as they read the selection and help them in learning to set their own purposes for reading. Guided silent reading requires much planning on the part of the teacher to insure its effective use.

Part of the development of comprehension may be having a child read segments of the passage orally to prove an answer, or to encourage children to hypothesize about what might happen next. This technique allows for purposeful oral reading and still further develops students' thinking strategies.

Follow-up.   The fourth phase of the DRTA is the follow-up. This is the section of the lesson where background is extended, more language is developed, ideas from the story are enriched, or the students just do something for fun related to their reading. The purpose of the follow-up phase is to help the child enjoy what has been read and develop the attitude of wanting to read again because it's fun. The follow-up activity should "leave a good taste" with the child so he/she will want to engage in reading more and more as he/she develops reading ability. Further motivation is the key to follow-up and is therefore very important in the development of a Directed Reading/Thinking Activity.

A Directed Reading/Thinking Activity is very appropriate for use with small groups as well as individuals. According to Stauffer (14) a group DRTA has a number of distinguishing features:

1. Pupils are grouped for a DRTA on the basis of reading appraisals that have placed them at about the same level of competency.
2. The group is limited to eight to ten pupils to promote participation and interaction.
3. All pupils in a group read the same material at the same time. This permits each member to compare and contrast her/his predictions, paths to answers, and evaluations with those of her/his peers.
4. Purposes for reading are declared by the *pupils.* The art of asking insightful questions is probably the best mark of a scholar. Each pupil must learn how to raise questions if he/she is to become a reading-thinking scholar.
5. Answers to questions are validated. Proof is found in the text and tested, with the group judging whether or not the proof offered is trustworthy. Immediate feedback helps develop integrity and a regard for authenticity.
6. Teacher direction of a DRTA by means of provocative questions that require the children to interpret and make inferences from what they have read is a must. The teacher serves as a directing catalyst (14, p. 34).

AN INSTRUCTIONAL SKILLS MODEL

Throughout the discussion of the DRTA we referred to Teach-Practice-Apply; these are the basic steps of effective reading skills instruction. For a reading skill to be effectively developed it must be systematically taught, given sufficient practice to help the student master it, and finally applied in a real reading situation. Too often teachers leave out parts of skill instruction, gloss

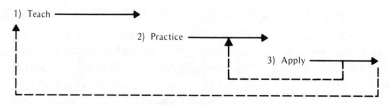

FIGURE 8-1. The Instructional Skills Model.

over them, or simply ignore them. By utilizing the DRTA along with the instructional skills model presented here one will do a more effective job of teaching reading. These parts of the skills model are illustrated in Figure 8-1.

Teach

The Teach step is the portion of the lesson where a new skill is taught. Within this step, the child or entire reading group is instructed by a teacher or teacher substitute such as a tape player, record, etc. The teacher demonstrates, illustrates, shows, or guides the child in using the skill. In this step the teacher is always involved as a facilitator in the learning process. Within the Teach step too, the child is introduced to the skill but has not yet developed or refined the skill to be used independently. This step can involve the teaching of such skills as recognizing initial consonants, determining main idea, or using the card catalog. The skills to be taught will be determined from the scope and sequence of the reading program. All skill instruction must include this Teach step from the instructional model.

Practice

The second step in the instructional skills model is practice. In this step the child is encouraged to use the skill independently, relying less and less on the teacher for assistance. The Practice step draws direct attention to the skill that has just been taught and allows the child to reinforce the skill. The form of practice can be any activity such as a workbook page, skills worksheets, learning center (5), or game.

The one important thing that must be remembered is that the Practice step cannot occur until the reading skill has been taught. Practice gives the child an opportunity to use the skill and begin to feel more comfortable with it. Practice allows the child to gain confidence in his/her reading ability. Sometimes if a child has difficulty using the skill at the practice level, the teacher might find it appropriate to return to the Teach step and *re*teach the skill.

Apply

The Apply step is the final phase of the instructional skills model and is where the child has the opportunity to use the skill in a meaningful situation. The Apply step is most often implemented in the guided silent reading part of the DRTA. A teacher must provide the reading material in this step that is interesting and motivating to the child and still contains the skill under concern.

A child who is ready for the apply step will use the skill automatically without hesitation or delay. A child who has been taught to use the long *a* sound and has completed several practice activities successfully will be able to read long *a* words without much hesitation or faltering. This shows that the skill is being internalized and can be used effectively in the guided silent-reading phase of the DRTA. Another example could relate to the area of study skills. A child who has been taught how to make an outline and given adequate practice experiences will meet few difficulties and apply the skill of outlining when asked to prepare an oral report about a topic in science. This student will, on his/her own, prepare an outline as an aid in making that oral report. In the Apply step, all the skills of reading should be applied in such a way as to encourage as close to real life reading experiences as possible for the child.

Since guided silent reading is the place in which a teacher is most likely to check for application of skills taught, it is important that this step of the DRTA be given much attention. The questions asked by the teacher as he/she guides the students' silent reading will let him/her know whether the skill has been applied.

USING THE INSTRUCTIONAL SKILLS MODEL AND THE DRTA

Within the three steps of the instructional skills model the child moves from a "can't do" in the Teach step through a "can do with assistance" in the Practice step to a "can do independently" in the Apply step. Since each child reacts differently to the learning situation, some may need very little teaching while others may require an extended Teach step with very few practice activities. The importance of individualization within reading group instruction is that the needs of each learner must be taken into consideration (13). The DRTA and the instructional skills model fit together as integral parts of effective reading instruction.

Writing a Lesson Plan

To assist teachers in understanding better how the Directed Reading/ Thinking Activity and the Instructional Skills Model fit together within a lesson plan format several sample plans are included here. These plans (illustrating the

Group _____   Date _____

Inst. Level—Primer   Material: Harper and Row, *Around the Corner*, pp. 93–98

Skill and Objective	Materials and Procedures	Results
I. Skill Building A. Teach The students will recognize the e	1. Say: How do these words *sound* alike? (bell, leg, ten, set, bed) Discuss e sound: do not isolate the sound. Point out that the sound in the middle of all these words is the same. Say: Are these words alike or different when you listen to the middle sound? (get-leg; get-got; wig-let; fed-ten, men-fell)	
Students will associate sound and symbol.	2. Show words from step 1. Ask students to point to e in words which contain that sound. Distribute cards with short e words written on them. Have students circle the e sound with their pencils. Determine where e sound appears in each word. (in middle of word)	
Students will read new words when e is substituted in known words. Students will be able to tell what e sounds like and where it is usually found.	3. Substitute e sound for the middle vowel in: pot, man, pin, bag, full. Students say those "newly created" words. 4. Ask what short e sounds like. Discuss where it is usually found by analyzing short e words used in steps 1 and 2.	
B. Practice Student will be able to do activity which reinforces short e	Feed the puppy activity. Members of the reading group will be given word cards. If they have a card that contains a short e sound they must pronounce it correctly and "feed" it to the puppy. Those students experiencing difficulty with previous activity will do the following: Ladders containing words with e will be presented. Students will try to climb the ladders by saying the words correctly. (They will exchange ladders with a member of their reading group.) Practice could also be an exercise from the reading workbook. Story containing new e words	
C. Apply Students will be able to read a story containing short e sound words. (This could be deferred to Guided Silent Reading).	will be presented. Students will read story to themselves to find out: 1. Who went on a trip? (Ben & Ted) 2. How did the two boys go? (by jet) 3. What color slacks did Ted wear on the trip? (red) Read the sentence that proves your answer.	
II. Readiness (for Guided Silent Reading A. Sight Vocabulary	1. Show words in sentences. Point to new word and ask if student knows word. Example: The *calf* was in the barnyard. The newborn had weak *legs*, etc.	

FIGURE 8-2. Sample DRTA with Emphasis on a Word Recognition Skill.

Skill and Objective	Materials and Procedures	Results
1. Teach Student will recognize and say the following words in context: legs, calf, tail, colt	2. If students do not know words, read the sentence(s) to them. Have one student read the sentence and point to the new word *or* have the word analyzed, using skills the students have already mastered. 3. Discuss meanings of words. Point out importance of context to figuring out unknown words. 4. Select group members to use words in a new sentence. 5. If necessary, present new words in new sentences. Have students read sentences and point to new word.	
2. Practice	Students will be given tic-tac-toe boards with new vocabulary words written in the squares. Students will take turns picking card out of container— reading word and using it correctly in sentence. As word is pronounced the other group members will cover square containing word on tic-tac-toe board.	
3. Apply	Deferred to Guided Silent Reading	
B. Motivation Encourage and develop interest in the new story.	Pictures of colts, lamb, and calf are shown and discussed. Students offer ideas about living on a farm.	

III. Guided Silent Reading
 	
Students will be able to read and answer the question given.
	Purpose Quesion: Ask students to read page 93 to find out what the little lamb did.
	(Have student read page 93 silently, re-ask purpose question)
	
	Ask a student to prove his answer to the purpose setting question by reading a passage from page 93.
	
	What does the word machinery mean?
	    (meaning vocabulary)
	What did the lamb ask the colt?
	   (literal comprehension)
	Why was the colt so unhappy?
	  (inferential comprehension)
	Prove your answer
	
	Do you think this story could really happen? Why or why not?
	    (critical reading/thinking)
	
	Continue the discussion of the selection in this manner.	

IV. Follow-up The students will enjoy talking about the farm animals and then drawing pictures of which animals they would like to be.	Discuss farm animals and allow time for students to create pictures.	

FIGURE 8-2. (*Continued*)

Group _____   Date _____

Inst. Level— 3   Selected portions of *Charlotte's Web*

Skill and Objective	Materials and Procedures	Results
I. Skill Building A. Teach Students will understand concept of antonyms. 1. Concept Level.	1. Say to students: What do you think is special about these pairs of words? (show words on flashcards: hot, cold; up, down; nice, mean; happy, sad) Teacher will discuss with students how the words are opposite. Students will pronounce the pairs of words.	
2. Listening Level.	1. Read the following sentences to the students and ask them to make the sentence have an opposite meaning by changing the key words. a. Pam brushes her teeth *after* she eats. b. The doctor went *up* in the elevator to get to his office. c. A *big* dog scared the cat. d. Mrs. Tarver *started* working at 8:00 this morning. e. The light was *off* in the baby's room. f. Pam's grandmother is *older* than Pam. 2. Read "Company at Fuller's Store" to the students (p. 35, *Along Friendly Roads Study Book*, T 1372–374.) Ask students to decide antonyms for designated words. Teacher will then use the antonyms in the story.	
3. Reading Level.	1. Show sentences on screen using overhead projector. Have students read the sentences and then choose the proper antonym of the underlined word. Teacher and students will discuss why choices are correct. a. *Remember* to get your lunch money before you go to school. (study, forget) b. The road was very *narrow* at the top of the mountain. (wide, weak) c. Pam can really *catch* that ball. (throw, smash) (continue with sentences such as these)	
B. Practice	Students will play Spider-Antonym Game.	

FIGURE 8-3. Sample DRTA with Emphasis on Comprehension.

Skill and Objective	Materials and Procedures	Results
	Students will read a story on the chalkboard and fill in the proper antonyms written on small spiders. If teacher deems necessary, the students can make up stories of their own and exchange them among group members.	
C. Apply (This could be deferred to Guided Silent Reading.)	1. A story containing antonyms will be presented to the students. The students will be asked like the following after reading: a. Who flew near Charlotte's Web? b. Who flew away from the web? c. What did the fly want not to happen? d. What finally did happen? (continue with questions such as these)	
II. Readiness (for Guided Silent Reading A. Vocabulary 1. Teach Student will recognize and say the following words in context: fancy, expression, creature, gamble, scheming, doubts.	1. Show each word in a sentence. Point to new word and ask if students can read the word and the sentence. 2. If not, tell word or have students analyze words using skills already mastered; read the sentence to the student. Have selected students read the new words. 3. Discuss meanings.	
2. Practice	1. Have students make up an oral story using the new vocabulary words. Teacher begins the story and lets each student have a certain amount of time to make up the story parts.	
3. Apply	1. Deferred to Guided Silent Reading.	
B. Motivation	Discuss and show long (hard back) version of *Charlotte's Web*. Show pictures of spiders. Introduce the characters Wilbur and Fern to the students.	
III. Guided Silent Reading Student will be able to read and understand the story.	Purpose Question: Ask students to read pg. 1 to find out what "salutations" are. What was the spider's name? (literal comprehension) Who was talking to Wilbur? (literal comprehension) Name possible antonyms of the red underlined words in the story. (meaning vocabulary) How do you know that Wilbur is pleased with Charlotte? (inferential comprehension)	

FIGURE 8-3. (*Continued*)

Skill and Objective	Materials and Procedures	Results
	Prove your answer.	
	What do you think "nearsighted" means on pg. 6? (meaning vocabulary)	
Guided Silent Reading (continued)	After reading this story, do you think you would like Charlotte? Why or why not? (critical reading/thinking)	
	(continue with questions such as these until reading selection is completed)	
IV. Follow-up	Discuss friendship.	
Students will enjoy discussing their best friends.	Ask students to draw a picture of their best friends - as a spider.	
a. Why they are friends.		
b. What makes a good friend.		

FIGURE 8-3. (*Continued*)

use of word recognition, comprehension, and study skills) are constructed so as to be implemented with an individual child or a reading group. They are not intended to limit a person's teaching or stifle creativity but rather to provide examples of how the DRTA and the instructional skills model work together. Within these lesson plans please note that the skill being taught is taken through all the steps of the Instructional Skills Model (Teach, Practice, and Apply) *before* the guided silent reading takes place. The teacher needs continually to have the child use the skill through effective questioning techniques in the guided silent reading—e.g., proving answers—and always be aware of the child's use of the skill in a reading situation. Figures 8-2, 8-3, and 8-4 are sample lesson plans showing how the instructional skills model can be implemented within the DRTA format.

UTILIZING THE ADOPTED BASAL SERIES

As teachers use a basal series they find many helpful suggestions and activities contained in the teacher's manual. This manual can be of tremendous assistance if used properly. We feel that the teacher's manual should be used as a guidebook. It offers a suggested format for teaching a DRTA, practice exercises developing the skills of reading, comprehension questions related to each story, enrichment activities, and supplemental resources and references throughout. A diagnostic-prescriptive teacher will find many activities in the basal readers to be appropriate for her/his instructional needs.

Because the teacher's manuals are filled with a wide variety of well-

Skill and Objectives	Materials and Procedures	Results
I. Skill Building A. Teach Students will understand concept of card catalog.	1. Teacher will introduce concept of a card catalog—its purpose and how it can be used in a library. Also discussed will be the three types of cards—author, subject, and title. 2. Teacher will take group to media center and show them a card catalog and specific examples of the author, subject, and title cards.	
B. Practice	1. Students will play a card catalog game. They will be divided into teams and each student will draw a card that contains certain information concerning the card catalog. Examples: Locate a book written by Dorothy Hamilton. Locate a book about frogs. Locate a book called—*The Fact Book about Trees* Locate a book about Abraham Lincoln. (continue with statement cards such as these.) The team to complete its cards is declared the winner.	
C. Apply	1. Deferred to Guided Silent Reading.	
II. Readiness for Guided Silent Reading Students will be prepared to complete reports on selected topics.	1. The idea of oral reports will be presented to the group. 2. A discussion of the procedure of making oral reports and locating information will be held with the students. 3. The procedure of outlining will be reviewed and discussed.	
Motivation	Students will be informed that they will be presenting these reports for other classmates.	
III. Guided Silent Reading Students will be able to read silently and understand the material.	1. Students will select topics for oral reports. Such topic choices are: Abraham Lincoln George Washington Famous Football Stars Ballet Birds of the North Racing Cars (etc.)	

FIGURE 8-4.   Sample DRTA with Emphasis on a Study Skill.

Skill and Objective	Materials and Procedures	Results
	2. Once the students have decided on a topic and located the material by using the card catalog they will be asked to follow the guided silent reading questions such as:	
Guided Silent Reading (contined)	a. Look at the material, italicized print, subheadings, etc. State questions that you would like to discover about your topic.	
	b. Read the material to find out the important information contained in it and try to answer the questions.	
	c. Make an outline of the material in preparation for writing the report.	
	d. Write the report from the	
	(1.) questions that have been answered and (2.) outline that has been created.	
	e. Proofread the report with the teacher and make final copy.	
IV. Follow-up The student will enjoy the process of making the report for other classmates.	1. The teacher will allow each student to create a project to accompany the report. 2. The projects and reports will be presented to classmates.	

FIGURE 8-4. *(Continued)*

developed teaching material their use in the classroom is to be recommended. However, teachers should be cautious to *select those activities to be used in light of their students' needs.* With the large number of suggestions available in a manual it would be very difficult for a teacher to do each activity with every reading group. Teacher judgment therefore must play an important part in selecting those experiences that would be *most* valuable for the students.

In some cases teachers feel they must follow the teacher's manual explicitly from story to story using every activity suggested. Some suggestions relating to skill development, for example, might be quite inappropriate if the child or group of children has already mastered the skill. Therefore, the activities implemented in a classroom should be dictated by student needs and *not* by what appears next in the teacher's manual of a basal reader.

Changing a Student's Reader

Sometimes a teacher, through informal and formal diagnostic procedures (see Chapters 3 and 4), will find it necessary to change a student's basal reader.

This change can take place within a series in the form of 1) a vertical move or 2) a horizontal move. The vertical move occurs when a student is advanced to a higher level or moved to a lower level text in the same series. The movement is an "up and down" movement thus reflecting a definition of the word *vertical* as compared to *horizontal*. The horizontal movement of a child occurs within the same reading level at which he/she was originally reading. The placement in this case is usually to another basal reader that is at a *comparable* reading level.

For example, if a fourth grade student was still having difficulty with silent reading comprehension at that level then the teacher might find it appropriate to place the child in a different fourth-level reader of another series. However, the skills to be taught would be drawn from the initial series.

The danger in changing students to a different basal reading series is that a different skills sequence from story to story might be utilized in the new series. A change in basals must *not* also mean a change in scope and sequence and the fundamental approach used. A different basal will offer additional reading materials to the student and further suggestions and activities to the teacher, but it should *not* offer a new reading program. Continuity of instruction should be of utmost concern in this situation (see Chapter 5).

FLEXIBILITY IN USING A BASAL SERIES

In order to more effectively meet the needs of students, the format of a basal series may be altered by the teacher who has become familiar with the steps of the DRTA as that series presents them. For example, students may have mastered the skills being taught; therefore, the teacher could skip the skill-building section of the lesson. One group may have very good vocabulary skills and not need the pre-introduction of vocabulary. In such instances the teacher will want to skip that portion of the readiness for guided silent reading.

Another occasion to change the order of presentation might occur when a teacher is careful to consider student interests in reading. With a certain amount of experience, a teacher comes to know those stories in a basal that are more interesting, better written, contain more action, or are otherwise more appropriate than other stories. In fact, the teacher may decide not to read some stories at all with the students, if they lack interest in the subject matter or the story is somewhat weak compared to the other stories in the book. The next time the teacher uses that same basal, students may want to read that story first. Whatever the case, reading instruction certainly depends, at least to some extent, on the interests of the learners! One must also carefully consider whether or not continuity is being maintained in teaching.

Most basal series present skill development after a story is read. In such cases the skills taught after a certain story are supposed to be applied in stories that follow. Therefore the program is really teaching the skills before they are applied in the guided silent reading of later stories.

The teacher will also need to be flexible in the use of guided silent read-

ing. For less able readers teacher guidance will need to be almost paragraph by paragraph or page by page. For more capable students it will need to be over an entire story.

ALTERNATIVE APPROACHES TO THE BASAL READER

There are numerous other approaches to reading instruction besides the basal reader. Even though they are not widely used, they can provide alternatives for learners who do not succeed with the basal. Also, these approaches can be utilized in conjunction with the basal. Five of these approaches are briefly summarized with advantages and limitations presented.

The Language Experience Approach (LEA)

In the language experience approach the language arts (reading, writing, listening) are interrelated and combined with the experiences of children (2). These experiences provide the basis for reading materials for the students. The rationale for this method has been stated by Allen as

1. What I think about, I can talk about.
2. What I say, I can write (or someone can write for me).
3. What I can write, I can read.
4. I can read what I have written and I can also read what other people have written for me to read (1, p. 158).

The language experience approach allows students to "write material themselves by dictating stories in their own speech patterns and with their own vocabulary" (2, p. 300).

The children provide the content by discussing an experience and dictating a story to the teacher. This story is written down for the children to see and read. Words are taught from the story. Vocabulary is continually expanded according to the types of experiences and activities each child talks about. All types of comprehension skills can be developed through the language experience approach by using discussion techniques with the newly created stories. Many times when a school system uses the language experience approach it is implemented as a method of teaching beginning reading.

Since all children use a variety of spoken words—some as many as 20,000 in meaningful context—the bases for the language experience stories can be quite varied. Some experience stories are based on the family life of a child, trips enjoyed, special relatives, while other stories are based on school experiences such as a film, a field trip, poetry reading, listening to a record, or even painting a picture. Any of these experiences can serve as a springboard to

Children Enjoy Reading What They Have Talked About and Written.

further discussion and the creation of children's stories. Aukerman states that the real purpose of the language experience approach is to "lead the child into reading through the media of listening to poems and stories; expressing himself in pictures and in words and sentences; perceiving the relationship of words to each other in our language; perceiving the construction of words by means of spelling and writing; and embellishing his spoken and written language by hearing and reading a wide variety of stories and poems by other authors. . . . As the children author their own books, they build interest and need to read many books from other authors" (2, pp. 308, 309).

Advantages of the Language Experience Approach

The main advantages of the language experience approach are

1. *It uses the language of the children as the avenue for teaching reading.* Reading instruction that utilizes the language of the child obviously builds on what is known. It allows children to use their own stories thus encouraging them to feel good about themselves and proud of their accomplishments.

2. *Skills are presented to the child as they are needed.* The child does not merely *work* on skill after skill but is presented a skill only when it can be used and applied in contextual reading. The child gains a feeling of accomplishment as more skills are being applied in a reading situation. This also enables the teacher to make the reading program more individualized for each student.

3. *The child comes to recognize reading as one part of the communication/language arts process.* Children have the opportunity to read what they say and then even write what they say, thus realizing that it is possible to express ideas through writing. Children become aware of the fact that they can read and enjoy the ideas that others have written.

Limitations of the Language Experience Approach

Although this approach has received wide usage there are certain limitations. They are

1. *Lack of sequential skill development.* Teachers usually feel more comfortable with a scope and sequence of skills to follow in the classroom. With the language experience approach, the skills are developed as the child or group needs them and as the teacher decides, thus creating a more haphazard approach to the teaching of reading.

2. *Repetition may become boring.* In order for the words to be learned the reading passages must be repeated many times for practice. The repeating of this material may become boring for some students causing them to lose interest in the activity.

3. *Developing materials is time-consuming.* The teacher must develop and prepare most of the materials. Since the stories are developed by the children, the teacher must create the learning activities around the subjects or topics the children suggest. This requires the teacher to prepare any learning activities simultaneously as the reading material is being developed. Even locating appropriate skills sheets or workbook pages can be quite time-consuming for a teacher.

Individualized Approach

In the individualized approach the teacher presents skills as they are needed in reading. This approach centers around child-teacher conferences. These conferences are often based on the books which children have selected for their own reading (15). Teachers employing the individualized approach try to hold at least a weekly conference with each of their students to keep abreast of their

reading needs. Harris and Smith have identified a suggested format that could be followed for individual conferences.

1. Greet the child and engage him in a brief conversation about a matter of personal interest, for example: How are you getting along in Boy Scouts? (30–60 seconds)

    (Time estimates are approximate. Each conference is adjusted as necessary. Some steps may be skipped on occasion to make more time for other steps.)

2. Ask the child what he has read since the last conference and what he is currently reading. Invite a brief account of the material read. (60–120 seconds)

3. Have the child read a passage orally from the book he is presently reading. On occasion you select the passage; normally the child should anticipate that you will ask him to read a passage and should be prepared to do so. Note reading fluency and the difficulty level of what he is reading. Offer positive feedback and encouragement. (120 seconds)

4. Check a skill you reviewed or introduced at the last conference and correct the assignment given (see step 6). Praise the child for accomplishments. (120 seconds)

5. Review or introduce a new skill. (180 seconds)

6. Give a follow-up assignment to be checked at the next conference. (60 seconds)

7. Help the child set goals for what will be accomplished by the next conference (tell him when the conference will be, how much will be read, what skills will be practiced). (60 seconds)

8. If a new book will be needed soon, make several suggestions and describe each one briefly. (60 seconds)

9. Compliment the child on progress made, then dismiss him.

10. Complete your records of what was accomplished during the conference before turning to the next child. (60 seconds) (9, p. 363-364)

Advantages of the Individualized Approach

Among the advantages of this approach are that

1. *It allows the students to read motivating material that is of specific interest to them.* Each student has the privilege and the responsibility of selecting his/her own reading material, thus making him/her eager to read. The material can better relate to real-life situations than the material discussed previously with the other approaches.

2. *The learner can receive a more personal learning plan.* Each teacher must talk personally with each student. This encourages a healthy rapport between teacher and learner and also enables the teacher to determine specific needs of the student and adjust instruction accordingly.

Limitations of the Individualized Approach

There are those authorities who feel that the individualized approach has the following limitations:

1. *Keeping abreast of the wide array of reading materials is quite time-consuming for the teacher.* Since the children are encouraged to read all types of materials on varying subjects, the teacher must be knowledgeable about the material to enable the most beneficial conference.
2. *A large assortment of reading materials must be provided.* This material, ranging in interest/subject matter, reading level, type, and so on, must always be available for student use. It is not only expensive to gather such a quantity of material, but also difficult to house it in a convenient spot.
3. *The classroom teacher must provide a mini-reading program for each student.* This requires the teacher to gather and organize the material and to keep careful records of how it is being used and who is using it.

Extending the Individualized Approach—Programmed Instruction

One approach to individualizing instruction is called the *programmed approach.* Programmed instruction "presents instructional material in small, sequential steps, each of which is referred to as a frame" (3, p. 221). As the pupil responds to each frame he/she is immediately reinforced as to the correctness of the response and then directed to a following frame.

The approach offers a very controlled vocabulary and also presents skills in a definite sequence. The Sullivan and Associate programmed materials and the *Systems 80* Program of Borg-Warner are two examples of available programmed material.

With this approach, a child might listen to a tape for instructional purposes, then follow step by step a series of learning activities in a workbook or participate in any number of individual activities. The material is so designed to allow a child to move ahead to more difficult lessons or move back to review lessons if he/she responds incorrectly to certain questions. The teacher is free to move around the room taking note of progress and looking for any problems

that might arise. A sample of some programmed reading material appears in Figure 8-5.

Advantages of the Programmed Approach

The major advantages of the programmed approach are that

1. *Behaviorally stated objectives are employed.* These programs are so designed as to guide the child very systematically through the specific reading skills. Progress can be measured by comparing the child's work to the stated behavioral objectives.
2. *The learner is encouraged to work at his or her own pace.* With the program designed on an individual basis, the child never feels pressure to be at a certain place at a certain time. This latitude allows the more advanced learner to continue at a faster pace and the less able learner to move along slower and with hopefully less frustration.
3. *Immediate feedback is provided to the learner.* As the child responds to the questions, he/she learns the correct answer immediately just by looking in the designated place. This approach provides immediate feedback to the learner and offers much positive reinforcement on a consistent basis.
4. *The program presents skills in a sequenced, highly structured format.* It is developed based on research related to the teaching of reading and skill presentation. Because of its individualistic design this program allows for students to be exposed to every skill contained in the material. Even if a child is absent he/she can return to school and begin the program where he/she previously was working rather than at the point to which the "reading group" has progressed.

Limitations of the Programmed Approach

The limitations of such an approach include the following:

1. *The learner may become bored with the presentation of the material.* With the information being presented in the same format consistently, this approach offers very little change or excitement to the child. A common experience with programmed material is that once the excitement of the "newness" wears off, the child actually lacks motivation to complete the materials. Since the progressive learning steps are very small the learner becomes bored too with the slow progress of the program itself.

fed

fed

bird

pet

ferns

after

fern

fern

fern

Meg led / fed the birds.

Ted f___d the birds.

A big b_____d sat on Ted's finger.

Rip ran into the ferns. Ted ran after him.
Rip led Ted into the ferns.

Rip is Ted's pen. / pet.

Rip ran into the f___rns.

Ted ran aft_____ his pet.

I'll dig it up and give it to Meg.

Rip led Ted to a big fer___.

Ted will dig up the ___ern.

Then Ted will give the f___ ___n to Meg.

FIGURE 8-5. Sample Programmed Reading.

Source: Harris and Smith. *Reading Instruction: Diagnostic Teaching in the Classroom*, 3rd ed. (New York: Holt, Rinehart & Winston), 1980, p. 363.

2. *Some feel the changed role of the teacher is a limitation to this approach.* With the programmed approach the teacher takes on the role of observer or question answerer instead of the more traditional role of teacher. The teaching is actually being done by the material itself.

3. *Slower students are at a disadvantage.* Because slower students usually experience difficulty with reading and reading-related tasks, they find programmed materials quite difficult since they require so much reading to complete. In some cases, the programmed material actually adds to the learner's frustration.

Computerized Instruction

"Computer literacy—defined as whatever a person needs to know about and be able to do with computers in order to function completely in our society—is fast becoming a basic survival skill" (17, p. 312). Microcomputers are now being used in classrooms across the country for all types of instruction from the language arts to mathematics and science. The uses of these computers are only limited by the creativity of the students, teachers, and administrators, for their implementation has been found to be quite versatile (18).

Plato is a system developed at the University of Illinois by Donald Bitzer. This computer system, created in the 1960's, is composed of a large group of

Young Learners Find School More Exciting with the Microcomputer.

programs that allow teachers to develop learning modules very similar to programmed material shown in Figure 8–5. An elaborate machine, as compared to the microcomputer, is required to operate the Plato system. Therefore authorities tend to favor the microcomputer over the Plato system because of the more inexpensive operational costs of microcomputers. The microcomputers are much more portable than the Plato computers due to the latter requiring telephone lines for operation. Since the microcomputers can operate anywhere with no additional equipment, they can easily be used in the classroom as a teaching tool (6). One of the most popular microcomputers used is manufactured by the Apple Company. It is enjoying such popularity currently because of all the software (created programs) that has been produced for it.

Following is a brief discussion of a portion of the microcomputer instructional materials that are being offered to schools in the reading/language arts area. The programs listed are in the forms of disks that can be easily slipped into the computer and enjoyed by students (11).

Letter Recognition—Grades K–3
> Useful in reinforcing lower-case letter recognition, teaching number words, and helping to correct reversal problems.

The Micro-communicator—Grades K–6 and 7–adult
> Designed for those handicapped learners experiencing great difficulty in speaking or writing. Keys represent words and phrases, thus allowing the user to express an entire thought by pressing one key.

The Spelling Machine-Grades K–6
> Students, being shown preselected spelling words on screen, are asked to type them and then use them to fill in blanks in sentences. After a certain number of correct sentences the students are given fun and reinforcement games (on the screen) such as "Hangman."

Word Families—Grades 1–4
> Program consists of three word lists of 90–100 words that cover beginning consonant substitution, final consonant substitution, and medial vowel substitution. Teachers have options of creating new lists continually.

Elementary Language Arts—Grades 2–6
> Crossword puzzles, mazes, and word jumbles in endless variety. Teachers can make up puzzles by using their own word lists.

Story Builder/Word Master-Grades 4–6
> Program reinforces vocabulary and grammar skills by using all parts of speech in game formats.

Compu-Read—Grades 4–12
> Letters, words, and sentences are flashed more and more rapidly across screen while students are asked to recall all or some of what they see.

GUIDED READING

Have pupils place their markers below the title. Have it read aloud. Ask, "Who will be in this story? What kind of animal is Nat?"
Guide the silent reading of each sentence by using the suggested statement or question above it. At this early stage, oral reading should follow the silent reading of each sentence.

This story begins with a question about Nat.

The question starts here (Indicate) with the circle word *Is*. It ends here (Indicate) with a mark called a question mark. Read the question to yourself.

What is the answer to the question?

What does the last sentence say about Nat?

Discuss the story. Use these questions: "What is the answer to the question *Is Nat a cat?* What does Nat look like?" Tell pupils they will learn other things about Nat in later stories.
Proceed to the oral reading of the entire story, which may be done in unison by the group. Individual pupils may then read each sentence aloud. Encourage pupils to use normal stress and intonation in their oral reading.
Continue with the Skills Development on the next page at this time or the next day.

Sample Page from Linguistic Reader—Teachers Edition.
Source: Page T-13 from the Teacher's Edition of I CAN. Reprinted by permission of Charles E. Merrill Publishing Co.

SKILLS DEVELOPMENT

Before Reading Page 7

Comprehension: Capitalization

Write the following on the chalkboard:

Tell the pupils that *is* and *Is* are the same word. Tell the pupils that *a* and *A* are the same word. (Pronounce the word *a* as it is pronounced in natural speech, not as its letter name is pronounced.) Explain that the word remains the same when a capital is used for the first letter. Have the pupils read the words *is, Is, a,* and *A* as you point to them on the chalkboard. First point to the words in order, and then point to them randomly.
Write the following sentences on the chalkboard:

Is a cat fat?
A cat is fat.
Is Nat a cat?
Nat is a cat.

Have each sentence read a number of times by individual pupils. Point out the use of a capital to begin each sentence.
Review with the pupils that a capital is also used for the first letter in a name. Write the name *Nat* on the chalkboard. Have pupils read it. Point out the capital used for the first letter in the name *Nat.* Tell pupils that *Nat* is the title of the next story. Ask them what they think Nat looks like. Show the pupils Picture Card 5, a picture of Nat, and have them discuss it.
Have the pupils open their Readers to page 7. *Continue with the Guided Reading of the story on page 7.*

213

Microcomputers seem to frighten some users because the machines "look" complicated. People tend to think they must be math-oriented to use a computer effectively, but this is not the case. One must remember that the microcomputer is merely a tool that assists the teacher with classroom instruction.

The Linguistic Approach

Linguistics focuses on the science and study of human speech (3, 13). Proponents of this approach have "identified the sound units of the language, the meaning units of the language, and the patterns that occur in the language" (3, p. 223). There are many materials available (referred to as *phonics material* by some) that have been built around these linguistic principles. One such set of materials is the Merrill *Linguistic Readers* produced in 1975.

In this series sounds are presented moving from the regular patterns to the irregular ones. For instance, if the short *e* sound is presented, no other sound of *e* is presented until the first one is thoroughly learned. Words of the same spelling pattern are presented together in very simple stories for the beginning reader. A sample sentence from a story might be constructed as "Dan is a tan man"—with all short *a* words being grouped together.

Somewhat recently linguists such as Smith, Goodman, and Meredith have extended the linguistic approach from merely a word-recognition method. They now have included the language used in the reading material and the meaning it conveys. They state that "reading methodology must reflect an understanding of language, of learning, of children, and of children learning language" (12, 271). The total language approach has been derived from this belief.

SELECTING ALTERNATIVE STRATEGIES

Selecting alternative strategies in the classroom requires changing to a different approach for the teaching of reading. Student needs can merit such a change. If a teacher discovers that a student is experiencing failure to read after a reasonable length of time with one strategy, then perhaps a change of strategy is necessary. If one strategy is followed so rigidly that there is no room for change the students might become disinterested or bored, thus creating a need for a strategy change.

Any of the previously discussed approaches to the teaching of reading can be used with the Directed Reading/Thinking Activity. If, for example, a teacher desires to use the individualized approach, the DRTA can be easily implemented on an individual basis: the teacher can use the DRTA plan with the reading material selected by the child. The language Experience Approach can be utilized through the DRTA and the basal reader. The LEA could be very

effectively used when motivating a group or individual to read a story. The students could dictate to the teacher a group story centered around what they already know about the topic. This will help them learn vocabulary words and concepts which will in turn enhance their comprehension of the story. The LEA could also be enjoyable when used in the guided silent reading phase of the DRTA. At a certain point in the story, the teacher could have the students create their own endings for the story and then compare their stories to what actually happened.

The programmed approach and even the computerized activities can be implemented in the skill-building part of the DRTA. Both of these approaches lend themselves to offering useful practice activities as related to the practice step in the Instructional Skills Model.

Changing strategies in your classroom is an important decision and should not be taken lightly. If you are having difficulties with a specific strategy and in turn a certain approach, you should not change immediately. Seek help from other teachers or your building principal and give yourself a chance to be successful. Whichever strategy is employed, the teacher must make certain that a change in strategies is still accomplishing the given program objectives. Using alternative strategies does not indicate a change of program or an excuse to deviate from the accepted scope and sequence. A sound reading program is based on specific skills and objectives, and teachers must develop these objectives through the instructional strategy or strategies that have been selected. The management techniques for coordinating strategies and implementing approaches are presented in Chapter 9.

SUMMARY

The diagnostically based reading program must involve careful selection of the appropriate instructional strategies that will enable all students to improve their reading ability. Instructional strategies are referred to as an overall plan under which a teacher selects one or more approaches to the teaching of reading. A classroom reading teacher will implement certain instructional strategies according to the philosophy she/he possesses about how a child learns to read.

The selection of instructional strategies depends on several factors: (1) reading levels, (2) skill needs, and (3) interests. As an instructional strategy is selected in a classroom it must be judged against what the learners need and not what the teacher finds most convenient to utilize.

In utilizing the basal reading series the teacher will find the teacher's manual to contain many helpful suggestions and activities. This manual should be used as a reference and not followed step by step. Teachers should be cautious to select the activities in light of their students' needs. The presentation of the order of the stories can be altered in light of student needs after a teacher has learned to use the series. Student readers can be changed within a series by

either vertical movement or horizontal movement. When a change is instituted the teacher must make certain that the approach to reading instruction remains the same and the scope and sequence is still being followed.

A Directed Reading Activity (DRA) or a Directed Reading/Thinking Activity (DRTA) provides structure for teachers when planning instruction. The DRA or the DRTA consists of four basic parts: (1) skill building, (2) readiness for guided silent reading, (3) guided silent reading, and (4) follow-up. An instructional skills model divides the skill presentation into three steps—teach, practice, and apply. These steps can be used when creating lesson plans for the classroom.

Some alternative approaches to the basal reader are (1) the language experience approach; (2) the individualized approach; (3) the programmed approach; (4) computerized instruction; and (5) the linguistic approach including the total language approach.

Selecting alternative strategies requires changing to a different approach. This change becomes necessary when a student is experiencing failure or becomes disinterested in learning. Whatever strategy is employed, the teacher must make certain that a change in strategies is still accomplishing the given program objectives. Using alternative strategies does not indicate a change of program or an excuse to deviate from the adopted scope and sequence.

THOUGHT AND DISCUSSION QUESTIONS

1. Why does a teacher need a basic instructional strategy under which to operate in the classroom?
2. How do any of the instructional approaches discussed in this chapter enhance a reading program?
3. Which approach would you implement in your classroom? Why?
4. Why must there be alternative approaches to the basal reading approach?
5. What must teachers be aware of in selecting teaching material that accompanies certain instructional approaches?

APPLYING WHAT YOU HAVE LEARNED

1. Visit a curriculum library where basal reading series are stored. Examine the readers, teacher's guides, workbooks, and any supplementary material. Determine how vocabulary is actually controlled and in what order a lesson is developed in the teacher's guide.
2. Compare two different basal series. Describe the differences between them in skill presentation, lesson format, and vocabulary control.

3. Develop a short learning program using the programmed learning technique. Try it out with children to see if it is effective.

4. Visit an elementary school that uses the language experience approach. Prepare and execute a lesson using this approach with children.

5. Conduct an individual reading conference with a child by following the format offered in this chapter.

6. Develop a lesson plan following the Directed Reading Format. Use a basal reader and other material in developing this plan.

BIBLIOGRAPHY

1. Allen, R. V. "The Language-Experience Approach" in *Perspectives on Elementary Reading: Principles and Strategies of Teaching.* Robert Karlin, ed. New York: Harcourt Brace Jovanovich, Inc., 1973.

2. Aukerman, Robert C. *Approaches to Beginning Reading.* New York: John Wiley & Sons, Inc., 1971.

3. Burns, Paul C., and Roe, Betty D. *Teaching Reading in Today's Elementary Schools.* Chicago: Rand McNally College Publishing Company, 1980.

4. Cheek, Martha Collins, and Cheek, Earl H., Jr. *Diagnostic Prescriptive Reading Instruction.* Dubuque, Iowa: Wm. C. Brown Company, Publishers, 1980.

5. Cooper, J. David; Warncke, Edna W.; Ramstad, Peggy A.; and Shipman, Dorothy A. *The What and How of Reading Instruction.* Columbus, Ohio: Charles E. Merrill Publishing Company, 1979.

6. Countermine, Terry. Director of Microcomputer Laboratory, School of Education, Auburn University, Auburn, Alabama. Interview, 1982.

7. Duffy, Gerald G., and Sherman, George B. *Systematic Reading Instruction*, 2nd ed. New York: Harper & Row, Publishers, 1977.

8. Hall, Mary Anne; Ribovich, Jerilyn K.; and Ramig, Christopher J. *Reading and the Elementary School Child*, 2nd ed. New York: D. Van Nostrand Company, 1979.

9. Harris, Larry A., and Smith, Carl B. *Reading Instruction: Diagnostic Teaching in the Classroom*, 3rd ed. New York: Holt, Rinehart and Winston, 1980.

10. Heilman, Arthur W.; Blair, Timothy R.; and Rupley, William H. *Principles and Practices of Teaching Reading.* Columbus, Ohio: Charles E. Merrill Publishing Company, 1981.

11. *Scholastic Microcomputer Instructional Materials Catalog* (1981–82). P.O. Box 2002, 904 Sylvan Avenue, Englewood Cliffs, N.J. 07632.

12. Smith, E. Brooks; Goodman, Kenneth; and Meredith, Robert. *Language and Thinking in the Elementary School*, 2nd ed. New York: Holt, Rinehart and Winston, 1976.

13. Smith, Nila B., and Robinson, H. Alan. *Reading Instruction for Today's Children*, 2nd ed. Englewood Cliffs, N.J.: Prentice-Hall, Inc., 1980.

14. Stauffer, Russell G. *Directing the Reading-Thinking Process.* New York: Harper & Row, Publishers, 1975.

15. Veatch, Jeannette. *Reading in the Elementary School*, 2nd ed. New York: John Wiley & Sons, Inc., 1978.

16. Wallen, Carl J. *Competency in Teaching Reading*, 2nd ed. Chicago: Science Research Associates Inc., 1981.

17. Winkle, Linda Wyrick, and Mathews, Walter M. "Computer Equity Comes of Age." *Phi Delta Kappan*, **63** (Jan. 1982), 314–315.

18. Zucker, Andrew A. "The Computer in the School: A Case Study." *Phi Delta Kappan*, **63** (Jan. 1982), 317–319.

FOR FURTHER READING

Deno, Evelyn N., ed. *Instructional Alternatives for Exceptional Children.* Arlington, Va.: The Council for Exceptional Children, 1977.

Frazier, Alexander. *Teaching Children Today, An Informal Approach.* New York: Harper & Row, Publishers, 1976.

Hall, Mary Anne. *Teaching Reading As A Language Experience*, 3rd ed. Columbus, Ohio: Charles E. Merrill Publishing Company, 1981.

Howards, Melvin. *Reading Diagnosis and Instruction, An Integrated Approach.* Reston, Va.: Reston Publishing Company, Inc., 1980.

Kennedy, Eddie. *Classroom Approaches To Remedial Reading*, 2nd ed. Itasca, IL: F. E. Peacock Publishing, Inc., 1977.

Lamberg, Walter J., and Lamb, Charles E. *Reading Instruction in the Content Areas.* Chicago: Rand McNally College Publishing Company, 1980.

Pearson, P. David, and Johnson, Dale D. *Teaching Reading Comprehension.* New York: Holt, Rinehart and Winston, 1974.

Stauffer, Russell G. *Directing the Reading-Thinking Process.* New York: Harper & Row, Publishers, 1975.

Wittich, Walter A., and Schuller, Charles F. *Instructional Technology, Its Nature and Use*, 6th ed. New York: Harper & Row, Publishers, 1979.

chapter 9

managing the diagnostic reading program

objectives

As a result of reading this chapter one will be able to

1. Understand the concept of classroom management and relate it to reading instruction.
2. Know the essential components of an effective classroom management program.
3. Become aware of instructional activities and techniques to make ones management more effective.

overview

The concept of management related to diagnostic teaching will be developed. The components of the diagnostic reading program cannot be successfully implemented without the effective management of the classroom itself. A person interested in the operation and management of a classroom might ask: How should I begin my instructional day? How can I coordinate individual or reading group activities? How can I schedule my time? or What additional activities can I offer my students to enhance the management of my reading program? The thrust of this chapter will be to assist the teacher in developing an understanding of management and the procedures needed to implement an effective management plan in a classroom reading program.

In reading this chapter one should draw on one's knowledge of assessment and organization and how they are necessary prerequisites to a management plan. The knowledge and skills one develops will help one carry out steps 3, 4, and 5 of the diagnostic teaching process:

Step 3. Evaluate alternatives and select ones to carry out.
Step 4. Teach.
Step 5. Evaluate results.

MANAGEMENT—WHAT IS IT?

The concepts of organization and management are often regarded as the same. Even though the two are highly related, they are quite different. Management is an extension of classroom organization. It involves those procedures that one will employ to keep one's organization running smoothly. Once students have been diagnosed (assessed) and a systematic plan for instruction has been developed the components of management can be implemented. In other words, assessment and organization must come *prior* to management.

Doyle views management as a teacher's responsibility when he states, "From a management perspective, a teacher's immediate task is to gain and maintain the cooperation of students in activities that fill classroom time" (5, p. 6). Classroom time must not just be *filled*, but filled with activities that are profitable and productive. Teachers must develop a balance in the classroom in the face of disruptions, discipline problems, and other disturbances that might occur. An effective management plan helps maintain this balance and should enhance and encourage learning for children. Students who are working in a well-managed classroom are better able "to apply their abilities, talents, and energies to educational tasks" (7, p. 6).

How each teacher operates the reading group or individuals, coordinates activities, encourages independent student work, or continually evaluates his/her performance in the classroom is the essence of classroom management. Management includes all of those minute details that make an average teacher outstanding. Without an effective management plan, the diagnostic reading program cannot be considered complete. "The management that good teaching facilitates is that which occurs concurrently with the instruction. Much management activity takes place before and after instruction; such activity provides the basis for both good instruction and effective concurrent management" (6, p. 19).

Management, as related to effective reading instruction has three parts:

1. Preplanning and scheduling instructional activities.
2. Productively involving students in independent reading/language arts work.
3. Providing the very best learning environment for developing readers.

The teacher is the key to the overall management of the classroom. Without the implementation of good management techniques, the organization of a classroom would be of little use. Each teacher is ultimately responsible for the management of the classroom and therefore must devise a plan that will complement the teaching style used by that teacher, and yet be educationally sound.

Developing a Management Plan

Effective classroom management cannot be implemented in a haphazard manner. The following steps should help develop a sound management plan.

Become familiar with Overall Goals and Objectives for Reading. Many school systems or corporations have some type of overall goals and objectives included in what has been referred to earlier as a curriculum guide. These goals are statements that symbolize the philosophy of the school system and are often nonspecific. An example of a general goal might be the development of critical thinking/reading abilities in students with the product being more independent learners.

All the skills of reading can be developed under the overall goals. The activities that a teacher implements to develop the skills are highly related to the management plan that is created. It is the teacher's ultimate responsibility to relate his/her instruction to the development of the overall goals.

Teachers and administrators must interpret and internalize the general goals so they can be correlated to the actual classroom teaching situation. Building principals, at times, ask teachers to set more specific goals that are directly related to their own classrooms. These goals are referred to by some school systems as growth targets. No matter what these goals or objectives are called, they have one purpose: to lead to improved instruction.

By implementing effective management related to the predetermined activities centered around the goals, teachers *will* be able to improve instruction. For example, there is the overall goal of developing better critical thinkers/ readers and independent learners. In order to attain this goal, a teacher might set as his/her individual reading instruction goal to implement learning centers within the classroom. These learning centers could provide activities related to comprehension—specifically critical thinking and critical reading. In addition, students will develop into more independent learners and thinkers by having to make decisions about which centers to use while at the same time working individually to complete the center task, thus contributing to the accomplishment of the teacher's goal of developing independent learners. In turn, this goal accomplishment is attained through effective classroom management of learning centers. Hence, classroom management can and should be highly related to the instructional goals set by a teacher.

No matter what the reading goals are stated to be they can be created by a teacher so they are the most practical, useful, and workable statements that guide the teacher in planning the reading instruction and developing effective management. By referring continuously to these goals, the teacher can incorporate the proper instructional activities that should lead to the development and refinement of the identified reading needs. The selection of the proper activities makes management more effective.

Plan for Instruction. It has been found that teachers are more capable of creative input and high-quality thought when they are thinking about and planning for a teaching situation than when they are actually in the process of teaching (9). While a teacher is implementing a lesson with students, the teacher is not only concerned with the presentation, but also with the behavior of other children in the classroom, potential discipline problems, and other disturbances that could occur. For these reasons, teachers should plan *prior to* the implementation of learning activities. Prior planning will contribute to a smoother-flowing presentation with students. A teacher who is better prepared for a teaching/learning experience can contribute greatly to his/her management of that situation.

Prediction is often related to effective planning and classroom management (3). A teacher must learn to predict what *might* happen under certain circumstances or conditions and how children might react to those conditions. By making sensible predictions a teacher can avoid certain management problems. For instance, if a teacher realizes that a specific workbook page contains unclear directions then the teacher should plan to discuss the directions *before* it is assigned. Confusing directions (causing student questions and general restlessness) can upset some students quickly and do much to deter classroom management. Therefore, the prediction of a possible trouble area can do much to contribute to effective management. Prediction is also important in judging completion time for classroom tasks. A teacher who can predict how long it will take students to complete assignments will be able to implement the management with greater ease.

Effective classroom management calls for teachers to do many types of planning in the course of one school year (3). These include daily, weekly, term, unit, yearly, or special-event planning. All these different planning needs are important in keeping the days and weeks running smoothly. Teacher planning must be compatible with the situation in which the learning occurs and the teaching style of the teacher.

SCHEDULING THE INSTRUCTIONAL TIME

Effective classroom management depends to a great extent on using teaching time wisely. A schedule need not be so rigid that it creates problems, but it should offer a structure that will enable a teacher to do his/her best teaching. It is desirable for a teacher who is learning to manage instructional time to write out schedules with enough detail to make them useful for the teaching situation. A teacher's predicting ability will prove quite useful in planning a time schedule. By estimating the completion time of certain kinds of activities, the teacher can create a schedule that is more accurate and reflective of the stu-

dents' work time. The following suggestions will help one plan one's instructional reading time.

1. Decide on the amount of time one has for reading instruction. This may be set by the school and will vary according to the type of organizational pattern one has (language-arts block or separate reading class). Time allotments can vary for reading time anywhere from one hour to three hours. Usually the three-hour segment combines reading with English, writing, and spelling.

2. Decide the instructional time segments to use with one's class. Usually with primary grades the segments (lesson presentation times) are five or ten minutes in duration while the intermediate-grade time segments vary from fifteen to thirty minutes. When determining the time segments one should draw a schedule page with blocks as shown in the samples at the conclusion of this section.

3. Determine the group or individual where one will begin instruction. Begin deciding activities and lessons from that point.

4. Decide how to give directions to get one's reading period started. Certain groups or individuals might be working independently at their desks, others could be working at learning centers, some will be gathered for a reading group lesson, and so on. The decisions on what one's groups will be doing can be written in one's schedule.

5. Plan how to move from group to group. One should predict how long it will take the students to complete work. At this point in planning

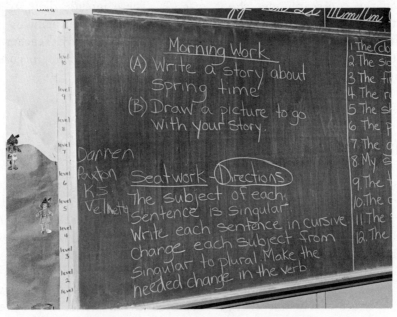

Clearly Stated Directions Are Essential for an Organized Beginning.

one will decide the next activities, being careful to coordinate them with other groups that are working. One must decide which groups or individuals with which to work directly in a reading instructional time and fill those in the blocks first.

6. Complete the schedule by filling in the needed independent activities. Once it has been determined when one will be working with specific reading groups and for approximately how long, independent activities can be included for those other groups working in the room without direct guidance.

The sample time schedules that follow illustrate the results of applying these six suggestions. It is necessary for most effective teachers to *write* a time schedule on paper rather than merely trying to remember it. Figures 9-1 and 9-2 follow a blocked format while Figure 9-3 uses a more open format.

Time in Minutes

Groups	20 Min.	10 Min.	20 Min.	15 Min.	25 Min.	15 Min	30 Min.	30 Min.
A Reading Level 1	Teacher reads portion of library book to all groups and holds brief discussion.	Teacher gets reading groups organized and makes appropriate assignments.	Independent practice activity on initial blends	TEACHER Teach sight words related to new story	Independent practice of new vocabulary words. Skill sheet using new words.	Recess and Reorganization	Independent skill practice from previous day	TEACHER Present new story and begin guided silent reading.
B Pre-Reading Readiness			TEACHER Reteach color words. Assign and explain independent activity on color words.	AIDE (if available) Check student progress on independent activity and assists where needed.	AIDE begins organizing students to participate in listening center activity.		Independent activity at listening center related to color words.	4 students attend speech class. Remaining students work with group D.
C Reading Level 2			Independent reading of story to detect main idea.	Short independent activity related to the main idea of the story.	Complete individually assigned learning centers related to diagnosed reading needs.		TEACHER Guided silent reading pp. 22–29 with accompanying discussion questions.	Independent activity related to story. Learning centers for remainder of time.
D Reading Level 2²			Independent practice sheet requiring the construction of simple sentences.	→	TEACHER Creative writing presentation: Motivate students to write short stories using the knowledge gained from previous activities.		Group does related art project to creatively illustrate stories.	Some students read stories and show illustration to group B students. Some finish art projects. Some work at skill review centers.

FIGURE 9-1. Sample Primary Time Schedule.

Time in Minutes

Groups	20 Min.	10 Min.	25 Min.	30 Min.	15 Min.	30 Min.	30 Min.
A Reading Level 4			Independent vocabulary exercise and word game from center. Complete library book for book report.	Continue work on book reports. Language independent assignment.		TEACHER Guided silent reading from story presented preious day. Oral discussion of story.	Independently answer discussion/comprehension questions related to the story (written exercise). Do center work if time permits.
B Reading Level 2	Oral book reports given by various group members.	Teacher gets students organized and makes appropriate assignments.	TEACHER Present new vocabulary. Allow independent practice. (check on other groups while B is working). Begin guided silent reading of story.	Independent silent reading of story followed by skills pages that are related.	Recess and Reorganization	Complete previous assignment. Do center work. Read library books in preparation for book report.	Continue reading library books. Plan shadow box illustrating book. Begin language assignment.
C Reading Level 6			Independent work on outlining a chapter in a social studies textbook.	TEACHER Briefly review outlining procedures. Individual group members are assigned topics for an oral report. Students are shown how to begin projects.		Independent work in library preparing oral reports.	Continue library work.
D Individualized			Continue comprehension practice activities from yesterday. Begin working from individual reading kits.	Independent center work developing critical thinking and critical reading skills.		Continue independent work. Prepare for individual conferences with teacher related to current library books being read.	TEACHER Individual conferences with students.

FIGURE 9-2. Sample Intermediate Time Schedule.

Figures 9-1 and 9-2 are probably the types of schedules needed as one begins to plan to manage one's time. As one becomes more proficient, the format in Figure 9-3 may be preferable to follow.

Many teachers feel that a daily routine for children allows them to realize what is expected of them as well as giving them a feeling of comfort and security. A general routine helps alleviate unneeded problems and confusion during transition periods when activities are changing during the instructional day. Routines can increase teacher efficiency and flexibility. This only serves to increase the stability of classroom activities.

A schedule should serve as a framework so that both teacher and the students know generally what to expect as the day moves along. Many times a

Time	Group I (Rdg. Lv. 3[1])	Time	Group II (Rdg. Lv. 4)	Time	Group III (Rdg. Lv. 5)
8:30	Vocabulary exercise and word game from center. (Be ready to bring work to reading group.) Finish library work or read library book for book report.	8:30	Read story from previous day and answer six discussion questions on worksheet 22. Skill work with centers. Students can read library books if time permits.	8:30 8:40	Finish skills sheets from previous day. READING GROUP WITH TEACHER Vocabulary presentation and concept development.
9:30	READING GROUP WITH TEACHER Review vocabulary, concept development, purpose setting questions. Silent reading if time permits.			9:10	Practice vocabulary with center activities. Workbook pages for developing vocabulary Read library book. Language assignment.
9:40	Workbook pages Skill extension Language assignment	9:40	READING GROUP WITH TEACHER Group discussion of worksheet 22. Review necessary skill work. Present new vocabulary and concept development.		
		10:10	Workbook pages (vocabulary development) Skill development Language assignment	10:10	READING GROUP WITH TEACHER Discuss vocabulary Present story to prepare for silent reading on next day.

FIGURE 9-3.   Sample Time Schedule.

schedule cannot be strictly adhered to every day but at least it will provide a basic structure of operation for the reading time. There are many predictable events that occur each day. Some of these might be opening-class time in the morning, recess, lunch, physical education, music, and art time, speech and language class for some students, and times when aides will be in one's room. All of these events affect reading time to some extent. Whatever is happening, all those involved should be familiar with the schedule. Even auxiliary personnel such as aides or assistant teachers need to be informed of the schedule and any schedule changes.

When beginning to develop a schedule for reading or for the day, the following points should be kept in mind:

- The content difficulty of a lesson is crucial to its effectiveness. Any time a teacher presents material that is too difficult for the students, the teacher is

increasing the chances for student restlessness and eventual boredom. Perhaps this situation might even lead to some discipline problems. The same situation could develop too if the material is too easy for the student.

- The attention span of one's students will affect the length of the time blocks one can use for instruction. Younger children and less able learners frequently have shorter attention spans. A child's attention span is also highly related to the teacher's approach to the presentation of the material. At times children do not attend to a certain learning situation because the teacher has selected an inappropriate approach to implement with those children. For example, a teacher who encourages just round-robin reading in a reading group may unknowingly encourage restlessness or boredom because the students aren't actively involved. Whereas if a teacher uses the guided silent-reading approach in a reading group and asks children to read orally to prove answers and add to the discussion these students will be more consistently involved and in turn might be much more cooperative with the teacher.

- Diagnostic teaching and individualization of instruction do not imply that every child or every group should be seen by the teacher every day. Some individuals or groups may need to meet with the teacher only every other day. This will depend in part on the ability of the children to work independently.

- Less able learners need to meet with the teacher for shorter periods of time more frequently. But just because these slower learners need shorter periods of instruction time it does not mean that they should be taught less. They should have material presented to them in smaller units. Care should be taken that less able learners are provided with material that provides the proper balance between too-easy or too-difficult material.

ROOM ARRANGEMENT AND EFFECTIVE MANAGEMENT

The effective use of space will lead to more effective classroom management for reading instruction and a more efficient utilization of materials and resources. The way a room is arranged will either encourage or discourage student involvement in class activities. An independent activity, for example, will encourage more student involvement if each student has access to a complete set of materials rather than having to wait for or share mutual materials.

Some teachers arrange student desks in rows, some arrange them in tables of four desks to a table, some make one large square on the edges of the room, and some make circles with the desks. Whatever the arrangement, it must be suited to the type of activities that will be taking place. If reading groups are to be in operation in one corner, then students in another group need to be able to move to their group without disturbing others who are working at desks. If

centers are being used for skill development, the teacher might consider moving student desks away from that area because of possible distractions. One might also consider seating all the members of a reading group in the same area of the room. Then they will be in a convenient position for any oral directions or special activities. Sometimes teachers place special work on the chalkboards for groups, thus requiring the groups to be near certain sections of the board. Students can also change to other desks during reading time if it proves more convenient.

A seating arrangement can remain flexible according to the teaching/learning situation that is occurring or according to the objectives set by the teacher. If one objective is to have students learn to cooperate with each other and help one another, the desks should be close enough to encourage communication between students. On the other hand, if one's objective in a lesson is to have totally quiet work, the desks could be arranged with a little more space between them for the purpose of physically limiting communication between students.

If a teacher is going to operate with reading groups, it would be wise to locate that group work area in a place where the teacher can see the entire classroom. While the teacher is working with a small group at a table, he/she must be able to easily watch the rest of the reading students. Even when a teacher is dealing with one group or individual directly, the teacher is still responsible for the entire reading class and must continually strive to get maximum output from all students. By sitting in such a way as to see the entire class, the teacher can "keep an eye" on things, detect a problem, encourage some students to remain on task, and generally supervise the operation of the reading class.

Teachers must also be concerned about the student fitting the desk. A desk that is too large or too small for a student will be uncomfortable and inhibiting. A desk that fits a child in the fall of the year may be too small by January. Teachers must be aware of these possible problems and either change the student's desk or have a custodian, if possible, adjust the size of the desk.

The arrangement of all furniture in the classroom plays an important role in effective management of one's reading class. If desks are too crowded, independent work areas are not provided, materials are not readily available, or the teacher does not have an instructional space free from congestion and interruptions, problems will arise. *Poor preplanning for space utilization can lead to failure of the best teaching.*

STORING TEXTBOOKS AND SUPPLIES

Some classrooms in schools across this country are very well equipped with such conveniences as built-in shelving, enclosed closets, lockers, individual bookcases, and tables while other classrooms have nothing more than a bulletin board or chalkboard. If the latter is the case, there are still many organizational

Containers Such as These Will Keep Materials Organized for Easy Location.

An Organized Room Will Contribute to a More Effective Management Plan.

230

possibilities that can be carried out. For the more barren rooms, cement blocks can be stacked with slats of wood to make shelving. Neatly stacked cardboard boxes or three-gallon round ice-cream containers placed on their sides have also been used by several teachers to keep a room organized. Some have resorted to keeping all supplies and materials in the individual student desks because there is no additional room for storage.

Whatever the situation—limited facilities or ample facilities—teachers must decide where the most practical places for special materials and supplies could be. If a reading table is going to be used for reading instruction, the teacher will have to be careful what materials will be stored around or near it. It might be more sensible to store the reading texts on shelves by the table rather than placing art or science supplies there. Often these supplies are used independently in a classroom, so a teacher teaching a reading group at the table would not want students continually coming to these shelves and distracting the reading group. Also, if the reading texts are stored by the reading table it would be much easier to distribute them to students.

Some classrooms have sinks with counter space, tile on the floor, carpet-

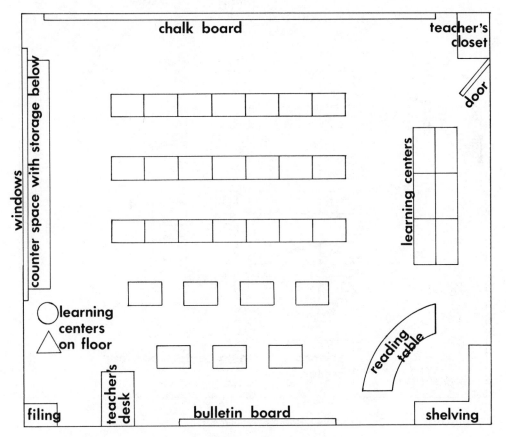

FIGURE 9-4. Self-Contained Room Arrangement.

ing in some areas, or a combination of all of these. The tiled areas by a sink lend themselves to "sloppier" activities such as art projects or science activities. Spilled water or paint can be much more easily cleaned from floor tile than it can from carpeting. Carpeted spaces can be used for quieter activities such as reading areas or learning center work. These areas can be created by obtaining carpet remnants or old carpet that is clean. Sheets of heavy plastic or linoleum can be put down for protecting areas. Many times local merchants will give one these materials free of charge.

One should organize the teaching materials so that they are at hand when one needs them. In planning one's lessons, decide what additional materials might be needed such as construction paper, paste, supplementary worksheets, special textbooks, or even just blank writing paper. Whatever it might be, it should be collected, stacked, or assembled so that when the time comes one can gather it together quickly and be ready to teach. This will contribute to a more effective management plan.

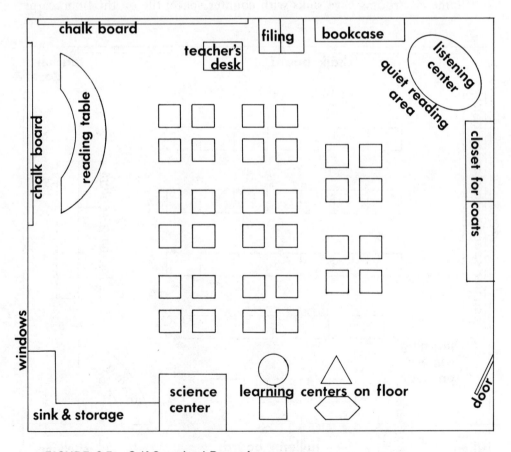

FIGURE 9-5. Self-Contained Room Arrangement.

The following diagrams illustrate what has been discussed in relation to arranging one's room. Figures 9-4, 9-5, and 9-6 present a space arrangement for various types of self-contained classrooms. Figure 9-7 shows a flexible space area arrangement in which space is shared by three teachers. These diagrams are merely suggestions, of course, and a teacher's own creativity will play a large part in the practical arrangement of any classroom.

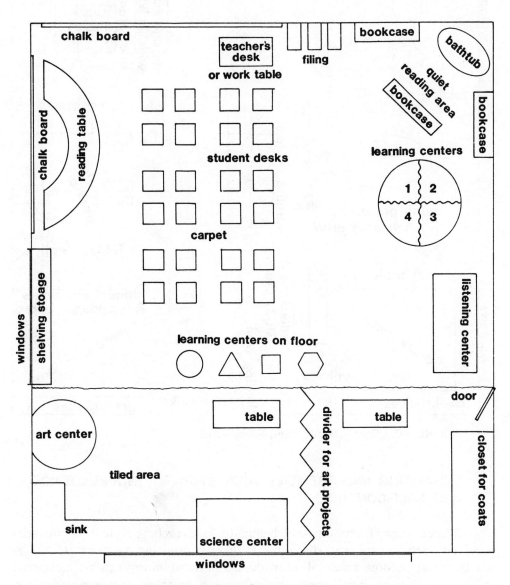

FIGURE 9-6. Self-Contained Room Arrangement.

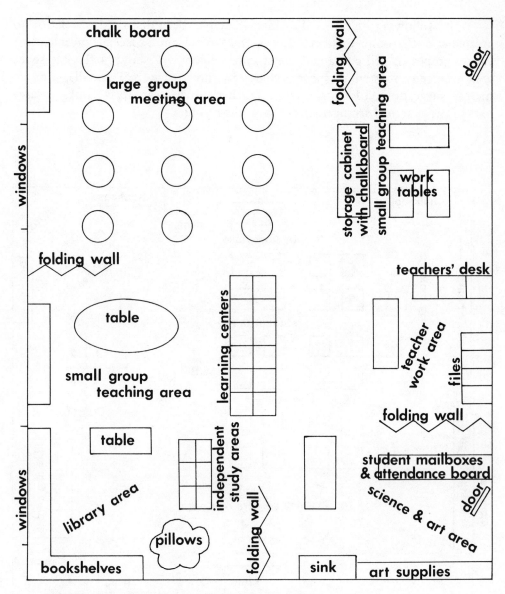

FIGURE 9-7.   Three-Teacher Flexible Space Area.

ENHANCING MANAGEMENT WITH STUDENT INDEPENDENCE AND SELF-CONTROL

Recent research studies have begun to link teaching style, student independence, self-control, and discipline with classroom management (1, 12). A teacher must become aware of all of these aspects to improve those managerial skills that are so essential to effective classroom teaching. It is more comfortable to think of discipline in a positive light rather than from a purely punish-

ment point of view. A teacher with effective classroom management techniques will probably be interested in developing self-discipline in students. After all, a child who is *in* control is usually more productive than a child who is merely *under* control.

Tanner refers to discipline as "the learner's constructive self-control and development toward self-direction and social responsibility" (11, p. 10). Teachers must provide the experience and activities for students that will guide them toward being more socially responsible within their own class unit. Just telling students what is expected of them has very little impact on their conduct (2). What does make a difference is that behavior can be generally modified because of teacher approval of certain forms of behavior. Studies are now showing that "the use of behavioral self-control procedures appears promising with on-task study habits and academic achievement" (12, p. 33).

A practical example might serve to illustrate this better. If a teacher wants the students in groups A and B to work quietly and independently (on a learning center, workbook activity, or written assignment) while one worked with group C, the teacher might want to discuss with groups A and B the importance of quiet work. One could also praise those who work quietly and efficiently so that others might want to try to do the same. With groups A and B now "going about their assigned tasks," the teacher could begin work with group C. This group might be engaged in a teacher-directed discussion, answering comprehension questions to a story, or some other type of activity that would be somewhat noisier than the other groups. Even though one has encouraged group C to talk or work together in some manner, thus "loosening up one's discipline for that session," this has not implied that everyone in the room is free to do or say what they want. While group C is conversing, the teacher should still be supervising, watching, and encouraging quiet independent work with groups A and B. Eventually the same thing can be done with any reading group while the other two are working quietly. This may not work immediately or every time but most students will eventually respond and strive to cooperate.

Kounin (8) has originated a term that he refers to as *withitness*. Withitness is defined as the method a teacher uses to communicate with students that he or she is knowledgeable about what is going on in all parts of the classroom. Such methods range from quick glances to actual physical contact with a student or group of students. Kounin has found that withitness or "the eyes in back of the head" syndrome does much to positively affect the behavior of children. Therefore, this should indicate to teachers that attending to the immediate teaching situation is not enough to insure effective classroom management. Being aware of trouble spots in the classroom, watching for students needing assistance on class work, and observing those students causing disturbances must all be taken into account.

One of the most important things to remember about establishing a positive, self-disciplined atmosphere in one's classroom is to let the students know *before* a specific activity takes place just what kind of behavior is expected of

them. Sometimes one might want to have the students discuss and decide what is appropriate for certain situations while at other times they must be expected to simply follow the teacher's instructions. Whatever the situation, the teacher must enforce her/his disciplinary decisions consistently with whatever criteria have been established. Building this type of classroom atmosphere will help to develop students who are more responsible and better able to cope with a class situation. One way to help them is by raising questions that will guide them to make their own decisions about how to operate as an independent productive learner.

Management of the reading program comes about more readily as students learn to develop their own independence and self-discipline. The teacher can help students build these much-needed qualities. The time one spends in continually developing these traits will in turn affect the quality and quantity of instruction that one can offer one's students.

A "Typical" Morning in the Classroom Reading Program

Now that the guidelines for developing a management plan have been presented, one should see how it all fits together. This section is included for the purpose of illustrating how three reading groups (it could have been four) can be coordinated and guided to effective classroom instruction by implementing appropriate management techniques. The examples and explanations offered assume that members of a reading group have not only been placed in the appropriate reading text, but also in an English/language text and spelling material to match the instructional reading level of the basal series being used.

Classroom Description.   Upon entering the classroom, the students turn over their names on an attendance board so that attendance can be taken by a student responsible for the task. After being greeted by the teacher, the students begin to get organized for the day. Each student has several choices or methods of getting involved in the day's work depending on the teacher's instructional techniques.

Students check the chalkboard for their own specific morning assignments. A sample of directions for the three reading groups in an elementary classroom follows:

Group I	Group II	Group III
Do vocabulary exercise and word game from reading center. (Be ready to bring work to reading group.)	Read story that was introduced yesterday and answer six discussion questions on worksheet 22.	Finish skills sheets from yesterday and be ready to begin a reading group in 10 minutes.

By looking at these sample directions carefully, one can see that Group I and Group II have been assigned work that will constructively occupy their work time. Group III has been given an assignment that will occupy a shorter amount of time and then allow them to begin a reading group. In other words, two groups will still have work to do while one group can be involved directly with a teacher. As the teacher finishes with the presentation and related work with Group III, he/she moves on to the next group (either I or II). Before leaving Group III, the teacher provides the students with a meaningful and appropriate assignment that will enhance or extend the intended instructional purpose. Perhaps Group III will be given (after purpose-setting) a story to read silently and a follow-up activity involving comprehension.

The teacher then proceeds to Group I and discusses the vocabulary words that the students have prepared and moves into purpose-setting for a new story. After the teacher introduces the story and sets a purpose for reading, he/she can allow the students to read it silently (perhaps applying a skill learned on the previous day). Soon members of Group II will probably be ready to discuss their story, become involved in some comprehension questions, and perhaps do some purposeful oral reading. The teacher then introduces a specific reading skill to the group (as diagnosed earlier) and assigns the students to do some independent practice, either written or in a manipulative/center situation or both.

By this time, approximately an hour and a half to two hours of class time have passed from the time the school day began. During this time, too, the teacher has provided a specific language assignment or activity to students who have completed their assigned reading group work. Learning centers, games, and other types of related activities coordinated to the objectives or skills being taught are available for those completing work before their reading group meets. These activities might or might not be done as part of the formal reading group instruction. Either way, they allow the students to work independently with as little teacher direction as possible. These activities are also self-checking so immediate feedback can be provided for the students.

Some teachers might like to have all of the assignments written on paper and distributed accordingly. These printed directions and assignments are sometimes called agendas. The agendas would contain vocabulary words, related exercises, comprehension work, skills practice, and enrichment activities. Reading group members could just continue working through their agendas during the morning preparing themselves for when their group will meet. The teacher, however, is still the key in making this all work effectively. The teacher must be involved in direct teaching of skills and concepts even though the agenda format is being used. A sample agenda, Figure 9-8, has been provided. Note the words *reading groups* listed on the agenda. This indicates to a student that when work is completed to this point, the teacher should call together a reading group for direct teaching purposes. If, by chance, all the students are not up to that place in the agenda, then they should be supplied with (prior to or at

General Takes the Cake

(Taken from the student
book *Whispering Ghosts*
Laidlaw Publishing Co.)

Name _____   Date _____

Follow the instructions given by your teacher.

General Takes the Cake

_____   Do English/language assignment pg. ____ (related to previously
presented skill)

_____   Do skills book page 52
(You may include any other related skill practice)

_____   Vocabulary Words—boast, chalkboard, double, fifty, leash, loose,
strawberry, tray, treat, weigh, wrap. (You may include a written
practice here or just do an oral activity)

_____   Skill development—T140
Sentences and Phrases

1) Jack *boasted* to his friends about *General.*

2) is as big as the *chalkboard*

3) eats *fifty strawberry* ice-cream cones

4) *weighs* more than a truck

5) causes *double* trouble

_____   (T141) Read to find out: (pgs. 124–125)

1) What had Jack planned to do on this particular day?

_____

2) How did Jack boast about his dog? _____

_____

_____   Reading Group (Discussion)

_____   (T142) Read to find out: (pgs. 126–127)

1) What was going on in the classroom while Carol waited outside
the door with General?

_____

2) Why had Jack told Carol to wait in the hall?

_____

(Continue stating questions in this manner throughout story)

_____   (T143) Reading for a new purpose.

_____   Evaluate - This section may be written or oral.

_____   (T144) Skills book: pg. 53

FIGURE 9-8. Sample Agenda for the Story.

_____ (T144) Skills book: pg. 54

(Include any other skills worksheets that would develop or extend
the introduced skill)

_____ Enrichment: Select an activity from the following choices: You may
want to do more than one.

* Write or tell a short story about another funny situation General
becomes involved in because of his size.

* Pretend that your school is having a Pet Fair. Make a list of
suggestions for handling pet visitors.

* Tell or write about a time when boasting may have gotten you into
some difficulty.

FIGURE 9-8. *(Continued)*

that time) a language assignment, or become involved in some sort of learning
center work. It will not be long before the teacher can gather the group, present the learning task, refer to the agenda, and move on with the next instructional activity.

Depending on the time that has been allotted to the language-arts block
each day the teacher could still have time in the morning to work with spelling
groups and/or language groups. There would even be enough time for some
type of library experience or oral reading to a class.

Now, in a practical sense, all these things cannot occur *every* day in the
elementary classroom. This is where the teacher is so important and crucial in
deciding needs, scheduling time, and setting priorities for the students. Sometimes these decisions can be made *with* the students and at times they must be
arbitrarily decided upon by the teacher. The teacher's "good sense" should dictate in either case.

Implementing Learning Centers as a Management Technique

A popular method of individualizing either singly or within small groups is
the learning center approach. Each learning center usually occupies a small area
in a classroom and can be done individually by students. Screens, table dividers,
cardboard, bulletin boards, or even material hanging from the ceiling can be
used to create a learning center space in a classroom. Each center is intended to
promote study in a particular skill area—word attack, comprehension, sustained
silent reading, creative writing, decoding skills (10). Some teachers eventually
broaden their approach and include science, social studies, math, music, and art
centers. No matter what type of center is being used, it must fit into and complement the instructional objectives previously set by the teacher.

The learning center approach to the reading program is an alternative to
the traditional concept of seatwork, either from ditto sheets or from the chalkboard and done at the students' seat. Using a learning center approach, few

children need to remain seated at their desks and the amount of ditto work is reduced, depending on the extent of center implementation determined by the teacher. The children do have some choice in the activities they do most days and they are sometimes given the opportunity to assume the responsibility for keeping a record of their completed work. Learning centers are often used as very appropriate practice activities but teachers should be cautious not to ignore the teach phase of a lesson presentation.

In planning a learning center the teacher should do the following:

1. Define the purpose.
2. Consider the characteristics of the students to be using the center.
3. Define the concepts or skills to be developed.
4. Outline the expected learning outcomes.
5. Select the appropriate activities and materials.
6. Evaluate the center.
7. Implement needed changes (4).

Learning centers can be set up in any area of a classroom. Corners can be partitioned from the rest of the classroom to give this special group or student just a bit more privacy. Even individual carrels can be provided for students. Quiet, private areas can be very effective for classroom work even if only one or two carrels can be provided for a class. Some teachers provide old bathtubs with cushions so that students can "escape" into their own private world, with a good book, for at least a few moments. Providing listening centers to students is wise also, not only because it is a valuable experience but because it offers a nice variety or change from the typical teacher-student lesson.

The material or ideas that are used for these centers can be gathered from the teacher's manual of the reading text, the reading workbooks, any old unused reading book, or the books currently published. Teachers find it very helpful to pay close attention to the reading skills that students need to develop and then make the centers fit these needs. After all, one of the purposes of a learning center is to further develop a specific skill.

Some teachers find the learning center approach a difficult one to implement because of the time required to prepare the individual centers. Not only is time required in beginning the center approach but a maintenance time is necessary in keeping the centers current for the students' needs. Teachers must keep replacing centers weekly, biweekly, or as frequently as they feel it is appropriate to get the best educational use from these centers. Sometimes, too, it is difficult to guide students into using centers in a classroom because of teacher disorganization or student attitude. If a teacher is not fully prepared to implement the centers or if the students have not been shown the procedure for their use, then many problems may arise. Usually with an adequate amount of preplanning, these problems can be avoided.

Listening Centers Contribute to the Further Development of Specific Reading Skills.

Centers have been used effectively in many classrooms. The following points favor the learning center approach:

1. Children are given some choice in planning their daily activities.
2. Language arts can be correlated with other subject areas.
3. Children are given a chance for purposeful movement. It is difficult for most young children to sit for long periods of time.
4. Children are encouraged to develop a greater sense of responsibility and self-discipline.
5. Self-evaluation is encouraged for all students.
6. A teacher can be freed from constantly creating daily seatwork assignments once the program is initiated.
7. Children can partake of a greater variety of activities.

Centers of all types and constructed for all purposes can contribute very effectively to the development of independent work habits. The students must learn to read the directions carefully and think them through step-by-step. This is a reading skill that more adults should learn! For those students not yet able to read, a taped message can be used or simple directional pictures can be posted. Tape players as well as audio-flashcard readers, computers, and so on can all be used effectively in well-planned learning centers.

Students Can Learn to Work Independently at Learning Centers, Freeing the Teacher for Small Group Instruction.

Even allowing and encouraging students to develop their own centers is enjoyable and also profitable. One interesting center was constructed by a fourth grader who was interested in feathers. She collected many varieties of feathers from actual animals, gathered identification books and pictures, and developed a picture-identification center. The creator of such a center might do specific research on a chosen topic and then carefully plan an accompanying learning center. Having the student write complete step-by-step directions for the center, decide those necessary materials to place with the center, actually construct or design the creation, and explain how to use the center to fellow classmates are all worthwhile skills for students to develop in a classroom setting.

No matter what center ideas are implemented, the teacher should continually evaluate the following concerns related to the use of centers in the classroom.

1. The difficulty level of the center.
2. The age of the students using the center.

Teachers Find Learning Centers to Be an Effective Management Tool.

3.   The interests and needs of the students.
4.   The students' developmental reading levels.

With continual consideration and evaluation of these major points about learning centers, the classroom teacher should experience many more successes with this management tool.

TIPS TO ENHANCE ONE'S MANAGEMENT PLANS

Once the teacher has developed a philosophy about management for the reading class and has the skills to make it all run smoothly, he/she should strive to keep improving. Good management techniques and sound teaching strategies are highly related. The following suggestions should be of help in enabling one to become not only a better teacher but a more efficient and productive manager of a classroom.

Add Variety to One's Instruction

Every classroom teacher needs to alter the instructional approach to the extent that classroom activities do not become totally predictable every day. If the students know that they are going to do the same types of activities, under

much the same conditions, at nearly the same time *every* day, they will undoubtedly become bored and disinterested with school activities. Often these conditions encourage discipline problems. A scheduled day is very important, but there are many ways to vary instruction and still not completely destroy a schedule. Some of these techniques to vary one's classroom instruction and related activities are quite easy to implement with just a small amount of pre-planning.

If there is a shady tree or trees near the school a reading activity could be held outside occasionally. Discussing the behavior expected in this situation will usually eliminate discipline-related problems. Another activity could be offering one's students either walking or bussed field trips to places of student interest. Visits to such places as grocery stores, factories, bakeries, ice cream shops, and butcher shops could be easily correlated with classroom reading instruction leading to many pleasant, productive activities. Inviting parents into the classroom to talk about their professions might also prove interesting. Introducing music into a reading lesson or creative writing into a language lesson will add a spark to one's instruction.

The following list provides more ideas that might give a variety to one's instructional plans:

1. If reading instruction is usually held in the morning, sometimes have it in the afternoon. Or if one always has math just before lunch or at the end of the day, change it to a different time.

2. Suggest special art projects that are correlated to a certain story. A papier-mâché puppy to accompany a story about dogs may be just enough stimulation for a student to want to read about dogs another time. Art projects must be sensibly planned so they can be completed in an appropriate amount of time and still be worthwhile enough to enhance the reading experience of the students. Students might also enjoy working on an art project either individually or in a small group for the duration of a few days. These students can work on the project in their spare time or during reading class or the teacher can assign a certain amount of time each day for the project. Either way, it offers the students a constructive activity and frees one to work with other students. Some art projects that might require several days to complete are diorama book reports in a shoe box, murals depicting story events, mobiles for related subjects, or individual books written and illustrated by students.

3. Organize a special play with a reading group. Two groups can work together for some plays. One can do the actual performing while the other group can make the scenery and organize the props. There are also programs to make, costumes to create, and invitations to distribute to other classes. All these different activities can provide valu-

Student Art Projects Enhance a Teacher's Reading Instruction.

able experience for the students as well as keep them productively occupied in a classroom.

4. Allow certain students to be teacher helpers. Students can do much to help each other if given the opportunity. They could be encouraged to help other children with practice sheets, assist in reading directions to center games, distribute papers, aid others in completing workbook pages, locate information in the library, and many more tasks.

5. Invite other students to join certain reading groups. There are many subjects/topics in the basal readers that would be very enjoyable for students other than those directly placed in the reading group through diagnostic procedures. The teacher can invite, once in a while, all those students interested in airplanes, to read about, listen to, or discuss a story about such a topic. Even if the story is not on the instructional reading level of each student, a few such experiences will prove quite enjoyable and all participants will gain from the occasion.

6. Altering one's room arrangement can be refreshing. Just changing the location of desks or other furniture in a room will give everyone some different scenery at which to look.

7. Provide independent work packets (previously referred to in this chapter as agendas) for students sometimes rather than always writing assignments and practice activities on the board. Include all work sheets, vocabulary words, comprehension questions, and enrichment activities in a packet for each student in a reading group. The agendas merely serve as a structure for independent activities related to reading group instruction.

Be Open to New Ideas

One's own creativity and instructional "good sense" provide unlimited ways to enrich instruction and keep it "alive" for the students. Every teacher can benefit from hearing or reading about new methods and ideas in the area of elementary reading instruction. Certain approaches or techniques seem to work more effectively, but there are still others that may be even better with which one is just not familiar. Thus, one should be flexible enough to seek new ideas or alternative approaches and attempt to implement them in one's reading class instruction. Of course, one should not try everything and anything that comes along, but at least one should attempt to implement those things that seem logical and sensible.

Attending professional meetings, listening to speakers, and reading from professional literature are just a few of the ways that a teacher might be introduced to new methods or ideas related to the teaching of reading and effective

classroom management. Some professional meetings that would prove beneficial to teachers would be sponsored by such groups as statewide teacher's organizations, the National Education Association, the International Reading Association, and the National Council of Teachers of English. There are numerous professional magazines such as *The Instructor*, *The Reading Teacher*, and *Language Arts* that would also be of interest to teachers. A teacher should take advantage of the professional literature and professional meetings to keep informed about new ideas or techniques. Talking with other teachers and even the principal about them might also help one to "sort through one's thinking" and decide how certain activities can best be implemented in the classroom. Teachers can also inform their administrative staff about outstanding programs that might be of interest to the entire faculty. By working together as an educational/instructional team, teachers and administrators can continue to improve the quality of the opportunities that are offered to their students.

Do Not Expect Miracles—Right Away

The items presented and discussed in this chapter on the subject of effective classroom management as related to reading instruction require much patience and time to implement to their fullest. Moving into new educational arenas should be done cautiously and slowly so that techniques and methods can be evaluated and assessed for their effectiveness. Also, it is important to remember that something that fails once may work beautifully in another situation or setting. It is also very difficult for a beginning teacher to attempt to implement all of these suggestions in one month at the beginning of school. It is better to select activities or ideas that seem appropriate, establish some guidelines for their implementation, and evaluate their effectiveness in the classroom.

ONGOING EVALUATION OF ONE'S CLASSROOM MANAGEMENT

An ongoing evaluation must take place for effective or lasting results to occur in any reading classroom. In addition to one's own professional judgment as to how one's management techniques are working for students, there are also more formal evaluation procedures to use. Included in Figure 9-9 is an evaluation form that teachers can use in evaluating their management techniques. The purpose of this form is to provide some structure and consistency in judging the management techniques that are being implemented.

The teacher's evaluation form was created to offer assistance to the teacher who is concerned with making classroom management more effective and ultimately to make reading instruction more effective. The form is primarily concerned with the management of reading instruction, including learning

center implementation, lesson planning, scheduling, and quality of independent activities. A teacher is given the opportunity to self-evaluate in the categories referring to how often certain conditions are implemented in the classroom: usually, sometimes, or never. For instance, one statement for the teacher to

Name	Date		
	Usually	Sometimes	Never
1. My students can work independently on center activities.			
2. My students can work quietly in small group activities when appropriate.			
3. I feel comfortable when coordinating my reading groups during instructional times.			
4. I can pace the work of my students to keep them productively involved.			
5. I keep records of my student's on-task behaviors.			
6. My learning centers and supplemental activities are correlated to my instruction.			
7. My lesson plans are written in advance of the day they are taught.			
8. I vary my reading instruction periodically.			
9. My students know the schedule and are informed of daily changes.			
10. I preplan for the effective use of my teacher aide.			
11. I provide appropriate independent activities to extend my instruction.			
12. I keep my room organized with supplies and materials kept in designated areas.			

FIGURE 9-9. Teachers Self-Evaluation Form for Management Techniques.

	Usually	Sometimes	Never
13. I search for and use ideas suggested in professional literature.			

Comments: _____

_____

_____

_____

Goals to be accomplished to help improve my management skills before my next evaluation.

_____

_____

_____

_____

Teacher	Principal

FIGURE 9-9. *(Continued)*

evaluate is "My students can work independently on certain activities." The teacher would mark a check in the box under the category usually, sometimes, or never, referring to how the students actually react to learning center work. If a teacher checks "never" and really wants to begin effective center work, the above statement might give the teacher some direction. Especially helpful to the teacher is to date the form when it is completed. If one form is completed in the first half of the year and another toward the end of the second half of the year a teacher could check to see if some or all areas show some improvement from the first evaluation to the second.

Students are individuals and it is very important to them that the teacher understand their needs and desires. Having built the student's confidence and gained respect, one can develop a positive cooperative attitude in the reading classroom. The teacher can set a good example and show students how hard work can be enjoyable, worthwhile, and productive. The students will usually look to the teacher to set an example, so one must create the type of "reading" atmosphere that will be most conducive for instruction. The teacher's goal is to not only inspire these students to become better people but also to help them develop into inquisitive skilled readers.

Teachers should provide activities that are educationally worthwhile and of high quality. Reading worksheets, comprehension games, or related activities require carefully worded directions so they are easily understood by the students. The displays should be attractive and current so that students can asso-

ciate or relate to activities. Some displays about popular singing groups or current movies spark more interest when correlated with a reading-skills practice of any kind. It is helpful and time-saving for the teacher to provide a variety of activities or displays that provide worksheets easily switched or replaced without a total display change.

Effective classroom management can be accomplished by the preplanning and implementation of sound educational practices. The ultimate purpose of good classroom management is to improve the reading ability of one's students. With proper direction from a teacher, the students can develop mentally as well as socially in a classroom environment that builds confidence and self-esteem. These management suggestions, if implemented consistently and wisely, can improve both the student's scholastic performance and thinking ability. Motivating students to reach toward the uppermost limits of their ability is a responsibility that concerns all educators. After all, a teacher who is an effective classroom manager develops students who are not only good readers and independent thinkers, but who are also interested, motivated learners.

SUMMARY

Classroom management involves many aspects of the teaching day. Once students have been diagnosed and their reading needs determined and organized into a systematic plan, the components of management can be implemented. How each teacher operates the reading group or individuals, coordinates activities, encourages independent student work, or continually evaluates his/her performance in the classroom is the essence of classroom management. In order to develop a management plan teachers must (1) become familiar with overall goals and objectives and (2) plan for instruction.

Effective classroom management depends to a great extent on using teaching time wisely. To plan instructional reading time teachers must (1) decide on the amount of time for reading instruction, (2) decide the duration of the instructional time segments, (3) determine the group or individual for whom instruction will begin, (4) decide how to begin their reading period, (5) plan how to move from group to group, and (6) decide on independent activities.

The effective use of space will lead to more effective classroom management and a more efficient utilization of materials and resources. Poor preplanning for space utilization can lead to failure for the best teaching. Proper storage of textbooks and supplies can also improve classroom management.

Effective management has also been linked to teaching style, student independence, self-control, and discipline. The time a teacher spends in continually developing these positive traits will in turn affect the quality and quantity of instruction. A reading teacher who is an effective classroom manager develops students who are not only good readers and independent thinkers but who are also interested, motivated learners.

THOUGHT AND DISCUSSION QUESTIONS

1. List the components that would be essential to effective classroom management. Compare your list to the discussion of classroom management in this chapter.
2. Why is it so important to be concerned with effective classroom management in a reading program?
3. What is the importance of a lesson plan in the teaching of reading?
4. How are student independence and self-control important in an elementary reading program?
5. What are the pros and cons of any new innovative idea in the teaching of reading?

APPLYING WHAT YOU HAVE LEARNED

1. Interview several elementary principals to examine their building goals and reading skills checklists. Do these written statements agree or disagree with your philosophy of reading instruction?
2. After working with a reading group, decide three specific goals or objectives that would benefit this entire group. How would you go about accomplishing these goals with this group?
3. Create your own classroom arrangement by drawing a scale model of a room setting. Explain how you will use each section of the room.
4. Interview elementary teachers to discover their viewpoint on discipline. Ask them how they control their reading classes—what techniques seem effective, what problem areas sometimes arise, how they develop self-control in their students, and so on.
5. View several elementary teachers' lesson plans to see how the more experienced teachers use the lesson plan approach.
6. Set up your own tentative schedule of a "typical" reading/language arts time. Be sure to coordinate at least three reading groups and include productive seatwork activities. Be ready to defend your decisions.
7. Referring to your newly created schedule, plan what you will say to your reading groups to get the reading/language-arts class started.

BIBLIOGRAPHY

1. Brophy, J., and Putnam, J. "Classroom Management in the Elementary Grades," in D. Duke, ed., "Classroom Management," in *Yearbook for the National Society for the Study of Education*. Chicago: University of Chicago Press, 1979, pp. 182–216.

2. Clarizio, Harvey F. *Toward Positive Classroom Discipline*, 3rd ed. New York: John Wiley & Sons, Inc., 1980.

3. Clark, Christopher M., and Yinger, Robert J. *The Hidden World of Teaching: Implications of Research on Teacher Planning.* Lansing, Mich.: Michigan State University, 1980. ERIC Document Reproduction Service No. ED 191 844.

4. "Designing the Science Learning Center." *Science and Children,* 14 (1976), 11–12.

5. Doyle, Walter. *Classroom Management.* West Lafayette, Ind.: Kappa Delta Pi, An Honor Society in Education, 1980.

6. Duke, David L., ed. "Classroom Management," in *The Seventy-eighth Yearbook of the National Society for the Study of Education.* Chicago: University of Chicago Press, 1970.

7. Johnson, Lois V., and Bany, Mary A. *Classroom Management.* New York: Macmillan Company, 1970.

8. Kounin, Jacob S. *Discipline and Group Management in Classrooms.* New York: Robert E. Krieger Publishing Company, 1977.

9. Peterson, P. L.; Marx, R. W., and Clark, C. M. "Teacher Planning, Teacher Behavior and Student Achievement." *American Educational Research Journal,* 15 (1978), 417–432.

10. Spache, George D., and Spache, Evelyn B. *Reading in the Elementary School,* 4th ed. Boston: Allyn & Bacon, Inc., 1977.

11. Tanner, Laurel N. "A Model of School Discipline," in Elizabeth Hirzler Weiner, ed., *Discipline in the Classroom,* 2nd ed. Washington, D. C.: National Education Association, 1980.

12. Workman, E., and Hector, M. "Self-control in Classroom Settings: A Review of the Literature." *Journal of School Psychology,* 16 (1978), 227–236.

FOR FURTHER READING

Allen, Roach Van, and Allen, Claryce. *Language Experience Activities.* Boston: Houghton Mifflin Company, 1976.

Clarizio, Harvey F. *Toward Positive Classroom Discipline*, 3rd ed. New York: John Wiley & Sons, Inc., 1980.

"Classroom Management: A Rule Establishment and Enforcement Model." *Elementary School Journal,* 78 (Mar. 1978), 254–63.

"Classroom Seating Arrangements: Instructional Communication Theory Versus Student Preferences." *Communication Education,* 27 (Mar. 1978), 99–111.

Doyle, Walter. *Classroom Management.* West Lafayette, Ind.: Kappa Delta Pi, An Honor Society in Education, 1980.

Duke, David L., ed. "Classroom Management," in *The Seventy-eighth Yearbook of the National Society for the Study of Education.* Chicago: University of Chicago Press, 1979.

Forte, Imogene, and Mackenzie, Joy. *Nooks, Crannies and Corners.* Nashville: Incentive Publications, Inc., 1972.

Gambrell, L. B. "Extending Think-time for Better Reading Instruction." *Education Digest,* 46 (Feb. 1981), 33–35.

Kaplan, Sandra; Kaplan, Jo Ann; Madsden, Sheila; and Taylor, Bette. *Change for Children.* Pacific Palisades, CA: Goodyear Publishing Co., Inc., 1973.

Kindsvatter, R., and Levine, M. A. "Myths of Discipline." *Phi Delta Kappan,* 61 (1980), 690–693.

Kounin, Jacob S. *Discipline and Group Management in Classrooms.* Huntington, N.Y.: Robert E. Krieger Publishing Company, 1977.

"Playing the Game: A Behavioral Approach to Classroom Management in the Junior School." *Educational Review*, **30**(Feb. 1978), 41–50.

Shrigley, R. L. "Strategies in Classroom Management." *Education Digest*, **45** (1979), 7–10.

"Ten Steps to Good Discipline." *Today's Education*, **66** (1977), 61–63.

Thomas, John I. *Learning Centers: Opening Up the Classroom.* Boston: Holbrook Press, Inc., 1975.

Tjosvold, D. "Control, Conflict, and Collaboration in the Classroom." *Education Digest*, **45** (1980), 17–20.

Weiner, Elizabeth Hirzler, ed. *Discipline in the Classroom*, 2nd rev. ed. Washington, D.C.: National Educational Association, 1980.

chapter 10

relating the reading program to all areas of the curriculum

objectives

As a result of reading this chapter one will be able to

1. Know the relationship between the diagnostic reading program and content teaching.
2. Utilize content textbooks as tools in reading instruction.
3. Employ appropriate techniques and methods that will assist students in reading content materials.
4. Construct unit plans that will combine reading and other subjects taught.

overview

The diagnostic/prescriptive reading program must encompass the content classes in the elementary curriculum. The concept of content teaching will be discussed in its relation to reading instruction. Practical suggestions will be presented and explained in regard to using content area textbooks, supplying additional help to students having difficulty reading the texts, and writing units of study that combine all the subjects taught in an elementary classroom with reading.

In reading this chapter the teacher can draw on knowledge of the

previous chapters presented in this text, for without the understandings of assessment, organization, and management one's content area teaching cannot be as effective as it could be. Relating to the content areas will involve all five steps in the diagnostic teaching process:

1. Gather relevant information about each student.
2. Generate alternative action.
3. Evaluate alternatives and select ones to carry out.
4. Teach.
5. Evaluate results.

The content areas of the elementary curriculum are those subjects other than reading, such as social studies, science, or mathematics. They are referred to as content areas because they contain the subject matter (content) information that is included in the elementary curriculum. Content teaching can be described as teaching the content that is contained in these special subject areas.

Content teaching requires the utilization of subject area textbooks and includes the active involvement of all reading skills. Instruction in the content areas calls for the application of reading skills that have been taught and practiced during formal reading instruction. "Teachers tend to devote more attention to the concepts of social studies, science, and mathematics than to the reading skills necessary to comprehend these subject areas" (6, p. 287). An effective diagnostic reading teacher must become more aware of implementing the reading skills in content areas.

THE DIAGNOSTIC READING PROGRAM AND CONTENT TEACHING

Teachers should actively use the content areas in extending and applying reading skills. Students need to realize that reading is more than merely using a basal reader. A large number of basal reader stories are structured with an introduction, action of characters around a developed plot, and some sort of a conclusion. However, the newer basal readers do include subjects related to the content areas to some degree. In contrast to the basal reader, content texts contain mostly factual material about a subject that may or may not be familiar to the student. Figure 10-1 shows a few of the basic differences between basal readers and content textbooks.

Basal Readers	Content Textbooks
Controlled vocabulary	Technical vocabulary
Stories centered around plot and the action of characters	Information presented in straightforward manner
Subjects or story content related to reader background and experience	Content/concepts often abstract and not related to reader background and experience
Readability levels controlled	Because of technical vocabulary and concept density per page readability is generally above intended grade level
Pictures enhance stories	Charts, graphs, and figures explain

FIGURE 10-1. Differences Between Basal Readers and Content Textbooks.

Content textbooks may require that the teacher assist students in using the technical vocabulary and in comprehending the information (6). Therefore, when one plans lessons in the content areas, they should be structured so they will be of the utmost help to the students. In this chapter are suggestions to help present content material so that it is meaningful and useful to students.

Reading skills can be applied in the content areas. Such activities as using an outline for an oral report in social studies, making graphs and charts to illustrate a science project, or using the card catalog in collecting material for a health report will all reinforce the idea that reading skills can be used in situations other than basal reading groups. Reading and understanding the newspaper can illustrate to a child how important one's own reading skills are in interpreting the events happening every day.

Accounting for Students' Reading Levels in the Content Areas

As mentioned previously, the teacher must be continuously aware of the reading levels of the students. "[They] must be able to understand 75 percent of the ideas and 90 percent of the vocabulary in a social studies selection in order to read it at an instructional level" (5, p. 5). These percentages must be even higher if the reading is to be at a student's independent level. Bormuth found "that 65 percent of the students in the intermediate grades gain little information from content textbooks" (1). This fact alone should offer a motivation to make content teaching as effective as possible.

Many times it is necessary to alter the already existing content material to make it easier to read for students experiencing difficulties. Either rewriting the material or using different reading material are two alternatives to the problem. In rewriting the material one should simplify it by decreasing the number of technical vocabulary words, replacing certain words in the sentences with those containing fewer syllables (changing beautiful to pretty, for example), and decreasing the number of words or phrases in the sentences. Thus one can offer material that will be more easily understood by the student. This process is time-consuming and not often done by classroom teachers but it is a worthwhile way to provide material at an appropriate reading level.

Even material that is rewritten to a lower level will still present problems for some less able readers. Rewriting will sometimes simplify a passage to such an extent that important concepts are excluded, thus robbing readers of necessary information. When this happens, one must teach the content through other means. It is possible to present important concepts by showing a movie or filmstrip. This makes the concepts quite vivid for the viewer and helps him/her attach meaning to vocabulary words as well as concepts and ideas. The teacher and the students can engage in productive discussions before and after the films, thus guiding the thinking and learning of the students.

Allowing less able students to listen to a tape recording of content material has also been found to be a desirable technique for helping them compre-

hend materials more effectively. Tapes can be made by a teacher's aide, other students, or volunteer parents. The material to be recorded can be read into the tape player, with the person reading into the tape making certain to speak distinctly so all listeners can easily understand the words. Some taped material offers discussion of vocabulary words and concepts as a means of assisting the listener in comprehension.

It might be helpful to read key material containing important facts aloud to the students. By doing this, all students will be exposed to the same material on which one might base a discussion or small group activity. The teacher must be careful to (1) pose purpose questions before the oral reading so students will know why they are listening and (2) continue discussion and questioning during the oral reading to improve the students' comprehension of the material. Reading aloud as described is not the same as round-robin reading. It is not suggested that the students take turns reading aloud. Rather, the teacher should read *specific* material aloud and lead students in a profitable discussion of that material.

Small-group activities may also be very productive for students (see Chapter 6 for a discussion of grouping). By combining more capable readers with less able readers in one small group, students are encouraged to learn from one another. The better readers, in working within the group, can read or interpret more difficult terms and concepts and can guide the group in report making or other relevant activities. The less able reader can play an important role in the group by assisting in locating additional materials or in creating art projects to accompany a report. Students of varying abilities can work together productively with the proper guidance.

In adjusting reading material to lower levels one must not forget to provide a proper challenge to the more capable readers. Supplying reading material at their instructional or independent level will do much to keep them interested. By encouraging the preparation of supplementary reports and/or projects or having them compare information written by several authors, one will enable students to delve into content topics more thoroughly and then share their information with less able readers. It is important to provide capable students with appropriate activities or assignments from which they will profit. Unfortunately, some teachers feel that making the same assignment for the entire group with the capable students only having to do "more of the same" an appropriate challenge. "Appropriate challenge" implies differentiating assignments and activities to benefit a variety of reading abilities.

Using Study Guides

Differentiating assignments and discussion questions among students of varying reading levels can also be done with study guides. A study guide is simply a guide to study. It is a set of questions or activities designed to direct a student's study. Usually a study guide is considered a practice tool to be used

<u>Work on a Dairy Farm</u>

Pages 18–21

Directions:

Everyone should answer questions with no *.

Group 1 answers questions with one *.

Group 2 answers question with two **.

1. What is a dairy farm?_____
   _____

*2. List the three steps in bottling milk.

   1. _____

   2. _____

   3. _____

**3. Why is milk pasteurized in a bottling plant?_____
    _____

TRUE or FALSE: Place on the blank an F for False, T for True.

___4. Dried milk is a powder.

___5. Evaporated milk is spoiled.

Complete each blank.

6. List two uses for milk.

   _____

   _____

7. What kinds of workers are used in bringing the milk from the dairy?

   farm to your table?_____
   _____

FIGURE 10-2. Differentiated Study Guide—Science.

by a teacher in guiding a discussion. A study guide offers guidance to students as they read content material. One major reason for using study guides is to direct the learner's study and help him/her draw out the points that the teacher believes important. A second purpose is to direct the student's reading and assist him/her in reading the given material more effectively (2).

Differentiating thought and discussion questions on a study guide is an excellent method of assisting less able readers as well as challenging more capable students. The questions for the less able readers should more specifically cover given amounts of material. The activities might direct better students to read only certain sections whereas the activities for other students might require them to read the same material but use more critical reading skills. This is illustrated in the following examples:

For Less Able Readers. Read the first two paragraphs on p. 21 and list the three ways that man will be able to use rockets.

For More Able Readers. After reading p. 21, select one of the three ways man will be able to use rockets and explain how you feel it will affect his life.

The first activity is more directed and assists the less able reader in locating the main points of the paragraph. In the second example the student is required to go beyond the point of merely obtaining facts and to do some critical thinking.

Study guides can be used with elementary students in all areas of the content curriculum. There are single-group guides that can be used with small groups, multilevel guides that develop primarily all the levels of comprehension and are quite similar to the differentiated type, and skill-practice guides that focus on one particular reading skill. These guides can be constructed in a question format, fill-in-the-blank format, crossword puzzle format, matching format, or any combination of all of these. The guides can be created for primary students as well as intermediate readers. Figures 10-2, 10-3, and 10-4 illustrate portions of the various study guides discussed.

When preparing a study guide for student use, several points must be kept in mind. Figure 10-5 is a teacher checklist to help one construct the most useful study guides possible.

The Civil War

Pages 46–53

As you read these pages, your group should use the following questions to guide it's reading. After you read, as a group, decide the answers to the questions and write them in the blanks.

1. List the three major causes of the Civil War.

    A. _____

    B. _____

    C. _____

2. What does the term "prejudice" mean? _____

    _____

3. How did Lincoln play a part in the history of the Civil War? _____

    _____

    _____

4. How did the Civil War affect our country today? _____

    _____

FIGURE 10-3. Single Group Guide—Social Studies.

Settling the New Land

Chapter 8, pgs. 126–142

Sequence:

Number the following from 1 to 6 as they appeared on the Santa Fe Trail.

Use page 133 of your book.

____ Wagon Train went to Dodge City.

____ They climbed the foothills and crossed to Santa Fe.

____ Traders loaded their wagons with goods from the east.

____ Most wagons took short cuts across the Cimarron Plain.

____ Made a ten day trip across the prairies to Council Grove.

____ Began at a point along the Missouri River.

Classifying:

Mark the following with either a "1" if the statement means the Mormons were like other settlers in this way or a "2" if the Mormons were unlike other settlers in this way.

____ The Mormons decided to settle in the Great Basin. (138)

____ They crossed the Great Plains and Rocky Mountains. (138)

____ They chose a place to live with water. (139)

____ Individual families owned no land. (139)

____ Each man had more than one wife. (140)

FIGURE 10-4. Skill Practice Guide—Social Studies.

USING A CONTENT TEXTBOOK EFFECTIVELY

The reading of a content textbook must be guided by the teacher with just the amount of assistance needed to make the reading most beneficial. Study guides, as mentioned, provide some assistance, but study guides do not provide the total solution. One technique that guides the reading and thinking of students quite effectively is the Directed Reading/Thinking Activity (DRTA) as it applies to content material.

Employing a Directed Reading/Thinking Activity Model in Content Areas

The DRTA format can be a guide to the teacher in the presentation of content material. The format can be used with entire chapters or with selected information covering just a few pages. Study guides can also be used within the DRTA format.

I.   Presentation and General Format

       Are sub-topics listed?

       Are page numbers present for easy referral?

       Is the guide legible?

       Is it appropriate for the intended grade level?

       Is the guide easy to follow?

II. Directions

       Are directions clearly and precisely stated?

       Are they included at the beginning of the guide and anywhere

       else that is necessary?

III. Organization

       Is there a sequence to the guide?

       Are vocabulary words, comprehension questions, and enrichment

       activities included?

IV. Variety of Questions

       Are there factual and inference/critical thinking questions

       included?

       Are there matching questions included?

       Can some questions be answered with just one word?

       Do some answers need to be written in complete sentences?

V.   Usefulness

       Does study guide fulfill purpose of writer (class discussion,

       outlining, test preparation, etc.)?

FIGURE 10-5. Evaluation of a Study Guide.

• *Skill Building.* During this step the teacher might want to review a specific skill prior to its use in the content material, such as recalling factual information, inference of main idea, or outlining. The students will not be able to use a skill until they have been taught it and allowed to practice it. This skill-building step, even when using it with content material, is a crucial component of the DRTA, uses the teach and practice parts of the Instructional Skills Model, and should not be overlooked.

• *Preparation for Guided Silent Reading.* The vocabulary and other special terminology are presented. A sample showing new terms presented in written context follows. The science chapter being read for this example is in the area of space and the solar system.

New Words
>revolution
>planet
>solar system
>lunar
>orbit

Possible Sentences
>A *revolution* is the turning of an object.
>One *planet* is considered a part of the entire *solar system.*
>*Lunar* refers to something related to the moon.
>The *orbit* is the path by which the earth travels.

These new words can be discussed. An appropriate practice activity would be to have the students create their own sentences using the new words either orally or written. The students could also do a short activity at their desks involving the matching of the new words to their definitions. Any brief practice activity would be appropriate to make certain that the students recognize and understand the new terms. This practice activity could also be included in a study guide.

Essential in this step of the DRTA is the preparation phase, in which the teacher motivates the students to read the content material—in this example, space—and builds background. The motivation could be a movie or filmstrip about planets or the moon walk. An appropriate discussion might be one in which the students share what they know about the topic of space and what additional information they would like to learn. These activities "set the stage" for the minds of the learners.

Students need to know what to expect from reading content material and what to look for in the process of reading. Purpose statements or questions provide such structure and offer guidance to the student doing the reading. They are structured in such a way as to assist the student in thinking and remembering as the reading is being done.

The following are examples:

—Read pages 216 to 218 to find out the important parts of a flower.

—How would you feel if you were stuck on a glacier? Read to find out what life on a glacier might be like.

—Read Chapter 3 to discover
   1.   The different forms of travel.
   2.   The advantages and disadvantages of each kind of travel.

These statements encourage the students to begin reading and continue until they discover or locate the answers. In doing this their thinking is being guided and in turn comprehension is facilitated.

The purpose statements or questions can be placed on a study guide and used as a basis for discussion of the material after the silent reading takes place.

Students can respond to the questions and locate specific facts in the material to support their answers.

● *Guided Silent Reading.*   Since this is the "heart" of the reading lesson the teacher will want to devote more time and energy to this step. Following is a sample dialogue with a purpose statement that would be appropriate for the content teaching of space and related topics:

Teacher: Now that you have talked about the solar system and shared what you already know about it, read pages 136 and 137 to find out just what is considered as a part of the solar system.

After silent reading the teacher might restate the purpose statement in the form of a question, and then continue with a variety of comprehension questions:

1.   How many planets are in the solar system? (literal comprehension)
2.   Which planet is the largest? (literal comprehension)
3.   What does the word solar mean? (meaning vocabulary)
4.   Who can tell me a synonym for orbit? (meaning vocabulary)
5.   Why must astronauts wear special equipment like in the picture on page 137? (inferential comprehension)
6.   Do you think it is wise for our government to spend so much money on the space program? Why or why not? (critical thinking/reading comprehension)

Such questions could continue throughout the entire reading passage. Younger children might be able to read only one page at a time while more advanced learners could complete an entire chapter for their guided silent reading experience. Teachers must remember, too, to include opportunities for productive oral reading and allow students to read specific facts, prove their answers to questions, or just share interesting sections for others' listening enjoyment. The guided silent reading step should continue for the duration of the reading material. This could mean one class session or several sessions depending on the length of the passage. In the unit plans offered later in this chapter, one can see how guided silent reading has been intertwined with large- and small-group activity work and related written activities. The questions used in this example of guided silent reading would be appropriate for use in a study guide as well.

● *Follow-Up.*   This step is for the purpose of providing further enjoyment about the topic being studied. Here are some sample follow-up activities related to space and the solar system:

1.   Individual or small-group reports on the different planets.
2.   Writing science-fiction books about space.

3. Constructing a scale model of the solar system in the classroom.
4. Making a bulletin-board display on a related topic of interest.
5. Creating a "simulated" trip to outer space.
6. Creating "future" robots that do specially selected chores.

The list could go on and on. However, one should remember to provide a follow-up activity that is both educationally beneficial and at the same time enjoyable for the student.

Introduce Book Parts

It is very important that children in an elementary reading program become familiar with the parts of a textbook and how to use each part. A child who can locate a topic in a textbook, find where certain chapters begin, or demonstrate understanding of a copyright page is well on his/her way to developing independent learning skills. The content textbook can be used effectively for teaching the parts of a book.

Students of all ages and grade levels need to begin learning about such items as the title page, copyright dates, table of contents, glossary, index, and a wide variety of tables, charts, and graphs. Incorporating these book parts into the actual learning activities will demonstrate how important they are to the child. Once children become acquainted with the different book parts, they will begin to read more comfortably and have more confidence in dealing with other books—either in the media center or in other content subjects. The parts of a book are included in the area of study skills and need to be taught, practiced, and applied just as one would do with any other reading skill.

One way to improve children's comprehension abilities is to help them realize how the headings and titles within a chapter can guide their thinking and reading. Whenever a title or subtitle is used, it indicates what is to follow in the written text. Some students develop the habit of skipping over titles and subtitles. They must be helped to realize that these special parts of a chapter do assist them in better understanding of that material.

Chapter introductory questions serving as purpose questions might be included. It is always profitable for students to develop the habit at the end of reading a section to return to the introductory questions and try to answer them. This assists learners in remembering what they have read and also in selecting the most important points from a section or chapter. Some examples of these questions follow:

What are hardwood trees? What does a natural hardwood forest tell you about soil and climate?
Could a village in colonial days grow very large without good farming land nearby? Explain.
Why were the large forests important to the shipping industry?

Special words and terms in boldface print or in italics may appear in a chapter. These are words the author feels are quite important to the understanding of the chapter and should prove helpful for the child. Usually these terms can be presented and reviewed in the vocabulary teaching section of the directed reading lesson. It is a desirable practice, too, to engage the students in using these words as they answer questions during the guided silent reading portion of the lesson. The following is an example of a special vocabulary word as it appears in a paragraph:

> People who do not drive to work need *public transportation*—buses, subways, and the rapid transit. If a city's public transportation is good, it is easier for people to get to work. If it is easier for people to get to work, more businesses will build offices and factories in the city. If public transportation is bad, do you think new businesses will move to progress?

Content textbooks can be utilized in all types of reading/learning situations. Figure 10-6 is a teacher checklist that summarizes some of the considerations that must be made when using content texts with students. In selecting material and incorporating it into one's plans, it might be helpful to answer the questions contained in this checklist.

Specialized Study Skills

The use of content materials can offer many opportunities to teach such special study skills as outlining, note taking, and caption reading. The ability to use these skills can assist the student in comprehending and remembering what is read. One must *teach* these skills before students can *practice* them.

1. Is the reading material appropriate to the objectives of the lesson?

2. Is the reading material suited to the reading levels of my students?

3. Can my students use the textbook effectively—table of contents, index, title page, etc.?

4. Am I aware of the special vocabulary appearing in this text?

5. Do I prepare my students in advance of reading the special vocabulary?

6. Have I decided how to differentiate instruction for this text material?

7. Have I provided supplementary material that is below grade level and above grade level?

8. Have I taught my students to use appropriate reference materials?

9. Can I use this textual material within the DRTA format?

FIGURE 10-6.   Checklist for Using Content Textual Material.

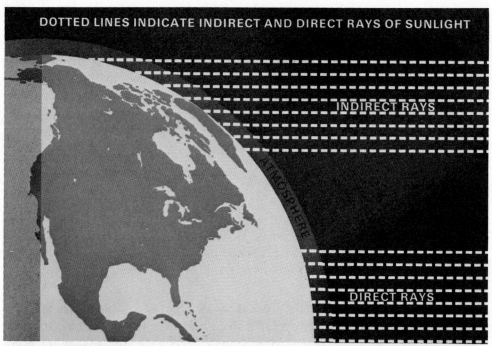

DOTTED LINES INDICATE INDIRECT AND DIRECT RAYS OF SUNLIGHT

INDIRECT RAYS

ATMOSPHERE

DIRECT RAYS

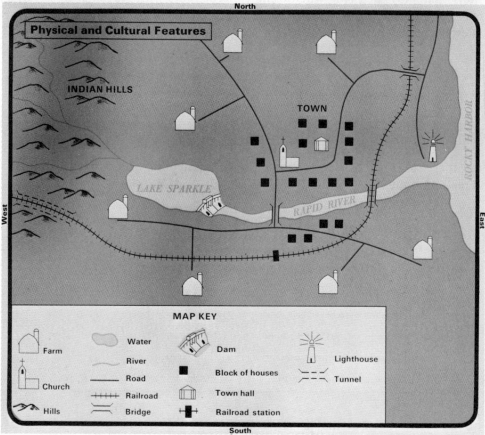

North

Physical and Cultural Features

INDIAN HILLS

TOWN

LAKE SPARKLE

RAPID RIVER

ROCKY HARBOR

West

East

MAP KEY

Farm

Church

Hills

Water

River

Road

Railroad

Bridge

Dam

Block of houses

Town hall

Railroad station

Lighthouse

Tunnel

South

Understanding Captions and Maps Will Improve a Child's Comprehension of Social Studies Material.

Outlining must be demonstrated to students before they will gain the skills to do it independently. The same is true for note taking. By using an overhead projector, for example, one can show students how to begin the process of either note taking or outlining. By encouraging them to take notes or outline a short segment of material with the teacher's guidance, one will build their ability and their confidence with the skills.

Reading and understanding the captions under pictures, charts, illustrations, and graphs will improve the comprehension of material. Young readers (and adult readers) need to be encouraged to use these extensions of the text and not be allowed to skip them in their reading. The teacher should present special lessons to the students dwelling on the captions, what they say, and how they add to the textual material. One can also include the discussion of pictures, charts, and graphs within the guided silent reading so students can come to realize their full importance.

IMPLEMENTING THE CONTENT TEXT INTO INSTRUCTIONAL PROCEDURES

For many teachers the textbook is the primary source used for content teaching. Because of this it is suggested that the content text be incorporated into the unit (resource) plan approach. A unit plan, or resource plan as it is sometimes called, is a unit of study centering around one content-related suject. The subjects could be a variety of topics from "the foods we eat" to "the history of California." Any content subject can be developed into a unit that can be used with students. A unit pulls together both content instruction and reading instruction under one organized plan. "As its name implies, a resource unit is a collection of materials, activities, and resources related to an area or topic and organized in a functional way, which a teacher uses in planning and developing a unit of work" (3, p. 437).

Steps in Unit Planning

Described in this section are the steps in constructing a content unit with emphasis on reading. After the steps have been presented and discussed, examples of units will be shown.

Step. 1. Identify Objectives.   Once a general topic has been decided upon by the teacher or teacher and students cooperatively, the unit objectives need to be identified. These objectives will guide the teacher in developing special learning activities. "Specialists in instructional design generally advocate thinking about objectives in behavioral terms" (4, p. 254). This means that teachers need to describe the observable behavior that would indicate mastery

of the stated objective. These objectives should be written for the purpose of developing specific content areas as well as specific reading skills.

One general objective for a social studies unit might be to develop skill in map reading. In behavioral terms a more specific statement of this objective would be "The student will tell what direction the Great Lakes Region is from Alabama." In this objective the student must know how to use a map (symbols, orientation, and so on—a skill of reading—and locate specific places—a skill related to the content area.

Step 2. Select Activities. The activities selected and lessons created must be appropriate to develop both the content and reading objectives identified in Step 1. If several teachers are working together to create a unit they might use a technique called brainstorming. They identify a topic such as "Growing Seeds" (see Figure 10-7), list all the content areas as well as the language arts around this topic, and proceed to brainstorm activities relating to seeds that can be done with students. These activities can be evaluated and placed in an order of presentation by the participating teachers. The same brainstorming approach can be used by one teacher in unit planning also.

Once all the kinds of activities are listed, the teacher(s) must decide specifically which ones will be used for the unit. For instance, Figure 10-7 shows experience stories listed under language arts. At this point the teacher(s) would identify what "experience" can be provided that is related to growing seeds. Could it be an experience of planting a garden? Or could it be a field trip to a garden nursery? Either activity could become the "experience" for which the students could write.

Step 3. Identify Needed Materials. Once a variety of activities has been identified the next step is to gather the appropriate materials that will prove to be the vehicles in teaching the unit objectives. Teachers must first check the inventory lists of their own classrooms to see what appropriate material might be available, such as content textbooks, supplementary books, reference books, reading books, games, charts, maps, and many other items.

In gathering material the teacher can delve into the resources available in her/his media center, from other teachers, throughout the school system, or in the community. Card catalogs contain information that is available from most of these sources. This material must be gathered and organized so that one can select the most appropriate information for the learning activities identified.

Step 4. Develop Timeline for the Unit. With all the activities decided and the materials organized in a sequential order of presentation, one must decide the exact time schedule for the unit. A time schedule need not be rigidly adhered to but it does offer a structure for teaching and helps one pace the learning activities. A time schedule encourages one to preplan and think through the activities carefully before they are presented to students. Deciding

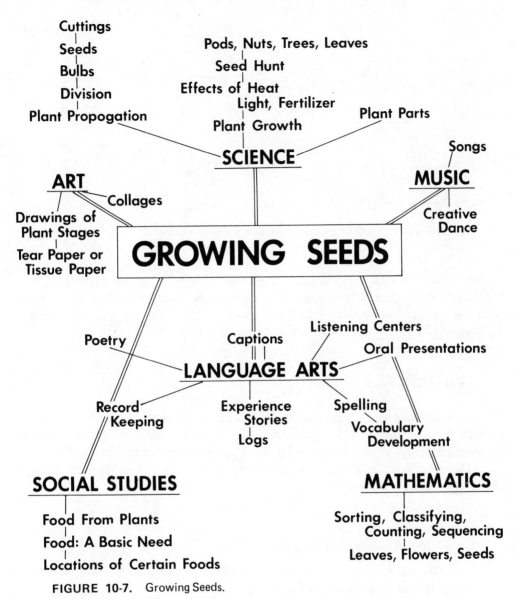

FIGURE 10-7.   Growing Seeds.

the duration of one unit will also indicate to the teacher approximately when a new unit should begin. Some units may last for two weeks while others may take two or even three months to complete.

Step 5. Plan Evaluation Procedures.   Every activity worth doing in a classroom is in turn worth some type of evaluation and this applies to a unit. The evaluation procedure must be planned in advance so that the chosen objectives can properly prepare the students. Teachers who create units around behavioral objectives can easily measure the child's performance against each

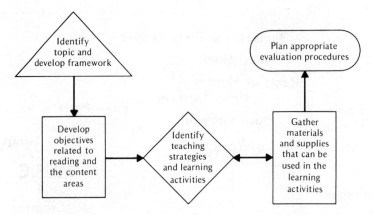

FIGURE 10-8. Flow Chart for Developing a Resource Unit.

stated objective. Other evaluation procedures might be implemented in the form of written tests, individual or small-group projects, or general discussion with the teacher. A summary in the form of a flow chart appears in Figure 10-8 identifying the steps to follow in developing a unit.

Sample Unit Plans

Included in this section are samples of unit plans that have been implemented in classrooms. The organizational techniques used in the writing of these plans were formed so as to offer the utmost assistance to the teacher.

The first sample is an excerpt taken from a science unit dealing with chemistry-related subjects.

Compounds, Acids, Bases
6th-grade level, 29 students

General Objective: The student will observe and participate in activities that deal with compounds, acids, and bases.

Individual Session Outline:

Specific Objective: Given models of selected elements, the student will demonstrate the theory of how atoms combine to make compounds.

Activities:

1. Observe formulas of several common compounds. Discuss meanings of letters and numbers and how elements combine in specific ways to make compounds.
   Materials and supplies: Overhead projector, pens.

2. Students will cut out models of different elements and combine them to make compounds. They will write the formulas for these compounds.

    Materials and supplies: Scissors, sheet with models of elements for each student, paper, pencil (activity 20, pp. 130–131 in *Science and You*).

3. Guided silent reading of page 129 in text. Using models, review how compounds are made. Have students make an outline of how compounds are made.

    Materials and supplies: Student-made models of compounds, notebook papers, pencils, and student textbooks.

Evaluation of Session: Given models of four elements (H, Na, Cl, O), the student will demonstrate the theory by which these atoms combine to make compounds.

The next example will illustrate how objectives can be written and used as the basis for development of the unit. The first portion of the outline lists the specific content to be studied.

A. Broad Area Title: "All About Our Bodies" (foods and nutrition).
B. Specific Sub topics in Support of Broad Area.
    1. Parts of the body and their purposes.
        a. Functions of organs.
        b. How organs work together.
    2. Foods in relation to a healthy body.
        a. Basic food groups.
        b. Deficiencies.
    3. Foods from other countries.
C. Understandings (what you want the student to know).
    1. The student will know the four basic food groups.
    2. The student will know the following body parts and their functions:
        a. Brain.
        b. Teeth and mouth.
        c. Heart and lungs.
        d. Stomach.
        e. Skeleton.
    3. The student will know the value of food in relation to good health.
    4. The student will know how the habitat in which people live affects the food one eats.
    5. The student will understand the relationship of economics to the food one eats.

    6.   The student will learn to prepare her/his own well-balanced breakfast.

    7.   The student will learn the effects of a poor diet.

C.   Attitudes.

    1.   To appreciate the value of the proper foods.

    2.   To appreciate the human body and its functional operations.

    3.   To recognize food differences among cultural regions with empathy.

    4.   To recognize the cost of food.

D.   Evaluation measures.

    1.   The student will locate and describe the important organs of the human body on a worksheet.

    2.   The student will keep a three-day record of everything eaten. This record will be evaluated according to the four basic food groups.

    3.   The student will list the four basic food groups and write several examples of each group.

    4.   The teacher and student informally evaluate discussions and student ability to complete activities and assignments.

Sources Used

A.   Filmstrips.
The Food We Eat
Food Comes from Many Places
Food for Big City
Food, Fuel for the Body
Human Factories

B.   Films.
Food and Nutrition
Citrus Fruits
Food Around the World

C.   Sound Filmstrips.
How Food Becomes You
Food Makes the Difference

D.   Books.
Food (Ames)
Food Is for Eating (Podendorf)
Food for People (Riedman)
Food Industry and Trade (Graham)
Food Service (Baker)
This Hungry World (Holfman)
The Human Body (Wilson)

This example not only offered sample objectives but also demonstrated how sources for the unit could be listed. It is sometimes beneficial, too, to have

listed the source of the films, books, and so on for easy and convenient locating when they will be used in the unit.

The next excerpt from a sample unit plan entitled "Occupations of the Town and Country" will show how each class session was planned and written into the unit. The teacher should note how reading and writing skills were integrated within the listed sessions.

DAILY SESSIONS

Session 1: Students will begin thinking about different occupations. They will write a paragraph and create an illustration of what their fathers and mothers do for a living. Students will discuss why their parents' respective jobs are important and what service they provide for the community.
Orally define:

> work
> pleasure
> employment

Discuss briefly and use in sentences.
Homework assignment: Students will bring in pictures of different jobs or people working at those jobs.

Session 2: Students will think about "What I would like to do when I grow up" and make an illustration and write a few sentences telling about the occupation, why they selected it, and how it helps the community.

Session 3: Students will show and discuss the pictures collected from the assignment in Session 1. The following terms will be presented in context and discussed:

> a. services
> b. producers
> c. goods
> d. agriculture
> e. manufacturing

The pictures will then be classified into two types: services and producers. Mobiles and murals will be made with the pictures.

Session 4: Guided silent reading on pages 2–7 in *Industry: Man and Machine.* Discussion questions relating to goods and services will also be presented.

Session 5: Have students decide the category (agriculture, manufacturing, services) for each parent occupation. On the chalkboard tabulate the occupations for each category.

Discussion questions related to session 5:

Is each of the three categories represented? If not, why not?

Are more parents in manufacturing than in services? Why or why not? Explain the chart on page 7.

Session 6: All students drink glasses of Kool-Aid and discuss the concept of consumer. Terms such as supply and demand will be related to discussion.

Question: What would happen if each person had to go to a well to get a drink of water? (demand)

Discussion will lead to the importance of industrialization. Relate past learnings (Inventors and Pioneers) to problem of supply and demand. Students will make a list of things that are consumable.

(There was a total of 38 sessions in this unit.)

Evaluation by Teacher

Through observation of people at work students will be able to classify occupations and tell in what area they belong, using vocabulary words learned in the unit.

By using terminology and new words learned, the students will question people in the community about their respective occupations.

Students will demonstrate their knowledge of an assembly line by participating in a mock "canning factory" work situation.

Students will understand the concept of profit and loss in business through an evaluation of a classroom crafts fair.

Students will score about 80 per cent on a written test.

These examples, representing a variety of topics and levels, should serve to illustrate how content material can be used to develop thinking and reading activities with children. Content textbooks can be used with children who possess a wide range of reading abilities. Children not only represent varied reading levels but they also have many different interests and attitudes. By selecting interesting, appropriate, and motivating content material, teachers can do much to improve the quality of the learning experiences they offer children.

Grouping Procedures

The grouping of students is just as important in content teaching as it is in reading instruction. Teachers must be aware of student abilities, needs, and in-

terests in planning instructional activities. For this reason, teachers might group their students in a variety of ways: by subject, reading levels, topics of interest, or skill application opportunities.

One obvious method of grouping is to organize students according to the subject they are studying. By placing together all those students who are interested in airplanes, or insects, or pioneers, one can more conveniently plan learning activities. One can use small resource units with the smaller groups and decide activities session by session. The activities will have to be coordinated with teacher-directed sessions combined with independent student work sessions. Referring to the sample topics given earlier, the teacher can create three social studies/science groups that could all be working simultaneously in the classroom: (1) airplanes, (2) insects, and (3) pioneers.

A teacher who is new to the area of content teaching might feel more comfortable with only one topic at a time being identified for one large group or class. Large group or total-class activities worked into a resource unit can be carried out with specific textual material serving as reading and discussion material.

When students are grouped by reading levels they must be provided with reading material at their independent or instructional level. The teacher provides a variety of textbooks—perhaps the same series of a social-studies book but at different levels—so each student will profit from the reading experience. If multiple texts are not available then the process of grouping by reading levels lends itself to the use of study guides, which have already been discussed.

Teachers have also grouped students at certain reading levels among several classrooms. For example, three fourth-grade teachers in the same building might group one class of third-level readers, one class of fourth-level readers, and one of above-level readers for content instruction. Each teacher would provide content material on the same subject but at the appropriate reading levels.

Grouping by interests is another method to use with students. Students who are allowed and encouraged to work in an area of interest are often more motivated learners. A teacher who groups by interests must be ready and willing to provide a variety of activities to accompany those interests. Some students might want to study insects, while another small group or individual will want to study the solar system, and others might be interested in famous inventions. The lists of interests, of course, is endless and limited only by the teacher's resources and creativity.

Another method of using children's interests in content teaching is to develop those interests around a certain theme or topic. An example might be to engage in a unit around a state theme such as Indiana. The children would then decide on an area of Indiana history that would be of particular interest to them such as the glacial development, the Indianapolis 500, or the sand dunes on Lake Michigan. Any of these interests could be further developed through content material in textbooks as well as all types of other material available.

A content lesson centered around the interests of children would offer many opportunities for specific reading-skill application. In developing oral re-

ports to accompany a topic in social studies or science, children would use reading skills such as outlining, note taking, or any of the comprehension skills.

LEARNING CENTERS THAT COMBINE READING WITH CONTENT MATERIAL

Learning centers (see Chapter 9) conveniently lend themselves to use with resource units. Activities can be created in a learning center that are related to reading as well as all areas of the language arts (7). When learning centers are used effectively special topics of interest can be presented in a variety of ways other than by a teacher or in a book. In the remaining section of this chapter several examples will be presented of how learning centers not only develop content-area subjects but also the skills of reading.

The first example employs research skills from reading with science and social-studies topics. Within the center are worksheets and learning activities that include questions about topics of interest to the students. Along with the worksheets in the center is a collection of reference books and supplementary materials representing a variety of reading levels. The worksheets can be placed in folders according to the reading-group name so that students know which activity to select according to their reading level.

The next example involves comprehension skills such as sequencing, following directions, and remembering factual information. The students are of-

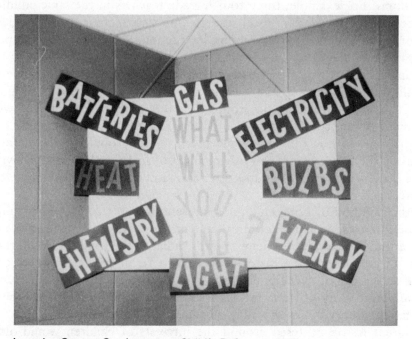

Learning Centers Can Improve a Child's Reference Skills.

Science Topics Can Be Easily Correlated with Reading Skills.

fered a variety of science experiments (collected from different science texts from all reading levels, 1–6) from which they can select one interesting to them. The students must gather the necessary equipment for the selected experiment and then must complete it following the step-by-step directions.

Centers Can Also Develop the Critical Thinking Ability of Students.

Another center involving the use of writing skills is called "Pollution Solution." In this center the students are asked to create an antipollution device and to write a description of how it will help our society.

SUMMARY

This chapter related the diagnostic reading program to the area of content teaching—subjects such as social studies, science, or mathematics. They are referred to as content areas because they contain the subject matter (content) information that is included in the elementary curriculum. Content teaching requires the utilization of subject-area textbooks and includes the active involvement of all reading skills. Often it is necessary to alter the already existing material, obtain other material written on the desired level, show a film or play a tape related to the material, read passages aloud to the students, or establish small working groups where students can assist each other. Study guides of all types can be used with students in the content areas to guide their reading and thinking.

When using a content textbook effectively, one must employ the Directed Reading Lesson Format (DRTA)—skill building, preparation for guided silent reading, guided silent reading, and follow-up. Students need to become familiar with the parts of a textbook and how to use each part. Reading and understanding the captions under pictures, charts, illustrations, and graphs will improve the comprehension of material.

A content text can be used very effectively in a unit or resource plan—a unit of study centering around one content-related subject. A unit pulls together both content instruction and reading instruction under one organized plan. The steps in unit planning are to (1) identify objectives, (2) select activities, (3) identify needed materials, (4) develop a timeline, and (5) plan evaluation.

The grouping of students is just as important in content teaching as it is in reading-group instruction. Students can be organized according to the subject they are studying, by reading level, by topics of interest, or by skill application. Learning centers lend themselves to being used with resource unit plans.

THOUGHT AND DISCUSSION QUESTIONS

1. How does content teaching relate to diagnosis?
2. How does content teaching relate to reading instruction?
3. What pros and cons exist in the correlation of reading skills and content subjects? Explain each.
4. What is the most important skill a child can learn from content-related teaching?
5. How does the unit-plan approach take into consideration those students of varying reading ability?
6. When does reading instruction become content instruction and vice versa?

APPLYING WHAT YOU HAVE LEARNED

1. Obtain some examples of unit or resource plans from several school systems. Compare the structure and format of the plans to the ones offered in this chapter.
2. Create several behaviorally written objectives about a selected topic in a content area.
3. Rewrite a small portion of a content textbook on a different reading level from what it is presently.
4. Develop a directed reading lesson using a content-area textbook.

5. Create a unit (resource) plan around a selected content topic.
6. Create a learning center that correlates reading with a content area of your choice.

BIBLIOGRAPHY

1. Bormuth, John R. "Literacy in the Classroom." Paper presented at the University of Chicago's Annual Reading Conference, 1972.
2. Cooper, J. David. "Using Study Guides to Improve Reading in Content Areas." Monograph, Ball State University, Muncie, Ind., 1978.
3. Hanna, Lavone A.; Potter, Gladys L.; and Hagaman, Neva. *Unit Teaching in the Elementary School.* New York: Holt, Rinehart and Winston, 1963.
4. Hennings, Dorothy Grant; Hennings, George; and Banich, Serafina. *Today's Elementary Social Studies.* Chicago: Rand McNally College Publishing Company, 1980.
5. Herman, Wayne L., Jr. "Reading and Other Language Arts in Social Studies Instruction: Persistent Problems," in Ralph Preston, ed., *A New Look at Reading in the Social Studies.* Newark, Del.: International Reading Association, 1969.
6. Stoodt, Barbara D. *Reading Instruction.* Boston: Houghton Mifflin Company, 1981.
7. Thomas, John I. *Learning Centers.* Boston: Holbrook Press, Inc., 1975.

FOR FURTHER READING

Barth, John L. *Elementary and Middle School Social Studies Curriculum Program, Activities, and Materials.* Washington, D. C.: University Press of America, Inc., 1979.

Breyfogle, Ethel; Nelson, Sue; Pitts, Carol; and Santich, Pamela. *Creating a Learning Environment.* Santa Monica, Calif.: Goodyear Publishing Company, Inc., 1976.

Cooper, J. David; Warncke, Edna W.; Ramstad, Peggy A.; and Shipman, Dorothy A. *The What and How of Reading Instruction.* Columbus, Ohio: Charles E. Merrill Publishing Company, 1979.

Crutchfield, Marjorie A. *Elementary Social Studies.* Columbus, Ohio: Charles E. Merrill Publishing Company, 1978.

Friedman, Myles I., and Rowls, Michael D. *Teaching Reading & Thinking Skills.* New York: Longman, Inc., 1980.

Hanna, Lavone A.; Potter, Gladys L.; and Hagaman, Neva. *Unit Teaching in the Elementary School.* New York: Holt, Rinehart and Winston, 1963.

Hennings, Dorothy Grant; Hennings, George; and Banich, Serafina Fiore. *Today's Elementary Social Studies.* Chicago: Rand McNally College Publishing Company, 1980.

Herber, Harold L. *Teaching Reading in the Content Areas*, 2nd ed. Englewood Cliffs, N. J.: Prentice-Hall, Inc., 1978.

Lamberg, Walter J., and Lamb, Charles E. *Reading Instruction in the Content Areas.* Chicago: Rand McNally College Publishing Company, 1980.

Rieks, Angela S., and Laffey, James L. *Pathways to Imagination.* Santa Monica, Calif.: Goodyear Publishing Company, Inc., 1979.

Thomas, John I. *Learning Centers.* Boston: Holbrook Press, Inc., 1975.

Victor, Edward. *Science for the Elementary School*, 4th ed. New York: Macmillan Publishing Co., Inc., 1980.

bibliography

"A Comparison of Punishment and Positive Reinforcement Group Contingencies in the Modification of Inappropriate Classroom Behaviors." *Canadian Journal of Education*, **3** (1978), 21–36.

"A Handicapped Kid in My Class?" *Social Studies*, **69** (1978), 18–20.

"A Pupils' Eye View of Teaching Performance." *Educational Review*, **30** (1978), 125–137.

Alexander, J. Estill, et al. *Teaching Reading.* Boston: Little, Brown and Company, 1979.

Allen, R. V. "The Language-Experience Approach," in Robert Karlin, ed., *Perspectives on Elementary Reading: Principles and Strategies of Teaching.* New York: Harcourt Brace Jovanovich, 1973.

Allen, Roach Van, and Allen, Claryce. *Language Experience Activities.* Boston: Houghton Mifflin, 1976.

Aukerman, Robert C. *Approaches to Beginning Reading.* New York: John Wiley & Sons, Inc., 1971.

Aukerman, Robert C. *The Basal Reader Approach to Reading.* New York: John Wiley & Sons, Inc., 1981.

Aukerman, Robert C., and Aukerman, Louise R. *How Do I Teach Reading?* New York: John Wiley & Sons, Inc., 1981.

Balow, Irving H., et al. *Metropolitan Achievement Tests: Reading Survey Test.* New York: Psychological Corporation, 1978, 1979.

Barth, John L. *Elementary and Middle School Social Studies Curriculum Program, Activities, and Materials.* Washington, D. C.: University Press of America, Inc., 1979.

Beldin, H. O. "Informal Reading Testing: Historical Review and Review of the Research," in William K. Durr, ed., *Reading Difficulties: Diagnosis, Correction, and Remediation.* Newark, Del.: International Reading Association, 1970, pp. 67–84.

Bennie, Frances. *Learning Centers, Development and Operation.* Englewood Cliffs, N. J.: Educational Technology Publications, 1977.

Betts, Emmett Albert. *Foundations of Reading Instruction.* New York: American Book Company, 1957.

Block, J. H. *Schools, Society and Mastery Learning.* New York: Holt, Rinehart and Winston, 1974.

Bloom, B. S., et al. *Handbook on Formative and Summative Evaluation of Student Learning.* New York: McGraw-Hill Book Company, 1971.

Bond, Guy L., and Dykstra, Robert. The Cooperative Research Program in First Grade Reading. *Reading Research Quarterly*, **2** (Summer 1967).

Bond, Guy L.; Tinker, Miles A.; and Wasson, Barbara B. *Reading Difficulties: Their Diagnosis and Correction*, 4th ed. Englewood Cliffs, N. J.: Prentice-Hall, Inc., 1979.

Bormuth, John R. "Literacy in the Classroom." Paper presented at the University of Chicago's Annual Reading Conference, 1972.

Breyfogle, Ethel; Nelson, Sue; Pitts, Carol; and Santich, Pamela. *Creating a Learning Environment*. Santa Monica, Calif.: Goodyear Publishing Company, Inc., 1976.

Brophy, J., and Putnam, J. "Classroom Management in the Elementary Grades," in D. Duke, ed., "Classroom Management," in *Yearbook for the National Society for the Study of Education*. Chicago: University of Chicago Press, 1979.

Burns, Paul C., and Roe, Betty D. *Teaching Reading in Today's Elementary Schools*. Chicago: Rand McNally College Publishing Company, 1976.

Burns, Paul C., and Roe, Betty D. *Teaching Reading in Today's Elementary Schools*, 2nd ed. Chicago: Rand McNally College Publishing Company, 1980.

Bussis, Anne M.; Chittenden, Edward A.; and Amarel, Marianne. *Beyond Surface Curriculum*. Boulder, Colo.: Westview Press, 1976.

Chall, Jeanne. *Learning to Read: The Great Debate*. New York: McGraw-Hill Book Company, 1967.

Cheek, Martha Collins, and Cheek, Earl H. Jr. *Diagnostic Prescriptive Reading Instruction*. Dubuque, Iowa: William C. Brown Company, Publishers, 1980.

Christenson, Adolph. "Oral Reading Errors of Intermediate Grade Children at Their Independent, Instructional, and Frustration Reading Levels," in J. Allen Figurel, ed., *Reading and Realism*, 1968 Proceedings, Vol. 13, Part 1. Newark, Del.: International Reading Association, 1969.

Clark, Christopher M., and Yinger, Robert J. *The Hidden World of Teaching: Implications of Research on Teacher Planning*. Lansing, Mich.: Michigan State University, 1980. (ERIC Document Reproduction Service No. ED 191 844)

Clarizio, Harvey F. *Toward Positive Classroom Discipline*, 3rd ed. New York: John Wiley & Sons, Inc., 1980.

"Classroom Management: A Rule Establishment and Enforcement Model." *Elementary School Journal*, **78** (1978), 254–263.

"Classroom Seating Arrangements: Instructional Communication Theory Versus Student Preferences." *Communication Education*, **27** (Mar. 1978), 99–111.

Cole, Ann, et al. *I Saw a Purple Cow: 100 Other Recipes for Learning*. Boston: Little, Brown and Company, 1972.

Coltheart, Max. "When Can Children Learn to Read—and When Should They Be Taught," in T. Gary Waller and G. E. Mackinnon, eds., *Reading Research: Advances in Theory and Practice*, Vol. 1. New York: Academic Press, Inc., 1979.

Cooper, J. David. "Using Study Guides to Improve Reading in Content Areas," monograph. Muncie, Ind.: Ball State University, 1978.

Cooper, J. David, et al. *Decision Making for the Diagnostic Teacher*. New York: Holt, Rinehart and Winston, 1972.

Cooper, J. David; Warncke, Edna W.; Ramstad, Peggy A.; and Shipman, Dorothy A. *The What and How of Reading Instruction*. Columbus, Ohio: Charles E. Merrill Publishing Company, 1979.

Copperman, Paul. *The Literacy Hoax*. New York: William Morrow and Company, Inc., 1978.

Countermine, Terry. Director of Microcomputer Laboratory. School of Education, Auburn University, Auburn, Ala. Interview, 1982.

Crutchfield, Marjorie A. *Elementary Social Studies*. Columbus, Ohio: Charles E. Merrill Publishing Company, 1978.

Deno, Evelyn N, ed. *Instructional Alternatives for Exceptional Children*. Arlington, Va.: Council for Exceptional Children, 1977.

DeFranco, Ellen B., and Pickarts, Evelyn M. *Parents, Help Your Child to Read: Ideas to Use at Home.* New York: Van Nostrand Reinhold Company, 1972.

"Designing the Science Learning Center." *Science and Children*, **14** (1976), 11–12.

Dishner, Ernest K.; Bean, Thomas W.; and Readence, John E. *Reading in the Content Areas: Improving Classroom Instruction.* Dubuque, Iowa: Kendall/Hunt Publishing Company, 1981.

Division of Pupil Personnel Services, Department of Public Instruction, State of Indiana, Indianapolis. "Family Educational Rights and Privacy Act of 1974," memo interpreting P.L. 93-380.

Doyle, Walter. *Classroom Management.* West Lafayette, Ind.: Kappa Delta Pi, An Honor Society in Education, 1980.

Duffy, Gerald G., and Sherman, George B. *Systematic Reading Instruction*, 2nd ed. New York: Harper & Row, Publishers, 1977.

Duffy, Gerald G.; Sherman, George B.; and Roehler, Laura R. *How to Teach Reading Systematically.* New York: Harper & Row, Publishers, 1977.

Duke, David L., ed. "Classroom Management," in *The Seventy-eighth Yearbook of the National Society for the Study of Education.* Chicago: University of Chicago Press, 1970.

Dunfee, Maxine. *Social Studies for the Real World.* Columbus, Ohio: Charles E. Merrill Publishing Company, 1978.

Durkin, Dolores. *Teaching Young Children to Read*, 3rd ed. Boston: Allyn & Bacon, Inc., 1980.

Eames, T. H. "A Frequency Study of Physical Handicaps in Reading Disability and Unselected Groups." *Journal of Educational Research*, **29** (1935), 1–5.

Ekwall, Eldon E. *Diagnosis and Remediation of the Disabled Reader.* Boston: Allyn & Bacon, Inc., 1976.

Ekwall, Eldon E. "Informal Reading Inventories: The Instructional Level." *Reading Teacher*, **29** (Apr. 1976), 662–665.

Ekwall, Eldon E. "Should Repetitions Be Counted As Errors?" *Reading Teacher*, **27** (Jan. 1974), 365–367.

Ekwall, Eldon E. *Teacher's Handbook on Diagnosis and Remediation in Reading.* Boston: Allyn & Bacon, Inc., 1977.

Ellis, Arthur K. *Teaching and Learning Elementary Social Studies.* Boston: Allyn & Bacon, Inc., 1977.

Epstein, Charlotte. *Classroom Management and Teaching: Persistent Problems and Rationale Solutions.* Reston, Va.: Reston Publishing Company, Inc., 1979.

Falletta, John, and Sheffield, James. *Pupil Reading Achievement in New York City.* New York City Public Schools, Dec. 1978.

Farr, Roger. *Reading: What Can Be Measured?* Newark, Del.: International Reading Association, 1969.

Farr, Roger, and Blomenberg, Paula. "Contrary to Popular Opinion . . . ," in *Thoughts on Reading.* River Forest, Ill.: Laidlaw Brothers (June 1979), No. 7.

Farr, Roger; Tuinman, Jaap; and Rowls, Michael. *Reading Achievement in the United States: Then and Now.* Bloomington, Ind.: Indiana University, 1974.

First Year Teacher Evaluation. Muncie, Ind.: Teachers College, Ball State University, 1977, 1978, 1979, and 1980.

Forgan, Harry W., and Mangrum, Charles T. II. *Teaching Content Area Reading Skills*, 2nd ed. Columbus, Ohio: Charles E. Merrill Publishing Co., 1981.

Forte, Imogene, and Mackenzie, Joy. *Nooks, Crannies and Corners.* Nashville: Incentive Publications, Inc., 1972.

Frazier, Alexander. *Teaching Children Today; An Informal Approach.* New York: Harper & Row, Publishers, 1976.

Friedman, Myles I., and Rowls, Michael D. *Teaching Reading & Thinking Skills.* New York: Longman, Inc., 1980.

Gadway, Charles, and Wilson, H. A. *Functional Literacy: Basic Reading Performance.* Denver, Colo.: National Assessment of Educational Progress, 1976.

Gallant, Ruth. *Handbook in Corrective Reading: Basic Tasks*, 2nd ed. Columbus, Ohio: Charles E. Merrill Publishing Company, 1978.

Gallaway, David. *Case Studies in Classroom Management.* London: Longman Group Limited, 1976.

Gambrell, L. B. Extending Think-time for Better Reading Instruction. *Education Digest*, **46** (Feb. 1981), 33–35.

Gates, Arthur I.; McKillop, Anne S.; and Horowitz, Elizabeth. *Gates-McKillop-Horowitz Reading Diagnostic Tests*, 2nd ed. New York: Teachers College Press, 1981.

Good, T. L., and Brophy, J. E. *Looking in Classrooms.* New York: Harper & Row, Publishers, 1973.

Goodman, Kenneth S. "A Linguistic Study of Cues and Miscues in Reading." *Elementary English*, **42** (Oct. 1965), 639–643.

Goodman, Kenneth S. "Analysis of Oral Reading Miscues: Applied Psycholinguistics," in Frank Smith, ed., *Psycholinguistics and Reading.* New York: Holt, Rinehart and Winston, 1973.

Goodman, Yetta M., and Burke, Carolyn. *Reading Strategies: Focus on Comprehension.* New York: Holt, Rinehart and Winston, 1980.

Goodwin, Dwight L., and Coates, Thomas J. *Helping Students Help Themselves.* Englewood Cliffs, N. J.: Prentice-Hall, Inc., 1976.

Guszak, Frank J. *Diagnostic Reading Instruction in the Elementary School*, 2nd ed. New York: Harper & Row, Publishers, 1978.

Guthrie, John T., et al. *A Study of the Locus and Nature of Reading Problems in the Elementary School.* Final Report, ED 127 568, 1976.

Hall, Mary Anne. *Teaching Reading As A Language Experience*, 3rd ed. Columbus, Ohio: Charles E. Merrill Publishing Company, 1981.

Hall, Mary Anne; Ribovich, Jerilyn K.; and Ramig, Christopher J. *Reading and the Elementary School Child*, 2nd ed. New York: D. Van Nostrand Company, 1979.

Hanna, Lavone A.; Potter, Gladys L.; and Hagaman, Neva. *Unit Teaching in the Elementary School.* New York: Holt, Rinehart and Winston, 1963.

Hanna, Lavone A.; Potter, Gladys A.; and Reynolds, Robert W. *Dynamic Elementary Social Studies*, 3rd ed. New York: Holt, Rinehart and Winston, 1973.

Hardin, Veralee B., and Petit, Neila T. *A Guide to Ecological Screening and Assessment.* Dubuque, Iowa: William C. Brown Company, Publishers, 1978.

Harper, Robert J., and Kilarr, Gary. *Reading and the Law.* Newark, Del.: International Reading Association, 1978.

Harris, Albert J., and Sipay, Edward R. *How to Increase Reading Ability*, 7th ed. New York: Longman, Inc., 1980.

Harris, Larry A., and Smith, Carl B. *Reading Instruction: Diagnostic Teaching in the Classroom*, 2nd ed. New York: Holt, Rinehart and Winston, 1976.

Harris, Larry A., and Smith, Carl B. *Reading Instruction: Diagnostic Teaching in the Classroom*, 3rd ed. New York: Holt, Rinehart and Winston, 1980.

Heilman, Arthur. *Phonics in Proper Perspective*, 4th ed. Columbus, Ohio: Charles E. Merrill Publishing Company, 1981.

Heilman, Arthur W.; Blair, Timothy R.; and Rupley, William H. *Principles and Practices of Teaching Reading*, 5th ed. Columbus, Ohio: Charles E. Merrill Publishing Company, 1981.

Hennings, Dorothy Grant; Hennings, George; and Banich, Serafina Fiore. *Today's Elementary Social Studies.* Chicago: Rand McNally College Publishing Company, 1980.

Herman, Wayne L., Jr. "Reading and Other Language Arts in Social Studies Instruction: Persistent Problems," in Ralph Preston, ed., *A New Look at Reading in the Social Studies.* Newark, Del.: International Reading Association, 1969.

Hoover, Sharon. "All The Records You'll Ever Need to Keep." *Instructor* (Aug. 1979), 86–91.

House, Ernest R., and Lapan, Stephen D. *Survival in the Classroom.* Boston: Allyn & Bacon, Inc., 1978.

How to Survive in the Open Space School. *Clearing House,* **51** (1978), 296–299.

Howards, Melvin. *Reading Diagnosis and Instruction, An Integrated Approach.* Reston, Va.: Reston Publishing Company, Inc., 1980.

Huitt, William G., and Segars, John K. "Characteristics of Effective Classrooms." Research for Better Schools, Inc., Philadelphia, Oct. 1980.

"Individualized, Success Oriented Instructions in Achievement and Self-Concept of First Graders." *Perceptual and Motor Skills,* **45** (1977), 721–722.

Jenkins, Jeanne Kohl, and MacDonald, Pam. *Growing Up Equal: Activities and Resources for Parents and Teachers of Young Children.* Englewood Cliffs, N. J.: Prentice-Hall, Inc., 1979.

Johnson, Lois V., and Bany, Mary A. *Classroom Management.* New York: Macmillan Publishing Company, Inc., 1970.

Johnson, Marjorie Seddon, and Kress, Roy A. *Informal Reading Inventories.* Newark, Del.: International Reading Association, 1965.

Johnson, Marjorie Seddon, and Kress, Roy A. "Individual Reading Inventories," In Leo M. Schell and Paul C. Burns, eds., *Remedial Reading: Classroom and Clinic,* 2nd ed. Boston: Allyn & Bacon, Inc., 1972.

Johnson, Richard A.; Kast, Fremont E.; and Rosenzweig, James E. *The Theory and Management of Systems.* New York: McGraw-Hill Book Company, 1963.

Kaluger, George, and Kalson, Clifford J. *Reading and Learning Disabilities,* 2nd ed. Columbus, Ohio: Charles E. Merrill Publishing Company, 1978.

Kaplan, Sandra; Kaplan, Jo Ann; Madsden, Sheila; and Taylor, Bette. *Change for Children.* Pacific Palisades, Calif.: Goodyear Publishing Co., Inc., 1973.

Karlsen, Bjorn, et al. *Stanford Diagnostic Reading Test: (SDRT).* New York: Psychological Corporation, 1978.

Kean, Michael M., et al. *What Works in Reading?* Office of Research and Evaluation, School District of Philadelphia, 1979.

Kender, Joseph P. "How Useful Are Informal Reading Tests?" *Journal of Reading,* **11** (Feb. 1968), 337–342.

Kennedy, Eddie. *Classroom Approaches to Remedial Reading,* 2nd ed. Itasca, Ill.: F. E. Peacock Publishing Inc., 1977.

Kindsvatter, R., and Levine, M. A. "Myths of Discipline." *Phi Delta Kappan,* **61** (1980), 690–693.

Kounin, Jacob S. *Discipline and Group Management in Classrooms.* Huntington, N. Y.: Robert E. Krieger Publishing Company, 1977.

Lamberg, Walter J., and Lamb, Charles E. *Reading Instruction in the Content Areas.* Chicago: Rand McNally College Publishing Company, 1980.

Lapp, Diane. "Individualized Reading Made Easy for Teachers." *Early Years,* **73** (Feb. 1977), 63–67.

Lapp, Diane, ed. *Making Reading Possible Through Effective Classroom Management.* Newark, Del.: International Reading Association, 1980.

Lapp, Diane, and Flood, James. *Teaching Reading to Every Child.* New York: Macmillan Publishing Company, Inc., 1978.

LaPray, Margaret H. *On the Spot Reading Diagnosis File.* West Nyack, N. Y.: Center for Applied Research in Education, Inc., 1978.

Levin, Harry, and Watson, J. "The Learning of Variable Grapheme-to-Phoneme Correspondences: Variations in the Initial Consonant Position," in *A Basic Program on Reading*, U.S.O.E., Project No. 639. Ithaca, N. Y.: Cornell University Press, 1963.

Loban, Walter. *Language Development: Kindergarten Through Grade Twelve.* Urbana, Ill.: National Council of Teachers of English, 1976.

Lunstrum, John P., and Taylor, Bob L. *Teaching Reading in the Social Studies.* Boulder, Colo.: ERIC Clearinghouse for Social Studies Education, 1977-78.

MacGinitie, Walter H., ed. *Assessment Problems in Reading.* Newark, Del.: International Reading Association, 1973.

MacGinitie, Walter H. *Gates-MacGinitie Reading Tests*, 2nd ed. Boston: Houghton Mifflin Company, 1978.

Madden, Richard, et al. *Stanford Achievement Test.* New York: Psychological Corporation, 1973.

Maeroff, Gene. "Reading Achievement of Children in Indiana Found As Good As in '44." *The New York Times* (Apr. 1976), p. 10.

Mann, Philip H., et al. *Teacher's Handbook of Diagnostic Inventories*, 2nd ed. Boston: Allyn & Bacon, Inc., 1979.

Marchbanks, Gabrielle, and Levin, Harry. "Cues by Which Children Recognize Words." *Journal of Educational Psychology*, **56** (Apr. 1965), 57-61.

McCracken, Robert A., and Mullen, Neill D. "The Validity of Certain Measures in an I.R.I.," in William K. Durr, ed., *Reading Difficulties: Diagnosis Correction, and Remediation.* Newark, Del.: International Reading Association, 1970.

McCracken, Robert A. "The Informal Reading Inventory As a Means of Improving Instruction," in Thomas C. Barrett, ed., *The Evaluation of Children's Reading Achievement.* Newark, Del.: International Reading Association, 1967.

Miller, Wilma H. *Reading Diagnosis Kit*, 2nd ed. West Nyack, N. Y.: Center for Applied Research in Education, 1978.

Muehl, Sigmar and King, Ethel. "Recent Research in Visual Discrimination: Significance for Beginning Reading." in *Teaching Word Recognition Skills*, compiled by Mildred A. Dawson, Newark, Del., International Reading Association, 1971.

"Observations of Classroom Space: Implications for Learning and Teaching Children in the Caribbean." *Caribbean Journal of Education*, **4** (1977), 112-145.

Oklahoma State Department of Education. *Oklahoma Educational Status Study: Reading and Math Grades, 3, 6, 9, 12, School Year 1978.* ED 179 587, 1978.

Oklahoma State Department of Education. *Oklahoma Educational Status Study: Reading and Math Grades 3, 6, 9, 12, Year 1978-79.* ED 179 587, 1979.

Osborne, Jean. "The Purposes, Uses and Contents of Workbooks and Some Guidelines for Teachers and Publishers." Champaign, Ill.: Center for the Study of Reading, August 1981, Report No. 27.

Otto, Wayne, et al. *Focused Reading Instruction.* Reading, Mass.: Addison-Wesley Publishing Co., Inc., 1974.

Otto, Wayne, and Askov, Eunice. *The Wisconsin Design for Reading Skill Development: Rationale and Guidelines.* Minneapolis: National Computer Systems, Inc., 1970.

Packman, Linda. "Selected Oral Reading Errors and Levels of Reading Comprehension," in Howard A. Klein, ed., *The Quest for Competency in Teaching Reading.* Newark, Del.: International Reading Association, 1972.

Pearson, P. David, and Johnson, Dale D. *Teaching Reading Comprehension.* New York: Holt, Rinehart and Winston, 1974.

"Peer Groups As Settings for Learning." *Theory Into Practice*, **16** (1977), 272-279.

Peterson, P. L.; Marx, R. W.; and Clark, C. M. "Teacher Planning, Teacher Behavior and Student Achievement." *American Educational Research Journal*, **15** (1978), 417-432.

Pilulski, John. "A Critical Review: Informal Reading Inventories." *Reading Teacher*, **28** (Nov. 1974), 141–151.

"Playing the Game: A Behavioral Approach to Classroom Management in the Junior School." *Educational Review*, **30** (Feb. 1978), 41–50.

Potter, Thomas C., and Rae, Gwenneth. *Informal Reading Diagnosis*, 2nd ed. Englewood Cliffs, N. J.: Prentice-Hall, Inc., 1981.

Powell, William R. "Reappraising the Criteria for Interpreting Informal Inventories," in Dorothy L. DeBoer, ed., *Reading Diagnosis and Evaluation*. Newark, Del.: International Reading Association, 1970.

Powell, William R. Validity of the IRI Reading Levels. *Elementary English*, **48** (Oct. 1971), 637–642.

Powell, William R. "The Validity of the Instructional Reading Level, in Robert E. Leibert, ed., *Diagnostic Viewpoints in Reading*. Newark, Del.: International Reading Association, 1971.

Prescott, George A., et al. *Metropolitan Achievement Tests*. New York: Psychological Corporation, 1978.

Reed, Shirley Anne. "An Investigation into the Effect of Prestated Purposes on the Silent Reading Comprehension of Good and Poor Readers Using an Informal Reading Inventory." Unpublished doctoral dissertation, Ball State University, 1979.

Rieke, Angela S., and Laffey, James L. *Pathways to Imagination*. Santa Monica, Calif.: Goodyear Publishing Company, Inc., 1979.

Robinson, Helen M. *Why Pupils Fail in Reading*. Chicago: University of Chicago Press, 1946.

Ruddell, Robert B. "Psycholinguistic Implications for a Systems of Communication Model," in Harry Singer and Robert B. Ruddell, eds., *Theoretical Models and Processes of Reading*, 2nd ed. Newark, Del.: International Reading Association, 1976.

Ruddell, Robert B. *Reading-Language Instruction: Innovative Practices*. Englewood Cliffs, N. J.: Prentice-Hall, Inc., 1974.

Rupley, William H. "Informal Reading Diagnosis." *Reading Teacher*, **29** (Oct. 1975), 106–107, 109.

Rupley, William H., and Blair, Timothy R. *Reading Diagnosis and Remediation*. Chicago: Rand McNally College Publishing Company, 1979.

Savage, John F., and Mooney, Jean F. *Teaching Reading to Children with Special Needs*. Boston: Allyn & Bacon, Inc., 1979.

Scholastic Microcomputer Instructional Materials Catalog (1981–82). P.O. Box 2002, 904 Sylvan Avenue, Englewood Cliffs, N. J. 07632.

Shipman, Dorothy, and Warncke, Edna W. *Group Assessment in Reading: Classroom Teacher's Handbook*. Englewood Cliffs, N. J.: Prentice-Hall, Inc., 1983 (in process at the time of this printing).

Shrigley, R. L. "Strategies in Classroom Management." *Education Digest*, **45** (1979), 7–10.

Singer, Harry, and Ruddell, Robert B., ed. *Theoretical Models and Processes of Reading*, 2nd ed. Newark, Del.: International Reading Association, 1976.

Spache, George D. *Investigating the Issues of Reading Disabilities*. Boston: Allyn & Bacon, Inc., 1976.

Spache, George D., and Spache, Evelyn B. *Reading in the Elementary School*, 4th ed. Boston: Allyn & Bacon, Inc., 1977.

Spiro, Rand J., et al., eds. *Theoretical Issues in Reading Comprehension*. Hillsdale, N. Y.: Lawrence Erlbaum Associates, Publishers, 1980.

Smith, B. Othaniel. *Research in Teacher Education: A Symposium*. Englewood Cliffs, N. J.: Prentice-Hall, 1978.

Smith, Frank. *Reading Without Nonsense.* New York: Teachers College Press, 1978.

Smith, E. Brooks; Goodman, Kenneth; and Meredith, Robert. *Language and Thinking in the Elementary School,* 2nd ed. New York: Holt, Rinehart and Winston, 1976.

Smith, Nila B., and Robinson, H. Alan. *Reading Instruction for Today's Children,* 2nd ed. Englewood Cliffs, N. J.: Prentice-Hall, Inc., 1980.

Stallings, June. "Allocated Academic Learning Time Revisited or Beyond Time on Task." *Educational Researcher,* **9** (Dec. 1980), 11–16.

Stauffer, Russell G. *Directing the Reading-Thinking Process.* New York: Harper and Row, Publishers, 1975.

Strang, Ruth. *Reading Diagnosis and Remediation.* Newark, Del.: International Reading Association, 1968.

Stoodt, Barbara D. *Reading Instruction.* Boston: Houghton Mifflin Company, 1981.

Tanner, Laurel N. "A Model of School Discipline," in Elizabeth Hirzler Weiner, ed., *Discipline in the Classroom,* 2nd ed. Washington, D. C.: National Education Association, 1980.

"Teacher Survival in the Classroom." *Journal of Research and Development in Education,* **7** (1978), 64–73.

"Ten Steps to Good Discipline." *Today's Education,* **66** (1977), 61–63.

"The Grand Plan: If I Only Had More Time!" *Instructor,* **88** (1978), 1–4, 16.

The Information Base for Reading. U.S.O.E. Mimeographed, Project Number 0-9031, 1971.

"The Politics of Classroom Organization." *Forum for the Discussion of New Trends in Education,* **20** (1978) 61–64.

Thomas, Ellen Lamar, and Robinson, H. Alan. *Improving Reading in Every Class.* Boston: Allyn & Bacon, Inc., 1979.

Thomas, John I. *Learning Centers: Opening Up the Classroom.* Boston: Holbrook Press, Inc., 1975.

Thorndike, Robert L., and Hagen, Elizabeth. *Measurement and Evaluation in Psychology and Education,* 4th ed. New York: John Wiley & Sons, Inc., 1977.

Tjosvold, D. "Control, Conflict, and Collaboration in the Classroom." *Education Digest,* **45** (1980), 17–20.

Tierney, Robert J., and Lapp, Diane. *National Assessment of Educational Progress in Reading.* Newark, Del.: International Reading Association, 1979.

Tinker, Miles A., and McCullough, Constance M. *Teaching Elementary Reading,* 4th ed. Englewood Cliffs, N. J.: Prentice-Hall, Inc., 1975.

Veatch, Jeannette. *Reading in the Elementary School,* 2nd ed. New York: John Wiley & Sons, Inc., 1978.

Venezky, Richard L., and Winfield, Linda F. *Schools That Succeed Beyond Expectation in Teaching Reading.* Final Report, NIE Grant, NIE-G-78-0027, University of Delaware, 1979.

Victor, Edward. *Science for the Elementary School,* 4th ed. New York: Macmillan Publishing Co., Inc., 1980.

Wallen, Carl J. *Competency in Teaching Reading,* 2nd ed. Chicago: Science Research Associates, Inc., 1981.

Wesley, Edgar Bruce, and Cartwright, William H. *Teaching Social Studies in Elementary Schools,* 3rd ed. Boston: D. C. Heath & Company, 1968.

Weiner, Elizabeth Hirzler, ed. *Discipline in the Classroom,* 2nd rev. ed. Washington, D. C.: National Education Association, 1980.

Weintraub, Samuel. "Auditory Perception and Deafness," in *Reading Research Profiles.* Newark, Del.: International Reading Association, 1972.

Weintraub, Samuel. "Vision-Visual Discrimination," in *Reading Research Profiles.* Newark, Del.: International Reading Association, 1973.

What Teachers Use to Teach Reading. Research in progress. Center for the Study of Reading. Champaign, Ill., 1980.

Wheeler, Alan. "A Systematic Design for Individualizing Reading." *Elementary English*, **50** (Mar. 1973), 445–449.

Williamson, Leon W., and Young, Freda. "The IRI and RMI Diagnostic Concepts Should Be Synthesized." *Journal of Reading Behavior*, **6** (July 1974), 183–194.

Winkle, Linda Wyrick, and Mathews, Walter M. "Computer Equity Comes of Age." *Phi Delta Kappan*, **63** (Jan. 1982), 314–315.

Wittich, Walter A., and Schuller, Charles F. *Instructional Technology, Its Nature and Use*, 6th ed. New York: Harper & Row, Publishers, 1979.

Wood, R. Kent, and Stephens, Kent G. "An Educator's Guide to Videodisc Technology." *Phi Delta Kappan*, **58** (Feb. 1977), 466–467.

Woods, Mary Lynn, and Moe, Alden J. *Analytical Reading Inventory*, 2nd ed. Columbus, Ohio: Charles E. Merrill Publishing Company, 1981.

Workman, E., and Hector, M. "Self-control in Classroom Settings: A Review of the Literature." *Journal of School Psychology*, **16** (1978), 227–236.

Younie, William J. *Instructional Approaches to Slow Learning.* New York: Teachers College Press, Columbus University, 1967.

Zucker, Andrew A. "The Computer in the School: A Case Study." *Phi Delta Kappan*, **63** (Jan. 1982), 317–319.

index

Visual discrimination, 29–30
Visual factors, characteristic signs, 29

W

Wallen, Carl J., 165, 217
Warncke, Edna W., 106, 217, 282
Wasson, Barbara B., 66
Watson, J., 124
Weiner, Elizabeth Hirzler, 253
Weintraub, Samuel, 67
Wheeler, Alan, 183
Williamson, Leon W., 106
Wilson, H. A., 25
Winfield, Linda F., 25
Winkle, Linda W., 218
Wisconsin Design for Reading Skill Development, 118–19
Wisconsin Tests of Reading Skill Development, 55

Withitness, 235
Wittich, Walter A., 218
Wood, R. Kent, 183
Woods, Mary Lynn, 106
Word attack, decoding, 38
Word-recognition responses, steps in analyzing, 95–96
Work habits, independent, 241
Workman, E., 252

Y

Yinger, Robert J., 252
Young, Freda, 106

Z

Zucker, Andrew, A., 218